THE RESURGENCE OF THE

Also of interest

Power and Security in the Information Age
Investigating the Role of the State in Cyberspace
Edited by
Myriam Dunn Cavelty, Victor Mauer and Sai Felicia Krishna-Hensel
ISBN 978-0-7546-7088-9

The Resurgence of the State
Trends and Processes in Cyberspace Governance

Edited by

MYRIAM DUNN
Center for Security Studies, ETH Zurich, Switzerland

SAI FELICIA KRISHNA-HENSEL
Center for Business and Economic Development
Auburn University, Montgomery, USA

VICTOR MAUER
Center for Security Studies, ETH Zurich, Switzerland

Routledge
Taylor & Francis Group
LONDON AND NEW YORK

First published 2007 by Ashgate Publishing

2 Park Square, Milton Park, Abingdon, Oxfordshire OX14 4RN
711 Third Avenue, New York, NY 10017

Routledge is an imprint of the Taylor & Francis Group, an informa business

First issued in paperback 2018

British Library Cataloguing in Publication Data
The resurgence of the state : trends and processes in
    cyberspace governance
    1. Information technology - Political aspects 2. Internet -
    Political aspects 3. Jurisdiction 4. Internet - Law and
    legislation 5. International relations
    I. Dunn, Myriam II. Krishna-Hensel, Sai Felicia III. Mauer,
    Victor
    303.4'833

Library of Congress Cataloging-in-Publication Data
The resurgence of the state : trends and processes in cyberspace governance / edited by
Myriam Dunn, Sai Felicia Krishna-Hensel, and Victor Mauer.
        p. cm.
    Includes bibliographical references and index.
    ISBN 978-0-7546-4947-2
    1. Information society--Political aspects. 2. Information technology--Political
aspects. 3. State, The. I. Dunn, Myriam. II. Krishna-Hensel, Sai Felicia. III.
Mauer, Victor

    HM851.R47 2007
    354.75--dc22

                                                                        2007003827

    ISBN 978-0-7546-4947-2 (hbk)
    ISBN 978-1-138-38371-5 (pbk)

Contents

List of Contributors

Ralf Bendrath is a researcher at the Collaborative Research Center 'Transformations of the State' at the University of Bremen. He has worked extensively on privacy, cyber-security, information warfare, international security policy, and peace research. He was chief editor of www.worldsummit2005.org, the leading civil society website on the World Summit on the Information Society (WSIS).

Myriam Dunn is Head of the New Risks Research Unit at the Center for Security Studies (CSS), ETH Zurich. Her field of expertise is the impact of the information revolution on security policy issues. She is the author of the *International CIIP Handbook*, a renowned publication analyzing critical information infrastructure protection policies in a range of countries. Apart from various articles on aspects of the information revolution, she is author of *Cyber-threats and Countermeasures*, a book analyzing the interplay between threat perceptions and state reactions to the threat (Routledge 2007).

Mika Hayashi is Associate Professor at the Graduate School of International Cooperation Studies, Kobe University. Her field of expertise is public international law and her published works cover security-related areas of international law such as international humanitarian law and disarmament treaties. She is a current member of the Executive Council of the Comparative Interdisciplinary Studies Section of the International Studies Association.

Sai Felicia Krishna-Hensel is Director of the Interdisciplinary Global Studies Research Initiative, Center for Business and Economic Development, Auburn University, Montgomery, and President and Program Chair of the Comparative Interdisciplinary Studies Section of the International Studies Association, United States.

Dirk Lehmkuhl is a Lecturer in the IR department of the University of Zurich. He studied political science and public administration at the University of Konstanz and achieved his PhD at the European University Institute in Florence. He was research fellow at the Universities of Konstanz and Bielefeld as well as at the Max-Planck Project Group Common Goods: Law, Politics and Economics in Bonn.

Victor Mauer is Deputy Director and Head of Research of the Center for Security Studies (CSS), ETH Zurich, and heads the Center's European Security and Defence Policy (ESDP) project. He specializes in European security, European integration, and transatlantic relations and has published on European and transatlantic affairs. He studied at the Universities of Bonn, Oxford, and Cambridge.

Jamal Shahin is a Lecturer at the University of Amsterdam and Vesalius College (Brussels), a Senior Visiting Consultant at the Danish Technology Institute, and a Senior Associate Fellow at the Institute of European Studies, Vrije Universiteit Brussel. Research and teaching interests include eGovernment and ICT policies in the EU and International Relations and the EU. He is the co-founder of the Unit for Internet Studies. His recent research work has focused on international, European, and local aspects of ICTs and their relationship with political institutions and citizens, where he has published several articles, book chapters, and studies. He is currently working on research into the role of the EU in international institutions.

Alexander Siedschlag is full Professor of Political Science at the University of Innsbruck/Austria. He is spokesperson of the working group 'Internet and Politics' in the German Political Science Association (DVPW). He has taught at the University of Munich and the Free University and the Humboldt University Berlin. His areas of specialization include: International security, German foreign and defence policy, NATO, ESDP, management of international conflict, digital democracy, internet communication and social/political change.

Introduction

Sai Felicia Krishna-Hensel

The notable changes in communication that occurred during the mid-twentieth century were the result of new technologies and concepts which were developed through a US government-sponsored collaborative research project to share defense-related information between industry, university researchers and government agencies.[1] The project evolved into a global network and communication system that has become central to the activities of the globalized world of the twenty-first century. This new communications network reflects both the complex and innovative technology on which it is based, as well as the visionary inspiration that led to the development of this phenomenon. The networked world is both a product of this world and has an existence that transcends this world, and it is affecting how we see ourselves and our environment in dramatic ways. By connecting the global system and transforming the way in which we view time and space, the internet has revolutionized the way we think, communicate, do business, learn, and go about various human activities. The network-based communication system has had far reaching consequences for societies all over the world, reaching into the remotest areas hitherto difficult to access. The disparities present between societies have not entirely impacted access to this network, although serious issues remain regarding the advantages it provides for the developing world.

Information technology policy has been presented with some unprecedented challenges resulting from the network-based system. Both the public and private spheres, in which the internet operates, have raised legitimate issues of regulation and governance. Traditionally, radio and television communication have been clearly geographically bound and hence easier to monitor, however the uniquely structured network of the new technologies has complicated the state's abilities to govern and regulate communications on a global level. The operation of the networks has caused us to confront fundamental questions about the power and reach of states and the rights of individuals and societies to freedom of expression untrammeled by controls. The new technology has empowered the individual in ways hitherto unimaginable, but it has also exposed the very real prospect of giving absolute controls to the nation-state. During the early stages of development of the internet, the primary effort was concentrated on expanding the network into a widely-available public resource. As a result, there was less attention given to traditional forms of governance based on general laws and regulations that were extended to other communications systems.

---

1 Rita Tehan, *Spinning the Web: The History and Infrastructure of the Internet*, Congressional Research Service Report 98- 649C (Washington, 1999).

This gave rise to the popular belief that the internet had created a unique borderless world controlled by users rather than governments.

On one level, the technologies have fostered idealistic scenarios presaging a complete revolution of the power equation that exists between governments and individuals. Technology is seen as a facilitator of the transformation of social and political relations in a new world. The realm in which this transformation is most dramatically visible is cyberspace – the alter ego of the real world. The relationship between two realms – the real and the virtual – has provided analysts with an opportunity to explore interesting and imaginative scenarios while simultaneously maintaining a realistic perspective on these issues.[2] What remains unclear is the extent to which communications technology can be credited with the restructuring occurring in the globalized world. The postmodern world is characterized by a high level of popular participation in public discourse and, to the extent that the information revolution has contributed to this development, it is a central force of this movement. The economic and ideological potential of this medium has not escaped the attention of governments or of individuals and groups. The challenge has resulted in vigilance and anticipation between the two opposing entities. While governments seek to control and limit expression and interaction in some instances, individuals and groups often seek to bypass the controls. The economic and political consequences of controls are being continually debated and reassessed in tandem with the rapidly changing technological and social environment. Technology appears to be moving faster than the policy debate. Governments are moving to use the rapidly developing technologies for information gathering, information blocking, and regulation. Simultaneously, the ability to circumvent supposedly secure systems also continues to develop, thereby providing a continuous challenge to the state. In this context, freedom of communications and civil liberties are precariously juxtaposed against the potential of increasing state control.

The blurred boundaries of regulating agencies date to the origins of the internet. The basis of resistance towards excessive control of this medium also has its origins in these beginnings, when the technological and academic origins of the internet gave rise to a reliance on self-regulation and minimal oversight on the part of governments. Most of the early attempts at self-regulation were technical responses to specific problems encountered by the new communications medium. The need for technological compatibility between signals and receivers was the impulse underlying standardization and eventually influencing the structuring of national, regional and global governance arrangements. Protocols governing the use of such technologies have ensured that information flows across national boundaries were in some measure regulated and controlled. As time progressed, legal responses applicable to proprietary commercial services, such as contract disputes and other specific matters were gradually developed. The impetus to formulate policies that would embrace the global net was still in its infancy and it is only the rapid growth of net technology, the ever-expanding user base, and the resulting regulatory challenges that created a need for a broader regulatory framework.[3]

---

2   Robert O. Keohane and Joseph S. Nye, 'Power and Interdependence in the Information Age', *Foreign Affairs*, 77/5 (September/October 1998): 81–94.

3   Edward A. Cavazos and Gavino Morin, *Cyberspace and the Law* (Cambridge, 1997).

The strong forces for global integration and expansion of communication across national borders have raised some compelling issues regarding the structure of controlling institutions in an increasingly integrated environment. The potential for global, regional, and national integration to cut across discrete political systems, ideologies, and cultures, presents extensive new opportunities for evaluating laws, and regulatory and controlling mechanisms and structures which have universal application in a borderless world. A discussion of borders and jurisdiction is central to understanding this issue. The global dimensions of internet management and governance pose a particularly interesting challenge to traditional areas of state sovereignty.

Beginning with the assumption that governance involves standards of regulation, control, and direction, we are faced with the issue of who should set these standards. Traditionally, policy regulation and enforcement have emanated from states. If, however, we were to separate standard-setting from regulation, then we would see that the state has not been the only actor. Standard-setting functions have reposed in both state institutions and in professionally-based organizations where the internet is concerned. Setting technical standards requires the work of technical experts, but it involves much wider issues than just technical ones. Standards often entail major political and economic issues. They are a means of protection and domination. Communications technology confers political advantage to whomever can control it, thereby facilitating and promoting its free use.

The location and sophistication of various elements of technology complicates the task of the policy maker, although they affect the technician somewhat differently. The positioning of satellites, such as the DBS (Direct Broadcasting Satellite) in realms that are not constrained by territorial boundaries, impacts on the ability to block or regulate incoming information.[4] The same holds true for information outflows. Many governments share the fear that unregulated information flows can compromise their ability to influence and govern their populations.

As the populations of the virtual world continue to grow and their exchanges spill over into interactions outside the networked world, one must consider the measures that states do and have taken to control networks. These network-based interactions impact a broad spectrum of social relations, commercial interests, and national security. Policy-makers in this new communications environment are faced with fundamental problems that transcend the earlier emphasis on self regulation, management, and protection of intellectual freedoms. The focus of much of the discussion of the governance of E-space relates to the perceived diminution of the influence of the nation-state and the concomitant rise of local and global initiatives. This premise is at the center of the conflicts surrounding DNS whose global character is often confronted by the national regulations of trademark laws.[5]

---

4   Rachel Anderson, 'Dishing up the Public Interest Programming: Noncommercial Networks on DBS', *The Benton Foundation-Digital Beat Extra* (2000), <http://www.internews.org/articles/2000/082900_benton_dbs.htm>, accessed July 2002.

5   Alexander Gigante, '"Domain-ia": The Growing Tension between the Domain Name System and Trademark Law' in Kahin and Keller (ed.), *Coordinating the Internet* (Cambridge, 1997).

The debate surrounding E-governance is often driven by the premise that there is not only something distinct and unique about the virtual world, but also that its character and its communities give rise to unique challenges which require a separate set of governance structures. Policies relating to censorship, cyber crime, protocols, and legitimate security interests are among the concerns that surround these discussions. The fact that these discussions have taken place against broader concerns about the effects of globalization, and the cooperative dialogues on international policy formulation between state agencies, the private sector, and civil society, have raised hopes that this will set a precedent for broader governance reform.

The growing emphasis on public regulation remains central to the current discussion of governance. As we have noted, the issues of E-governance give rise to a basic question as to whether the world created by new technologies reveals familiar challenges which can be met with existing policies, laws, and enforcement mechanisms, or whether we are looking at something entirely new which requires the development of new structures and new responses. The ultimate challenge facing regulators is how to police a technology-based network whose impact on traditional commerce, social values, and national security, is often generated by the interactions that occur within this environment of virtual reality. The question for analysts is to ascertain whether the existing structures and institutions are up to the challenge of the realm without borders and other traditional lines of demarcation and constraints. The global phenomenon, some argue, requires a global perspective, global institutions, and laws. Others examine the challenges and find them merely variations of existing situations which can be addressed within the structures of the nation-state. On one level, governance may be perceived as a set of 'internalized' controls, and on another level, as 'externalized' control. The protocols put in place by web developers have more in common with the first category, while legislation falls into the second category, without the ability, in many instances, of enforceability.

Internet governance routinely encounters the basic divide that exists between national political and legal imperatives and international priorities and objectives. The dilemmas faced by individual states which have membership in organizations which set international standards mean that they may encounter conflicts between their own rules and those of the supra-national bodies unless they happen to have a convergence of interests at the time. This would call for developing some measure of multilevel governance requiring an agreement regarding the issues that can be handled at the national level and those that would require intervention on a global level. National interests could prevail in the response at one level and would be subsumed in the interests of a wider polity in other instances. From the standpoint of enforcement, national rules clearly stand a better chance of being effective.

Models of a new governance structure would ideally be based on integrative principles, allowing for a wider participation in policy making and in policy implementation. The reorganization of the management structure of governance would involve a recognition that a multidisciplinary group of individuals, administrators, engineers, and visionaries may well need to work together to anticipate future challenges, as well as address ongoing issues. This restructuring would have to acknowledge that coordination would have to be an integral process of governance. There is a definite conflict of interest in internet governance, since the goal is to keep the networks functioning and not to enact so many rules that it cannot function. At the same time, the norms underlying governance differ from state to state and lack of consensual norms greatly inhibits policy formulation, coordination, and implementation. Many governments have begun to recognize some of these issues and have taken the first steps toward more integration in decision-making by appointing committees to achieve this. A common viewpoint among analysts is that, since the internet is a global phenomenon used by a global community, the public institutions responsible for its regulation should be international in scope. The presence of global bodies responsible for setting standards and enforcing international treaties, such as the UPU (Universal Postal Union), WHO (World Health Organization) etc., have often been cited as precedents for the growing need for coordination on global policies likely to impact the publics that lie beyond national boundaries. The Internet Corporation on Assigned Numbers and Names (ICANN) was set up as an unusual collaborative effort between public and private entities to function as an international regulatory body in a flexible, informal, and independent manner.

Responding to the need for a global strategy on internet governance, the World Summit on the Information Society (WSIS) which met in Tunisia in November, 2005, held important discussions on the rights to oversight and control of the internet including issues of freedom of expression, commerce, and information. The centre stage, however, was occupied by technicalities, such as domain name allocation and security against terrorism. The final decision by the negotiators, representing the one hundred plus countries, was to defer to the US control of the DNS system. This resolved for the moment the issue of US domination of this element of a global network, as well as the growing momentum for having some sort of international input and control of the network. A compromise solution left management of the global network in the hands of the US and ICANN, while simultaneously creating an international medium lacking the authority for enforcement, the Internet Governance Forum (IGF), which would engage in broad based policy discussion. A distinction that was emphasized during these deliberations was between 'soft' and 'hard' instruments, since a large proportion of the international guidelines related to the internet fell into the former category. The 'soft' instruments did not have the clear jurisdictional strengths of domestic legislation, but could be a spur for policy makers. Among other advantages cited for continued reliance on 'soft' laws was the opportunity to test out provisions informally without a formal adoption of these laws so that modifications could be made if necessary.[6] Scholars have pointed out that the challenge for drafting international documents of governance is that they would have to be couched in general terms which would be interpreted as the need arose. This could limit the effects of these laws in cases of unique and unanticipated events which are characteristic of the changing technology. The WGIG position took into consideration the fundamental character of ICT, that it was a broad based collaborative process, involving thousands of nodes, individuals and institutions, and that much of it was not proprietary, and neutral. The goal was to maintain these qualities with an emphasis on the effective operation of the network.[7] The issue of

---

6   Working Group on Internet Governance, Background Report, June 2005, pp. 54–55.
7   Ibid., p. 5.

E-governance replaced other items on the agenda, such as the digital divide which has been of concern as inequality of access to the global network continues to dominate the discourse on the future of the internet. Three perspectives dominated the discussion of governance. The first approach emphasized the continuation of self regulation with its emphasis on standardization protocols. The second view called for expanded intervention and control over a broader range of issues by international institutions. A third approach envisaged a visionary transformation driven by the forces of technology convergence that are currently set to transform communications as we know it. Bundling of services would be leading to obsolescence in many areas of broadcasting and communication

If we understand governance exclusively as state-level policy initiatives designed to achieve economic, political and social outcomes within the context of the existing policy framework, then the challenges of internet governance reflect an incomplete grasp of the evolving technology. The technology continues to make physical limitations irrelevant at best. So policy makers have to devise ways to manage a phenomenon that occupies a unique space. The problem often revolves around the institutions that are responsible for developing policy initiatives. The institutional structures and their relations with other regulatory agencies often determine just how much and what kind of recommendations they can make. It is increasingly clear that a fundamental reorganization is needed to effectively manage and govern the digital world. The reorganization would involve restructuring the entire decision making process to enable an accelerated response when needed. The decision making process differs according to the political system in place. Autocratic societies make policy without reference to the wider body politic and achieve speed and consensus by virtue of a doctrinaire process. Democratic societies, on the other hand, are relatively inclusive in setting policy and invest both time and effort into consultation, committee, hearings, and legislation. The interests and opinions of the public, interest groups, corporations, and other interested parties are included in making a final pronouncement. The result is often fair, but the process is slow and does not keep pace with the rapidly emerging threats and issues of the digital world. Reconciling the need for inclusiveness with the need for speed may be the ultimate challenge of governance.

The essays in this volume seek to provide an understanding of the internet world and its regulatory environment and the chapters approach the subject from a variety of perspectives and methodologies. The volume is the result of a joint undertaking by the Center for Security Studies at ETH Zurich and the Comparative Interdisciplinary Studies Section of the International Studies Association. The contributors to this volume have undertaken to explore the subject in a systematic and innovative manner.

Jamal Shahin's chapter begins with the assumption that, notwithstanding the transnational environment brought about by the information revolution, governments have been successful in maintaining their place in the new scheme of things. Examining E-governance within the framework of the discussion of the fundamental concept of governance, this analysis concludes by upholding the primacy of the nation-state in this debate on changing institutions in a digitized world.

Alexander Siedschlag argues that the transnational environment of cyberspace has obscured the traditional distinction between policy and execution of policy, or as he observes, 'between deliberation in terms of communication and decision-making in terms of action' thereby complicating the discourse and requiring us to re-examine the traditional concepts and tools of analysis. His examination of 'digital democracy' is presented in terms of a paradigm that transcends the divide between the virtual and the real and enables us to theorize more effectively. Focusing his argument around the main models of democracy associated with the internet, he explores the notion of E-publics and other transnational phenomena that continue to be analyzed with the context of an international system.

Mika Hayashi's essay approaches the subject of cyber governance from a legal perspective and examines the relevance of rules of jurisdiction developed in a territorially based environment to the borderless world created by the cyber revolution. She places her analysis within the context of the existing rules of jurisdiction in general international law, citing cases where extraterritorial principles have prevailed. Hayashi examines two classes of rules of jurisdiction, those reflected in general principles of international law and those found in treaties. Her argument revolves around whether the existing rules are retained in the context of cyber-crime (both civil and criminal), or whether they have they been modified. She concludes that the relevance of domestic law still dominates the discourse, notwithstanding developments such as the Cybercrime Convention which was organized as a universal instrument regulating cyberspace. Her assessment reinforces the common thread that runs through the chapters in this volume, namely that the role of the state has not substantively changed in response to the unique challenges posed by the borderless environment created by the information revolution.

Dirk Lehmkuhl's chapter introduces the concept of jurisdiction to compare the national approaches to protect trademarks with the movement towards having an internationally regulated system of internet domain names. In support of his approach, Lehmkuhl examines the concept of governance from three perspectives, the setting of rules, the sanctioning of rules, and the enforcement of rules, especially as they relate to the intellectual property disputes that characterize the issues of cyberspace. While trade names are usually issued according to national principles, the internet's structural design often goes beyond the governance boundaries related to national and territorial principles and, as in the case of the domain name system, requires a universal rule. By raising the issue of jurisdictional conflict, Lehmkuhl introduces the differing objectives between public and private actors at the international and the national level.

Ralf Bendrath's empirical study of the changing role of the state in cyberspace reinforces his thesis that the borderless world of the internet presents challenges to the structures of governance and contributes to their transformation. His analysis of cyber-data protection beginning in the 1980s, leads him to the conclusion that an increase of state regulation is counterbalanced by public participation in the development of policy and governance structures. He also notes that there is a synergistic confluence of state-regulation, private-public partnerships, and private self-regulation. His analysis supports the claim that globalization may have helped to elucidate the emerging role of the state as an influential actor in a multidimensional regulatory environment. The chapter emphasizes the interdependence and reliance of the state on other actors and exemplifies the complexity underlying the global governance debate. Bendrath observes that the predilection for global regulatory structures in Europe, contrasted with the self-governance approach favored in the United States which has dominated the regulatory dialogue, has given place to the current thinking of a more realistic state which recognizes that it can be most effective by opting for a more complex and multidimensional approach.

In the concluding chapter, Myriam Dunn and Victor Mauer expand upon a number of issues touched on in the volume, reinforcing the viewpoint that E-governance should not be seen as distinctive in itself, but rather as a variation of existing governance mechanisms. They emphasize the adaptation occurring within traditional governance policy in response to the forces of technological change and conclude that the nation-state continues to endure as a power player in the globalized world.

The authors collectively recognize that the changing global environment, which has facilitated the information revolution is simultaneously being shaped by it and conclude that problems of governance continue to be addressed by the institutional structures that are in place.

Bibliography

Anderson, Rachel. 'Dishing up the Public Interest Programming: Noncommercial Networks on DBS', *The Benton Foundation-Digital Beat Extra* (2000), <http://www.benton.org/news/extra/pm082900.html>, accessed 17 January 2007.

Cavazos, Edward A. and Gavino Morin, *Cyberspace and the Law* (Cambridge: Cambridge University Press, 1997).

Gigante, Alexander. '"Domain-ia": The Growing Tension between the Domain Name System and Trademark Law' in Kahin and Keller (ed.), *Coordinating the Internet* (Cambridge: Cambridge University Press, 1997).

Keohane, Robert O. and Nye, Joseph S. Jr., 'Power and Interdependence in the Information Age', *Foreign Affairs* 77/5 (September/October 1998): 81–94.

Tehan, Rita. *Spinning the Web: The History and Infrastructure of the Internet* Congressional Research Service Report 98- 649C (Washington, 1999).

Working Group on Internet Governance, Background Report, June 2005, <http://www.itu.int/wsis/wgig/docs/wgig-background-report.pdf>, accessed 17 January 2007.

Chapter 1

The Reassertion of the State: Governance and the Information Revolution

Jamal Shahin

Introduction

This chapter outlines a framework for understanding the role of the state in international affairs in the context of the information revolution. By looking at three main understandings of the concept of governance, this chapter will show that the information revolution has yet to live up to the promise of disintegrating national boundaries and borders. Despite the fact that the world has indeed 'changed' in many ways, this chapter reveals that governments have found ways to ensure that the nation state remains crucially important; the case of eGovernment is used to show how the ICT revolution is being garnered by states. The chapter starts with a discussion of governance as a concept, focusing on the main trends in the literature, with a particular focus on the impact of ICTs. This will then be related to the growth in attention by public administrations in eGovernment. Finally, the chapter will conclude with a summary of several issues relating to new conceptions and understandings of governance and their relationship with the information revolution.

Governance – Fuzzy Definitions

Governance is an ambiguous concept. Due to its fuzziness, agreement on a common definition is heavily contested. From a Public Administration perspective, Kooiman *et al* describe it as 'primarily a descriptive and analytical tool...a means through which we can search the pattern in which a particular social and/or political (sub-) system works and in which social forces are at work'.[1] From a political science perspective, governance is about 'steering' organisations.[2] Traditionally, in political science literature[3] the term governance has been identified with 'government', but the notion of government as the sole actor in politics no longer dominates mainstream literature: in the words of Jon Pierre: 'political institutions no longer exercise a

---

1   Jan Kooiman, 'Findings, Speculations and Recommendations', in Kooiman (ed.), *Modern Governance: New Government – Society Interations* (London, 1993), p. 258.

2   Paul Hirst, 'Democracy and Governance', in Pierre (ed.), *Debating Governance: Authority, Steering, and Democracy* (Oxford, 2000).

3   This chapter will not discuss the topic of corporate governance, but will focus particularly on governance issues involving public political institutions.

monopoly of the orchestration of governance.'[4] Governance, in the scope of this chapter, provides the link between politics and policy. In other words, governance is about both formulation and implementation of policy and the manner in which this is carried out. The debates surrounding governance attempt to provide explanations for the processes of change within existing political institutions and their relations with the outside world. Three main theoretical directions lie within this framework for understanding governance, which rely on both domestic and international considerations. This chapter will start by describing and analysing each of these in turn, with special reference to the role of ICT. This will be followed by a discussion on relevant dichotomies in the existing literature concerning the role of the state and the information revolution.

Democratic Governance

The first theoretical debate concerning governance revolves around the relationships between governors and governed. This could be labelled *Democratic Governance*.[5] Within this debate, new interpretations of democratic authority – the right to govern and the legitimate authority to do so – have been investigated.[6] Certain readings of governance literature fit into this definition by critically approaching one of the central activities of the modern liberal democratic state: that of providing democracy.[7] Democratic governance is more about the perceptions of the institutions from the citizens.

Encouraging awareness of the citizen's role in political affairs (or at least the knowledge that participation can make a difference) is one of the central problems of today's democratic systems. This has been called 'the crisis of political participation.'[8] It would seem that the crises in representative democracies such as the member states in the European Union could benefit from new developments in ICTs.[9] In the words of Macpherson: 'the ease of communication and access to information now and in the near future has led some observers to predict that a new public arena or 'agora'

4   Hirst, 'Democracy and Governance', p. 4.

5   Pippa Norris (ed.), *Critical Citizens – Global Support for Democratic Government* (Oxford, 1999).

6   Jens Hoff, Ivan Horrocks and Pieter Tops (eds.), *Democratic Governance and New Technology: Technologically Mediated Innovations in Political Practice in Western Europe*, Routledge/ECPR Series in European Political Science (London, 2000).

7   Hirst, 'Democracy and Governance', pp. 137–50.

8   Cathy Bryan, Roza Tsagarousianou and Damian Tambini, 'Electronic Democracy and the Civic Networking Movement in Context', in Tsagarousianou, Tambini, and Bryan (ed.), *Cyberdemocracy: Technology, Cities and Civic Networks* (London, 1998), p. 3; Richard Huggins, 'The Transformation of Political Audience?', in Axford and Huggins (ed.), *New Media and Politics* (London, 2001), p. 128.

9   Notis Lebessis and John Paterson, 'Evolutions in Governance: What Lessons for the Commission?', (Brussels: Forwards Studies Unit (European Commission), 1999); Agnes Hubert and Benedicte Caremier, *Democracy and the Information Society in Europe* (London, 2000); OECD, 'Issues and Developments in Public Management: Survey 1996–1997'.

will emerge to aid collective decision-making'.[10] Hubert and Caremier state: 'New ICTs change things somewhat, in that they offer new possibilities for cohesion and simultaneously further the fragmentation of society', which reveals the precarious nature of democracy in the information age.[11]

Unless states react constructively to the separation of economic and political geographies that is exacerbated by communications technologies, the 'erosion of democracy' becomes apparent.[12] Cerny questions whether 'liberal democracy' is 'realisable in a politically, socially and economically multilayered world characterised by internationalisation, transnationalisation and globalisation.'[13] And this has, to some observers already become apparent.[14]

Others believe that the internet and its associated technologies can have a very revolutionary 'net effect': the prospect of distributed, global communication also affects our notion of the local. Cities can become far more important: as networks develop, there will be central nodes of communication.[15] This is due to the decreasing costs of transmission, decoding and storage of information, which allows for development of distributed, as opposed to centralised or even decentralised, networks of communication.[16]

The roots of the 'technological emancipation' argument, claiming that citizens will evidently benefit from the implementation of new technologies are deep-seated. The Worldwide Web brought the internet into the spotlight in the mid-1990s with its user-friendly interface to the 'information utility' that had been foreseen by J.C.R. Licklider and others. This was firstly a phenomenon that was seen as giving global electronic commerce a gateway to individual users, but there were voices even in the early years of the internet's exponential (and commercial) growth that highlighted the importance of the internet and the Web upon democratic behaviour.[17] In years previous to the popularisation of the internet, other technologies had been accredited with the same status: studies included one on the use of multiple-party telephone lines in an experiment established by Kenneth Laudon, the subject of his book on democratic participation and communications technology.[18] In *The Victorian Internet*, Tom Standage highlights how the Telegraph was used for several

---

10 Michael Macpherson, 'Citizen Politics and the Renewal of Democracy', <http://www.snafu.de/~mjm/CP/cp2.html>.

11 Hubert and Caremier, *Democracy and the Information Society in Europe*, p. 84.

12 Philip G. Cerny, 'Globalization and the Erosion of Democracy', *European Journal of Political Research* 36 (1999): 1.

13 Ibid.: p. 4.

14 See, for example, Noreena Hertz, *The Silent Takeover: Global Capitalism and the Death of Democracy* (London, 2001).

15 Xiudian Dai, 'A New Mode of Governance? Transnationalisation of European Regions and Cities in the Information Age', *Telematics and Informatics*, 20/3 (2003).

16 Leonard Dudley, 'Communications and Economic Growth', *European Economic Review*, 43/3 (1999): p. 603; Paul Baran, 'On Distributed Communications Networks', Paper presented at the IEEE, Hot Springs, VA, November 1964.

17 Mark Poster, 'Cyberdemocracy: Internet and the Public Sphere', <http://www.humanities.uci.edu/mposter/writings/democ.html>.

18 Laudon, *Communications Technology and Democratic Participation*.

tasks, including capturing criminals and performing marriages.[19] The conclusion to be drawn from these examples is that new technologies are considered to offer the *potential* to deliver efficiency of public services to their users. However, the application of Videotex in Canada, and Minitel in France were considered to be of great value to public service delivery and democracy, but either died out or were eventually used for other purposes. Conclusions to be drawn from these applications were that although democracy was aided by such technology, it was also hampered by the limitations of the technology and the reticence of the users of the technology to change.

It seems, thus, that, along with our understanding of changes in government, our understanding of democracy also has the opportunity to evolve with the technological change. It is important here to stress that the idea of creating a 'push-button democracy', where government as well as governance will be carried out online, is not considered valid – it raises issues of possible 'democracy dissolution'.[20] But to imagine this as an ideal type of democracy provides us with a good basis from which to start. Macpherson believes: 'with modern technology it is theoretically possible to allow all citizens to inform themselves about public issues and to vote on them electronically'.[21] This may be theoretically possible, but not entirely desirable. On the contrary, Malerba believes that a blend of existing and new forms of democracy will be created.[22]

Institutional Governance

A different debate in governance studies focus upon *Institutional Governance*. Institutional governance looks from the inside at an institution's ability to govern. This is promulgated primarily by policymakers, who have started to use the term as well: the European Commission's *White Paper on Governance*[23] is one of the starkest expressions of the phenomenon. Likewise, other international organisations such as the OECD and the UN have also started using the term to describe their role in international affairs.[24] In many of these instances 'governance' refers to the acts of increasing legitimacy for existing institutions.[25]

---

19 Tom Standage, *The Victorian Internet: The Remarkable Story of the Telegraph and the Nineteenth Century's Online Pioneers* (London, 1999).

20 Michel Catinat and Thierry Vedel, draft chapter, 15 January 2000.

21 Macpherson, 'Citizen Politics and the Renewal of Democracy.'

22 Franco Malerba, 'Policies for Development and Employment in the Information Society', Paper presented at the XVI European Carrefour of Science and Culture, 15–16 October 1998.

23 Bram Dov Abramson, 'Media Policy after Regulation?', *International Journal of Cultural Studies*, 4/3 (2001).

24 OECD, 'Issues and Developments in Public Management: Survey 1996–1997 (Paris, 1997), Department of Economic and Social Affairs (United Nations), *World Public Sector Report: Globalization and the State 2001* (New York, 2001).

25 Helen Wallace, 'The Institutional Setting: Five Variations on a Theme', in Wallace and Wallace (ed.), *Policy Making in the European Union* (Oxford, 2000); Alberta M. Sbragia,

In the field of global communications, the role of the state still dominates mainstream literature. According to this 'materialist' approach, government is the central actor, dominating through regulation and legislation.[26] Although the infrastructure of global communications has been largely supported by the market, the liberalisation policies that made this possible have been supported by governments, with the recognition that regulation is necessary to ensure efficiency of the market. From such a perspective, one could say that the role of government has become more important as opposed to less: as well as the need to create efficient markets,[27] the question of public access to the technology is raised to ensure 'that sections of the community are not further marginalised and existing educational inequalities magnified'.[28] This topic is not limited to availability of access points, but also related to questions of accessibility: regulators and governments are still busy in the information age.[29] Contrary to the cyber-libertarian belief that the internet, and by extension the Information Society, cannot be regulated by traditional means, the liberalisation of infrastructure and subsequent reliance upon the markets is not the state giving up on regulation, but recognising that markets are more effective at delivering an efficient Information Society. Subsequent efforts to bridge the digital divide and provide computers in schools (for example) reveal that governments are taking action to develop the Information Society.[30] Similarly, content has been subject to varying degrees of regulation, which reflect national preferences for control of communication. Lukasik presents a strong case for governmental action in order to protect the 'global commons', which focuses upon the need for governments to act using varying methods (technical, legislative, regulatory) that will ensure that the infrastructure of public communications remains secure.[31]

Thus, there is some need for strong governmental action in terms of regulation and public service requirements, and even foreign policy. States can enter into agreements to liberalise markets also to protect their economies: this opportunity to rejuvenate the first world's economies and bring other economies into line with them is being taken by states *along with* new actors, such as private authorities and stronger international and regional organisations. One cannot simply announce the

---

'The Dilemma of Governance with Government (New York, 2002); Kooiman, 'Findings, Speculations and Recommendations'; Hirst, 'Democracy and Governance'.

26 Alexander Wendt, *Social Theory of International Politics* (Cambridge, 1999).

27 Stolfi and Sussman, 'Telecommunications and Transnationalism: The Polarization of Social Space'.

28 C. Charlton et al., 'Bringing the Internet to the Community', *Interacting with Computers*, 12/1 (1999): 51; David Zeitlyn, Jane Bex, and Matthew David, 'Access Denied: The Politics of New Communications Media', *Telematics and Informatics*, 15/3 (1998).

29 Thomas and Wyatt, 'Access Is Not the Only Problem: Using and Controlling the Internet'.

30 It is worthwhile noting that the decision to provide Internet access in all schools in the EU's member states emerged from a European Council meeting, which (however) was based on actions taken by individual states Michel Alberganti, 'Internet Pour Tous En Grande–Bretagne,' *Le Monde*, 6 November 1999, Simon Targett and Christopher Price, 'Internet Plan for Schools Unveiled', *Financial Times*, 8 October 1997.

31 Lukasik, 'Protecting the Global Information Commons'.

death of the state. Boundaries still play an important role. This is despite the effects of liberalisation of telecommunications markets, and the effects of global ICTs. Indeed, authors like Hulsink and Davies recognise the 'Janus-faced approach' of national governments towards telecommunications policy, and show that governments try to 'further their nation's particular interest by encouraging the rise of national champions'.[32] Besançon and Kelly have gone as far as to say that the liberalisation of telecommunications markets can help governments in many ways (through tax revenues, for example). There are many other issues touched upon by the growth of global communications; copyright, censorship, privacy, consumer protection, and security are just some of the issues that are raised by the internet, and these have their roots under national jurisdiction.[33]

The 'democratising' aspect of the internet has become a key motive for the deployment of new ICTs by governments in many states. It has been claimed that the introduction of the Worldwide Web and other applications will help empower citizens, rendering governments more accountable to their electorates and also increasing efficiency across the entire spectrum of government operations. However, the discussion on the changing face of public administration and democracy is sidelined, in the main, by the focus on increasing efficiency in public services that is clearly apparent in the eGovernment agenda. In doing so, governments are ignoring the broader questions raised by digital networks and are focusing on how to revive their own institutions.

Governance as a Mode of Coordination

The previous two directions in governance literature reveal that governance is indeed a moving target, but try to show how traditional understandings of the state and its responsibilities are treated within the contemporary literature. Another approach to understanding governance has been proposed, which treats the concept not as an action or a process in the traditional sense, but as a 'mode of coordination.'[34] This tries to avoid the normative aspects of the steering present in the previously mentioned definitions, and tries to introduce ideas of a crucial, but lesser role for governments in controlling states. The previous two approaches to the concept of governance focus on processes within, and actions of, institutions, which naturally identify a goal that is implicitly or explicitly derived from norms. Using governance to describe and analyse modes of coordination avoids such normative and ontologically biased presuppositions and enables an analysis of governance patterns that does not naturally reify either democratic principles or the role of institutions.

---

32 Willem Hulsink and Andrew Davies, 'The Emergence of National Champions in Global Telecommunications', *Telematics and Informatics*, 14/4 (1997): 356.

33 Laurent Besançon and Tim Kelly, 'Telecom Privatisations: The New Realism? (Geneva, 1996).

34 Renate Mayntz, 'Governing Failures and the Problem of Governability: Some Comments on a Political Paradigm', in Kooiman (ed.), *Modern Governance: New Government – Society Interations* (London, 1993), p. 11.

This understanding of governance as a mode of coordination requires us to rethink our understanding of political institutions. One example of a new approach towards this is provided by Ruggie, who described how the notion of 'unbundled territory' is useful for understanding the role of modern transformations in political institutions. 'Unbundling' territory has profound consequences for the understanding the notion of authority in both political and economic spheres.[35] Reinicke builds upon Ruggie's arguments, and uses the notion of unbundled territory to create a framework for understanding and explaining the role of the state in a globalised environment. The framework distinguishes between internal and external sovereignty, which enables creation of a scenario where the 'implications of globalisation for public policymaking…will be path-dependent and thus mediated by the primary form of political organisation in the world today; the modern and territorial democratic state'.[36] Thus even in a global environment, states will be the predominant arbiters of regulation. However, Reinicke sees that the only way for governments to achieve internal sovereignty 'is to pool, and thus share, internal sovereignty in those sectors in which globalisation has undermined the effectiveness and efficiency of internal sovereignty at the national level.'[37] This is making use of a mode of coordination on an international level.

Other actors are now increasingly important in decision-making processes at national and international levels. Ronit, for example, describes the role of private organisations in a framework of globalisation.[38] Claiming that the discussion over whether the state loses power or not is difficult to measure, Ronit looks to other forms of influence on global policymaking, such as civil society and private authority. These organised bodies provide substantial input into global governance, through self-regulation. This growth in private actors has also happened in the development of the Information Society. The future development of the internet, after intense interest from the commercial sector has meant that the societal aspects of the internet are generally subjugated to those of commercial concern, even by public administrations and governments. However the result of this apparent contradiction has been the increased involvement of commercial actors in social, cultural, and political issues,[39] and a decline in the importance of 'politics' for the citizen.

An understanding of the role of the state as the central point of authority in a global, ICT-enriched environment is rendered difficult through an analysis of dominant international relations theory, which causes us to look for answers in other areas. Through use of boundaries, these dominant theories attempt to locate authority at one single point, and yet, this has been shown to be increasingly difficult due to, amongst other factors, the Information Revolution. In effect, the impact of

---

35 John Gerard Ruggie, 'Territoriality and Beyond: Problematizing Modernity in International Relations', *International Organization*, 47/1 (1993): 138–74.

36 Reinicke, *Global Public Policy: Governing without Government?*, p. 53.

37 Ibid., p. 71.

38 Karsten Ronit, 'Institutions of Private Authority in Global Governance: Linking Territorial Forms of Self–Regulation', *Administration & Society*, 33/5 (2001): 557–78.

39 Macgregor Wise, *Exploring Technology and Social Space*, p. 151; Juliet Roper, 'Government, Corporate or Social Power? The Internet as a Tool in the Struggle for Dominance in Public Policy', *Journal of Public Affairs*, 2/3 (2002): 113–24.

ICT broadens the debate from being concerned with rules, regulations, norms, and principles (activities which are established by the state) to one of management, steering, and coordination (processes which can be established by states, but which generally involve other actors as well).

New Debates in Governance

Having laid out three main approaches to the governance debate, the discussion now turns to new issues that have been raised through this, and other relevant literature. One of the central contributions to the governance debate emerges from analysis of the development and deployment of new Information and Communications Technologies (ICTs). Digital technologies, as exemplified by the internet – which at its basic level is simply a network of digital data networks – are redefining the landscape upon which actors play their roles in most economic, social, and political spheres. Brian Loader defines the impact of ICTs as presenting a 'paradigmatic change' in relations between individuals, government and social institutions.[40] These changes are wrought in political, economic, and social spheres.

Inherent in all the recent discussions on governance are notions that several external factors affect, indeed to a large extent limit, contemporary practice of government by public institutions. These have been outlined by Pierre as an 'overburdened' mechanism of government, lack of financial power to maintain the (overburdened) public sector, problems of coordination, and the impact of globalisation.[41] Combined, these have led to questions such as: 'what new forms and shapes the pursuit of the collective interest can and should take and to what extent we need to rethink the traditional, liberal-democratic model of the state'? [42]

One element common to all these factors described by Pierre and Kooiman, of which a greater understanding may help answer the question posed by Pierre, is the role that technologies such as the internet play in helping shape forms and modes of governance.[43] Technology plays a great, if implicit and still understudied, role in current discussions on governance and the role of governments. Mathews states: 'The most powerful engine of change in the relative decline of states and the rise of nonstate actors is the computer and telecommunications revolution, whose deep political and social consequences have been almost completely ignored.'[44]

A wealth of critical literature on the impact of ICTs on society emerged around the time that the internet became popular.[45] There were some general themes

---

40 Brian D. Loader (ed.), *The Governance of Cyberspace* (London, 1997), p. 1.

41 Hirst, 'Democracy and Governance', p. 4.

42 Ibid., p. 5. See also Jan Kooiman, 'Governance and Governability: Using Complexity, Dynamics and Diversity', in Kooiman (ed.), *Modern Governance: New Government – Society Interactions* (London, 1993), p. 35.

43 Susan Strange, *The Retreat of the State: The Diffusion of Power in the World Economy* (Cambridge, UK, 1996), pp. 100–109.

44 Jessica T. Mathews, 'Power Shift', *Foreign Affairs*, 76/1 (1997).

45 Herbert S. Dordick and Georgette Wang, *The Information Society: A Retrospective View* (London, 1993); Webster, *Theories of the Information Society*; Gordon Graham, *The*

emerging from these debates which can be broadly divided into institutional[46] and democratic governance[47] 'camps'. These have been used to analyse and influence policies implemented towards use of the internet in society and particularly in political institutions. These studies attempt to understand where and how policies and institutions are located in domestic and international interactions. This literature identifies, in many cases, a complete change in societal interactions, and in others, it highlights continuity in social and political relations despite the profound change in patterns of communication.

Networks vs. Hierarchies

Notions of hierarchies in politics have to some extent been replaced by the discourse of packet-switched networks, connectivity, interactivity, digital media and hypertextuality.[48] Do these shifts from hierarchies to networks and from the Industrial to the Information Society lead to the decline of the governing capabilities of existing institutions? The environment in which government-organised activities take place is much evolved, and it is easy to believe some commentators when they question the future feasibility of current institutional structures. Despite the fact that policies and initiatives are established by national governments, legislation, and regulation are struggling to keep up with technology. States and governments 'are responding to the increasing permeability of borders, even though they are complicit in bringing it about'.[49] The logic of global free markets appears to be a

Internet:// a Philosophical Inquiry (London, 1999). Notable works had been written on earlier technologies and their impact on society and state relations, both in domestic and international politics: Ithiel De Sola Pool, *Technologies of Freedom: On Free Speech in an Electronic Age* (Cambridge, 1983); John Gerard Ruggie, 'International Responses to Technology: Concepts and Trends', *International Organization*, 29/3 (1975).

46 Saskia Sassen, 'Digital Networks and the State: Some Governance Questions', *Theory, Culture & Society*, 17/4 (2000); Robin Mansell (ed.), *Inside the Communication Revolution – Evolving Patterns of Social and Technical Interaction* (Oxford, 2002); Christopher May, *The Information Society: A Sceptical View* (Cambridge, 2002); William Dutton (ed.), *Society on the Line – Information Politics in the Digital Age* (Oxford, 1999); Robin Mansell, 'Communication by Design?' in Mansell and Silverstone (ed.), *Communication by Design: The Politics of Information and Communication Technologies* (Oxford, 1996); Kubicek, Dutton, and Williams (eds.), *The Social Shaping of Information Superhighways: European and American Roads to the Information Society*.

47 Darin Barney, *Prometheus Wired: The Hope for Democracy in the Age of Network Technology* (Chicago, 2000); Jerry Everard, *Virtual States: The Internet and the Boundaries of the Nation State*, ed. Talalay and Farrands, Technology and the Global Political Economy (London, 2000); Mowlana, *Global Information and World Communication*; Chris Freeman, 'Social Inequality, Technology and Economic Growth', in Wyatt, et al. (ed.), *Technology and in/Equality: Questioning the Information Society*, (London, 2000); John Macgregor Wise, *Exploring Technology and Social Space* (London, 1997).

48 Castells, *The Rise of the Network Society*.

49 Patricia M. Goff, 'Invisible Borders: Economic Liberalisation and National Identity', *International Studies Quarterly*, 44/4 (2000): 534.

self-defeating one.[50] At the international level, Kettl has stated that 'maintaining national sovereignty while effective pursuing international policy has become an increasingly difficult problem'.[51] This is occurring domestically as well. To look to governments for answers to certain questions is increasingly difficult. Concerning the subject of electronic fraud, Jack Straw MP, then Home Secretary in the UK, was quoted as saying 'we're using 19th Century tools to face a 21st Century problem.'[52] Perhaps he could have said that we are using 19th Century *institutions* to deal with a 21st Century problem.

In contrast, Monroe Price highlights the role of a state's foreign and domestic policy in managing global media, particularly in areas of content regulation.[53] Lukasik goes further, claiming that the internet 'is a domain for the exercise of sovereignty'.[54] The author outlines action to protect the global information commons, recommending that sovereign states take co-operative and competitive postures to ensure the stability of the global information commons.[55] The thrust of Lukasik's argument is that states can take action unilaterally as well as multilaterally to ensure that the stability of the internet (and thus the Information Society) is ensured. These actions are firmly rooted in international law.[56] However, Lukasik does maintain that alongside sovereign state activity, there are also specific roles for private organisations to undertake. Another commentator, David Rothkopf presents the tensions between state and market in the information age from a realist perspective.[57]

Zacher highlights the role of technology in creating emergent regimes, which subsequently contribute to the decay of the 'Westphalian temple' of state sovereignty.[58] These regimes are based upon authority accorded by the state, but often contribute to the decline of state autonomy in the international system. This understanding of global governance as a network relies not only upon the state as an important actor, but places the state within a network context. In other words, this network contains many other actors, as well as the state.

The concept of authority is challenged by the creation of these global markets which are, in part, facilitated by the development of digital networks. Authority

---

50 Wolfgang H. Reinicke, *Global Public Policy: Governing without Government?* (Washington, 1998).

51 Donald F. Kettl, 'The Transformation of Governance: Globalization, Devolution, and the Role of Government', *Public Administration Review*, 60/6 (2000): 489.

52 Clifford Krauss, '8 Countries Join in an Effort to Catch Computer Criminals,' *New York Times*, 11 December 1997.

53 Monroe E. Price, *Media and Sovereignty: The Global Information Revolution and Its Challenge to State Power* (Cambridge, 2002).

54 Stephen J. Lukasik, 'Protecting the Global Information Commons', *Telecommunications Policy*, 24/6–7 (2000): 519.

55 Ibid.: p. 520.

56 Ibid.: pp. 524–25.

57 David J. Rothkopf, 'Cyberpolitik: The Changing Nature of Power in the Information Age', *Journal of International Affairs*, 51/2 (1998): 341.

58 Mark W. Zacher, 'The Decaying Pillars of the Westphalian Temple: Implications for International Order and Governance', in Rosenau and Czempiel (ed.), *Governance without Government: Order and Change in World Politics* (Cambridge, 1992), p. 63.

'involves the surrender of private judgment and the recognition of the right to rule,'[59] and it is the state's right to rule that has been challenged in recent years, in part by the consequences of the internet's development along commercial lines.[60] The establishment of recognised authority is a crucial antecedent of any governance mechanism. As Baer notes, 'governance of the GII [Global Information Infrastructure] seems one element of a larger shift of authority from the political to the economic realm.'[61] The characteristics of the internet provide a concrete example of a shift in our understanding of the source of authority in the international arena.[62]

As with most technological developments, there is another opportunity provided by communications technologies. They can also act as a force for greater democratisation.[63] Using new technologies, interest groups dispersed over distances and beyond borders can communicate: more effectively than before.[64] Use of the internet by virtual communities, both those involved in policymaking and social activities, has reinforced the network as a basis for institution-building. As Powell notes, 'networks are particularly apt for circumstances in which there is need for efficient, reliable information. [...] The open-ended relational features of networks, with their relative absence of explicit *quid pro quo* behaviour, greatly enhance the ability to transmit and learn new knowledge and skills.'[65] Thus, in the digital age where information and knowledge are considered central, networks also present appropriate mechanisms for organisation of economic, social, and political interactions based upon knowledge and information: these are central to increasing legitimacy and efficiency. This change in communication paradigm has broad consequences for society as a whole, and particularly in the way that states organise governance.[66] 'Connexity' – defined as 'a new intensity of connections...[which] is forcing itself on to public consciousness through everything from global warming and the internet, to ever more intensive arguments about the virtues and vices of free trade' – describes one of the early ways of thinking about this change.[67] Transformation

---

59 A. Claire Cutler, 'Locating 'Authority' in the Global Political Economy', *International Studies Quarterly*, 43/1 (1999): 63.

60 Peter McMahon, *Global Control: Information Technology and Globalization since 1845* (Cheltenham, 2002).

61 Walter S. Baer, 'Will the Global Information Infrastructure Need Transnational (or Any) Governance', <http://www.rand.org/pubs/reprints/RP603/>.

62 Stephen J. Kobrin, 'Back to the Future: Neomedievalism and the Postmodern Digital World Economy', *Journal of International Affairs*, 51/2 (1998): 370–5.

63 Laudon Kenneth C Laudon, *Communications Technology and Democratic Participation*, Praeger Special Studies (New York, 1977) and Ferdinand Peter Ferdinand (ed.), *The Internet, Democracy and Democratization* (London, 2000) examine the arguments for use of ICTs in greater detail.

64 Wise, *Exploring Technology and Social Space*, p. 141.

65 Walter W. Powell, 'Neither Market nor Hierarchy: Network Forms of Organisation', in Thompson, et al. (ed.), *Markets, Hierarchies and Networks: The Coordination of Social Life* (London, 1991), p. 272.

66 Hamid Mowlana, *Global Information and World Communication: New Frontiers in International Relations*, 2nd ed. (London, 1997).

67 Geoff Mulgan, *Connexity: How to Live in a Connected World* (London, 1997), p. 3.

from hierarchical models of information provision to more distributed and even decentralised information sources leads to a questioning of authoritativeness and a 'demassification' of the mass media.[68]

The amount of information disseminated over the networks comprising the internet, at increasing speeds and decreasing costs, are 'reshaping the landscape of politics and international relations... and altering policy formulation and implementation.'[69] Effectively, traditional boundaries of domestic and international, often reified in dominant discourse, are being subsumed into networks that disregard territory and hierarchy as the most important driving principles. Governance of networks is emerging as a layer above and intertwined with older mechanisms for policymaking and politics.

New vs. Old Economy

The 'new economy' is highly dependent upon the creation and development of the digital networks that supposedly disregard territory and geography. This is defined by the OECD as showing some central characteristics: 'strong non-inflationary growth, low unemployment, a rapidly increasing role for ICTs, still-high stock-market valuations, particularly in the hi-tech sector, and continued restructuring of enterprises and markets'.[70] However, the impact of ICTs does not appear to have a similar impact on all national economies; the OECD notes large divergences between various countries. The main beneficiary of the development of the internet appeared to be the United States, where, 'since 1995 economic growth [...] has been partially driven by the commercialisation of the internet.'[71] On the other hand, it has been stated that the rolling out of digital networks worldwide would provide an opportunity for the developing world to participate in global economic relations.[72] Freeman and Louçã [73] show that the impact of networking on traditional economies has allowed the reorganisation of firms; citing Castells, they identify the basic unit of economic organisation as the '*network* composed of a variety of organisations. The 'glue' that holds the networks together is the 'spirit of information' itself'.[74] ICTs can 'bring about new opportunities for economic growth. New markets, new products, and new services are being created bringing with them new sources of

---

68 John Seely Brown and Paul Duguid, *The Social Life of Information* (Boston, 2000).

69 Mark W. Zacher, 'Capitalism, Technology, and Liberalization: The International Telecommunications Regime, 1865–1998', in Rosenau and Singh (ed.), *Information Technologies and Global Politics: The Changing Scope of Power and Governance* (Albany NY, 2002), p. 39.

70 OECD, 'Is There a New Economy? First Report on the OECD Growth Project' (Paris, 2000), p. 3.

71 Gordon L. Brady, 'The Internet, Economic Growth and Governance', *Economic Affairs*, 20/1 (2000): 13.

72 L. Press, 'The Role of Computer Networks in Development', *Communications of the ACM*, 39/2 (1996).

73 Chris Freeman and Francisco Louçã, *As Time Goes by – from the Industrial Revolutions to the Information Revolution* (New York, 2002).

74 Ibid., p. 326.

revenue'.[75]Furthermore, the consequences of the shift towards an 'e-conomy' will dramatically change the political sociology of communities of all kinds: 'indeed [we are told], the changes underway have the potential to radically change the very configuration and orchestration of social and political life.'[76]

In fact, the role of the information revolution in helping promote a 'new economy' is contested; the concept of a new economy is also under debate. Much of the discussion, as highlighted by the title of the OECD's report cited above (which raised the question *Is There A New Economy?* rather than stating that there is a new economy) is speculation. At the local level, the implications of digital networks may even be damaging: Charles Steinfeld and Pamela Whitten present the need for a research agenda that uncovers the community level impacts of electronic commerce.[77] And at the international level, the impact of new ICTs may not be as dramatic as we often hear: Grahame Thompson provides a critical analysis of the adherents of the profound change in the economy due to the development of digital networks (in particular, the internet), claiming that in terms of international trade, we are merely witnessing a 'new configuration of the system that was first established in the seventeenth century'.[78] Similarly, the impact of the internet is seen as leading not to greater competition, but concentration.[79] One of the most prominent aspects of the new economy, the widening of free markets, has been shown not to have a direct cause-effect relationship with the new economy in the telecommunications sector in research carried out in Europe.[80]

Furthermore, implementation of ICTs does not automatically incur economic competitiveness. The growth of new ICTs also raises new challenges for economic growth, particularly in the area of employment and skills, and these need to be governed effectively. Although Freeman agrees with 'those economists and technologists who saw in computer technology, information technology and the internet an enormous potential for new employment and a new wave of high investment and high growth' he states, 'all previous experience shows that when a new pervasive technology

---

75 Robin Mansell and Uta Wehn, 'Innovative 'Knowledge Societies' – Consequences of ICT Strategies', in Mansell and Wehn (ed.), *Knowledge Societies – Information Technology for Sustainable Development* (Oxford, 1998), p. 242.

76 John Zysman and Stephen Weber, 'Governance and Politics of the Internet Economy: Historical Transformation or Ordinary Politics with a New Vocabulary?', *BRIE Working Paper* (Berkeley, 2001), p. 20.

77 Charles Steinfeld and Pamela Whitten, 'Community Level Socio–Economic Impacts of Electronic Commerce', *Journal of Computer Mediated Communication*, 5/2 (1999).

78 Grahame Thompson, 'Networks of Complexity? Network Theory, International Economic Networks and the Development of ICTs', Paper presented at the EAEPE 2002: Complexity and the Economy, Aix-en-Provence, 7–10 November 2002, p. 17.

79 Andrew Graham, 'The Assessment: Economics of the Internet', *Oxford Review of Economic Policy*, 17/2 (2001).

80 Marc Bogdanowicz, 'The Social Impacts of Telecom Liberalisation in Europe. The Productivity Gains Hypothesis: How Do Corporate Users React?', *Telematics and Informatics*, 14/4 (1997). See also F. Stolfi and G. Sussman, 'Telecommunications and Transnationalism: The Polarization of Social Space', *The Information Society*, 17/1 (2001), who examine deregulation in the US.

enters the economic system, it can do so only after a prolonged social process of learning, reform and adaptation of old institutions.'[81] Whilst the creation of new jobs is apparent, the threat of jobs disappearing due to the impact of global, digital technologies is also of concern.[82] Similarly, as technology develops, users are still required to carry out aspects of work requiring human interaction, such as in the telecentre. This work often does not require highly-skilled personnel, and the development of further inequalities in the workplace are all too prominent.[83] 'The existence of the internet has not suspended the normal ways in which organisations operate,'[84] and instead of bringing the expected cost reductions, the internet might be responsible for a rise in these costs: certain activities need more skills, which become more expensive the more they are in demand.

Recognising that governments cannot govern the free markets of global commerce alone has led to partnerships between governments and businesses as governments try to maintain their role in some way. Liberalisation of the telecommunication sector provides a good example; this turned the tables on traditional client-producer relationships between government and users of telecommunications services. However, government did not disappear: it emerged as the main player in determining policy for the sector in which these companies now operated, and as one of the major users of telecommunication services.

In order to cope with the changes in the economy brought on by developments in digital networks, governments and other actors have developed new approaches to governance to ensure economic survival and to aspire towards economic prosperity. Institutional change is necessary to enact these changes: looking to what Geoffrey Hodgson calls the 'Creative Society', the author has outlined the argument that current policies do not go far enough to deal with the increasing complexity of society that is, to a large extent, brought on by technological developments.[85] In the field of telecommunications, Eli Noam recognises that a shift is required in telecommunications policy to 'assure an integration that permits the functioning of the emerging 'network of networks.''[86] Abramson notes that a shift in regulatory regimes has occurred in the context of media regulation: 'the state's regulatory

---

81 Graham Thomas and Sally Wyatt, 'Access Is Not the Only Problem: Using and Controlling the Internet', in Wyatt, et al. (ed.), *Technology and in/Equality: Questioning the Information Society* (London, 2000), pp. 159–60. The fact that one of the earliest applications of the new 'coordination' form of EU governance was in the sphere of employment is telling.

82 Peter Fleissner and Wolfgang Hofkirchner, 'The Making of the Information Society: Driving Forces, 'Leitbilder' and the Imperative for Survival', *Biosystems*, 46/1–2 (1998): 203.

83 Gavin Poynter and Alvaro De Miranda, 'Inequality, Work and Technology in the Services Sector', in Wyatt, et al. (ed.), *Technology and in/Equality: Questioning the Information Society* (London, 2000).

84 Graham, 'The Assessment: Economics of the Internet', p. 150.

85 Hodgson, 'Socio–Economic Consequences of the Advance of Complexity and Knowledge'.

86 Eli M. Noam, 'Principles for the Communications Act of 2034: The Superstructure of Infrastructure', *Federal Communications Law Journal*, 47/2 (1994).

role does not shrivel into nothing… But it shifts.'[87] This has been carried out by government under the guise of the so-called 'Promotional State'. Government itself sees its role as changing due to the impact of new technologies.[88]

There is a stronger argument to challenge the transformatory power of the information revolution, which is far more subtle. Whereas, in some respects, policy actions towards global commerce, at least in the Western world, seemed to be converging towards the 'new economy' and the free market, policies that deal with the internet and its associated technologies and services are also revealing particular national (and Europe-wide, but not global) responses, such as in the areas of employment policy and content regulation. Whereas certain borders might be dissolving, other borders based on cultural lines, are being created.[89] Despite the global environment, regulation is being implemented along these borderlines. In areas such as employment policy and content regulation, global activities towards the Information Society are not sustainable or desirable: this highlights the need for a study of regional responses, as opposed to one homogenous, global approach to the impact of ICTs.[90] The state provides the only mechanism allowing enforcement of such protections at present, as can be seen in Germany and the UK, where curbing of libellous material and pornography was tried through means of holding internet Service Providers responsible for the material posted on their servers.[91]

Therefore, technology is not just an independent variable in the governance matrix: it is also shaped by existing and new mechanisms of governance. Despite the role of new ICTs in introducing new actors and possibilities for action across space not bounded by territory and hierarchy, a distinction between domestic and international governance in dominant theoretical discourse remains. Territory and hierarchy are still important considerations in mainstream literature on the issue of governance: the development of the internet does not render these analyses useless. As Kevin Robins notes: 'the institutions developing and promoting the new technologies exist solidly in this world.'[92] With this in mind, it is important to understand the relationship between 'new' and 'old' forms of governance.

What is clear, however, is that governments are currently trying to 'find their feet' in the new environment in which they are placed, where they are not the only actors in the international and domestic arenas. The developments in our understanding of gover*nance* as opposed to govern*ment* are brought to light by digital networks such as the internet, and the subsequent blurring of many boundaries that emerge from application of such a technology. The internet has contributed to this debate on traditional explanations of international relations by re-presenting the paradox

---

87 Abramson, 'Media Policy after Regulation?' p. 316.

88 Ira C. Magaziner, 'The Framework for Global Electronic Commerce: A Policy Perspective', *Journal of Common Market Studies*, 51/2 (1998): 535.

89 Goff, 'Invisible Borders: Economic Liberalisation and National Identity'.

90 Shalini Venturelli, 'Inventing E–Regulation in the US, EU and East Asia: Conflicting Social Visions of the Information Society', *Telematics and Informatics*, 19/2 (2002).

91 Peter Norman, 'Concern at German Internet Verdict', *Financial Times*, 29 May 1998; Ian Burrel, 'Ministers Plan Internet Curb', *The Independent*, 25 June 1998.

92 Kevin Robins, 'Cyberspace and the World We Live In', in Dovey (ed.), *Fractal Dreams: New Media in Social Context* (London, 1996), p. 3.

of state action in global markets; in public administration, technology has provided an opportunity to re-examine the effectiveness of policymaking and policy implementation by the state. It no longer makes sense to focus upon the state or on state-based solutions to problems of global or domestic governance.

The other extreme is also not a feasible scenario for the future. Digital networking and changing communication paradigms do not automatically lead to the development of a democratic utopia based on an individual citizen's needs, rather than governmental desires. In fact quite the opposite is seen to happen according to Sassen, who claims that geography is changing, but not dispersing: 'the growing digitalisation and globalisation of leading economic sectors has further contributed to the hyper-concentration of resources, infrastructure, and central functions, with global cities as one strategic site in the new global economic network.'[93] Perhaps governments are still necessary institutions after all.

eGovernment and the State

The goals of the eGovernment agenda reflect the concerns of the perceived malaise in Western-style democracies regarding citizen trust and democratic participation in political institutions. The motivation for development of eGovernment programmes is thus politically oriented. It should be viewed separately from the implementation process that is inherently technological. The goals of many eGovernment initiatives outline the need for this separation. These have been ambitious in some cases, attempting to turn government 'inside out' and 'upside down' in order to rectify this perception of failing institutions,[94] and thereby challenging the Weberian notion of government as a hierarchical bureaucracy.[95] Traditionally, government departments worked in relative isolation to each other, whereas now, prevailing ideology from the eGovernment 'camp' wishes to show that government is one single entity. This makes it easier for citizens to contact their public administrations.

Much of the literature has alluded to the need to redesign institutions to improve the way in which governments can and should serve the needs of their citizens.[96] Governments are required to be more responsive to these needs, and are expected to respond to the changing demands that citizens have of their public administrations. Modern governments should be able to harness the new opportunities for better

---

93 Saskia Sassen, *Globalization and Its Discontents: Essays on the New Mobility of People and Money* (New York, 1998), p. 191.

94 Robert B. Denhardt, 'The Future of Public Administration', *Public Administration and Management*, 4/2 (1999).

95 Alfred Tat–Kei Ho, 'Reinventing Local Governments and the E-Government Initiative', *Public Administration Review*, 62/4 (2002): 435.

96 Robert D. Behn, 'The New Public Management Paradigm and the Search for Democratic Accountability', *International Public Management Journal*, 1/2 (1998); OECD, 'The E-Government Imperative: Main Findings' (Paris, 2003); Tat–Kei Ho, 'Reinventing Local Governments and the E-Government Initiative', Lawrence Pratchett, 'New Technologies and the Modernization of Local Government: An Analysis of Biases and Constraints', *Public Administration*, 77/4 (1999).

interaction with citizens through use of new communications channels such as the internet.

Much has been written on the role of governance in the place of traditional forms of government from a public management perspective.[97] This literature focuses upon the evolving role of the state in terms of public policy provision in a changed and changing world, which has followed two courses: globalisation and localisation. The focus in some of the literature has revolved around changing patterns of policymaking and political organisation at the national level. Kettl has claimed that 'Government has come to rely heavily on for-profit and non-profit organisations for delivering goods and services ranging from anti-missile systems to welfare reform', which has led to layering 'new challenges on top of the traditional institutions and their processes.'[98]

The focus upon technology has been apparent when examining the role of the internet and other ICTs in changing governance. The parameters of the debate are not about the need to readdress the discussion over the role of government but about the role of technology in improving current activity. Therefore, it is worthwhile to seek inspiration from outside of the technology-driven literature to examine how mainstream public administration literature deals with change. In an article written in 1995, Peter Drucker highlighted the need to reinvent government.[99] Drucker's critique of the Clinton administration's efforts to carry out a National Performance Review (NPR), whose name was later changed to the National Partnership for Reinventing Government (also with the acronym NPR), claims that it was 'trying to patch and to spot-weld, here, there, and yonder – and that never accomplishes anything.'[100]

Reinventing government has been given other titles in different countries: 'Joined-up Government' in the UK and 'In the Service of Democracy' in the Netherlands.[101] The common thread driving all these initiatives can be found in OECD literature, where the issue became prominent around the turn of the century.[102] These tend to look at the role of national government as a facilitator, or a coordinator, of many activities, rather than the central, sole, point of authority. Decentralisation of political

---

97 Mark Bevir, Rod A. W. Rhodes, and Patrick Weller, 'Traditions of Governance: Interpreting the Changing Role of the Public Sector', *Public Administration*, 81/1 (2003); Peter F. Drucker, *Post-Capitalist Society* (New York, 1994); Peter F. Drucker, 'Really Reinventing Government,' *The Atlantic Monthly*, February 1995; Kettl, 'The Transformation of Governance: Globalization, Devolution, and the Role of Government'; Rod A. W. Rhodes, *Understanding Governance: Policy Networks, Governance, Reflexivity and Accountability*, ed. Rhodes, Public and Policy Management (Buckingham, 1997).

98 Kettl, 'The Transformation of Governance: Globalization, Devolution, and the Role of Government', p. 488.

99 Drucker, 'Really Reinventing Government.'

100 Ibid.

101 Christopher Pollitt, 'Joined-up Government: A Survey', *Political Studies Review*, 1/1 (2003); Dennis Kavanagh and David Richards, 'Departmentalism and Joined–up Government: Back to the Future?', *Parliamentary Affairs*, 54/1 (2001).

102 See, for example, OECD, 'Impact of the Emerging Information Society on the Policy Development Process and Democratic Quality' (Paris, 1998).

activity in certain countries, and a resurgence in the ideas of the 'local' are testament to this.

From the traditional perspective of public administration, the impact of the internet upon the creation of *new* political arenas is limited, given that their discourse relates to the performance of these existing institutions. Whilst much was made of the creation of public agorae in cyberspace,[103] the need for concrete realities to these spaces is now seen as apparent. Although the internet does provide a new channel of communication, the ramifications for not-yet-existing political institutions are unclear, and new institutions are not likely to emerge for a while. This is especially apparent as governments learn to adopt their own practices to bring cyberspace down to earth. It is, at present, more realistic to talk about current political structures and the relationship between their governance and the internet.

In this context, it must be noted that the roles of traditional governance structures are normatively supported by most eGovernment agendas; the OECD and the EU (*via* the European Council) are both serving the needs and desires of the nation state in regenerating trust in political institutions in the era of the internet. The initiatives developed in the framework of the eGovernment agenda attempt to strengthen the role of existing institutions and mechanisms through use of new technologies. They do not take into account new possibilities to restructure the political system.

The discourse surrounding and supporting the introduction of the internet in governmental organisations contains many assumptions about the way that government should be carried out rather than how technology should be shaped to fit with the aims and ambitions of actors wishing to take full advantage of the new technology to 'improve' governance mechanisms. Institutions are keen to focus on sustaining themselves. Thus, if we were to accept the dominant aims of the eGovernment agenda alone, the internet would simply be one more layer of communication between a government and its citizens; it would be only a tool to enhance the way in which government already communicates with its 'clients'. However, there is another, more fundamental argument that highlights the need for governments to reinvent the way in which they communicate with their electorates. Tat-Kei Ho notes that traditional government bureaucracy is 'often criticised for its rigidity, proceduralism, inefficiency, and incapability to serve "human clients,"'[104] and this has been challenged, in part, by the new eGovernment and eDemocracy agendas. If global communications have a role to play in reviving democratic governance of existing institutions, it is in enhancing democratic practice: '[the] ongoing two-way communication between governors and governed.'[105] Until now, however, the focus has been more administrative. This is a consequence of the natural boundaries that emerged between politics and policymaking. When these issues are viewed through the lens of governance, the divisions no longer make sense.

---

103   Howard Rheingold, 'The Virtual Community: Homesteading on the Electronic Frontier,' <http://www.rheingold.com/vc/book/>.

104   Tat-Kei Ho, 'Reinventing Local Governments and the E–Government Initiative', p. 435.

105   Hirst, 'Democracy and Governance', p. 27.

When considering this revival, it is useful to refer to the example set by the US through its *Access America* (subsequently renamed as *FirstGov*) programme established in 1997.[106] Due to the vision of Vice President Al Gore, the US became one of the leading countries in eGovernment implementation. However, the road to an eGovernment platform was, and is, not always easy.

Jane Fountain, in supporting this argument, describes how 'the Internet does not lead to institutional transformation but is enacted to strengthen the status quo.'[107] A substantial amount of eGovernment literature is devoted to analysing how to improve current services, thereby enhancing the standing of existing institutions. The dominant vision of eGovernment places much stress upon the efficiency, effectiveness, and legitimacy of implementing tools and services that are already exist in offline forms. Scant attention is paid, in eGovernment policies and programmes, to the political implications of such technological implementations, particularly in the way that they impact upon the broader relations between citizens, civil society, the market, and governments. Governments are still determined to see government as the dominant actor in governance and thus act to rejuvenate existing political structures through their eGovernment agendas. Despite this fact, the shift from considering government as the sole authority, to considering government as one, amongst many authorities is apparent. Rather than showing a decline in the role of the state, this shows the continued importance of the institutions that make up the state.

Governance in an Era of Digital Networks: Conclusions

The connection between global communications and shifts in patterns of governance are debated at both the international and national levels. The changes which have occurred in both economic and social milieus have contributed to a more general change in perceptions of both democratic and institutional governance in and by political institutions. In an era that is characterised by 'transnational technologies, multinational stakeholders and global markets',[108] the internet is one of the most interesting subjects that can be studied when trying to analyse the shifts in governance.

These developments require change, or at least a reassessment of governance of states and institutions at a fundamental level. The debates raised above about economic, social, and political aspects of the decline and revival of institutions show that there are opportunities and challenges presented by the growth of ICTs for political institutions and indeed, the future of democracy.

Clearly, explanations that focus entirely on the state or on the role of supranational institutions are lacking in ontological constructs to deal with the tensions between

---

106 National Performance Review, Government Information Technology Services Board, and Al Gore, 'Access America: Reengineering through Information Technology' (Washington, 1997).

107 Jane E. Fountain, *Building the Virtual State: Information Technology and Institutional Change* (Washington, 2001), p. 12.

108 Baer, 'Will the Global Information Infrastructure Need Transnational (or Any) Governance?'.

the process of globalising and the level of institutional control when examining the impact of the global communications revolution on the nation state. The issues in question are both international and domestic, crossing borders as easily as the bits and bytes that surround them. The challenge remains to find an explanatory model that describes both aspects of the phenomenon of harmonisation and fragmentation in a world with distributed spheres of authority.

This chapter has outlined the context within which governance has become a dominant subject of discussion, and how new global communications technologies have been part of the trend towards governance not by governments alone due to the fact that they provide opportunities for the concretisation of abstract policy networks or institutions. For now, it appears that the nation state is still winning.

Bibliography

Abramson, Bram Dov, 'Media Policy after Regulation?', *International Journal of Cultural Studies*, 4/3 (2001): 301–26.

Alberganti, Michel, 'Internet Pour Tous En Grande-Bretagne', *Le Monde*, 6 November 1999.

Baer, Walter S., 'Will the Global Information Infrastructure Need Transnational (or Any) Governance', <http://www.rand.org/pubs/reprints/RP603/>, accessed 1 January 2007.

Baran, Paul, 'On Distributed Communications Networks', Paper presented at the IEEE, Hot Springs, VA, November 1964.

Barlow, John Perry, 'A Declaration of the Independence of Cyberspace.' <http://www.eff.org/~barlow/Declaration–Final.html>, accessed 1 January 2007.

Barney, Darin, *Prometheus Wired: The Hope for Democracy in the Age of Network Technology* (Chicago: University of Chicago Press, 2000).

Behn, Robert D., 'The New Public Management Paradigm and the Search for Democratic Accountability', *International Public Management Journal*, 1/2 (1998): 131–64.

Bell, Daniel, *The Coming of Post–Industrial Society. A Venture in Social Forecasting.* (New York: Basic Books, 1973).

Besançon, Laurent, and Tim Kelly, 'Telecom Privatisations: The New Realism?' (Geneva: International Telecommunication Union, 1996).

Bevir, Mark, Rod A. W. Rhodes, and Patrick Weller, 'Traditions of Governance: Interpreting the Changing Role of the Public Sector', *Public Administration*, 81/1 (2003): 1–17.

Bogdanowicz, Marc, 'The Social Impacts of Telecom Liberalisation in Europe. The Productivity Gains Hypothesis: How Do Corporate Users React?' *Telematics and Informatics*, 14/4 (1997): 357–63.

Brady, Gordon L. 'The Internet, Economic Growth and Governance', *Economic Affairs*, 20/1 (2000): 13–20.

Brown, John Seely, and Paul Duguid, *The Social Life of Information* (Boston, MA: Harvard Business School Press, 2000).

Bryan, Cathy, Roza Tsagarousianou, and Damian Tambini, 'Electronic Democracy and the Civic Networking Movement in Context', in Roza Tsagarousianou, Damian Tambini and Cathy Bryan (ed.), *Cyberdemocracy: Technology, Cities and Civic Networks* (London: Routledge, 1998), pp. 1–17.

Burrel, Ian, 'Ministers Plan Internet Curb', *The Independent*, 25 June 1998, p. 1.

Castells, Manuel, *The Rise of the Network Society*. 3 vols., vol. 1 (Oxford: Blackwell Publishers, 1996).

Cerny, Philip G., 'Globalization and the Erosion of Democracy', *European Journal of Political Research*, 36 (1999): 1–26.

Charlton, C., C. Gittings, P. Leng, J. Little, and I. Neilson, 'Bringing the Internet to the Community', *Interacting with Computers*, 12/1 (1999): 51–61.

Cutler, A. Claire, 'Locating 'Authority' in the Global Political Economy', *International Studies Quarterly*, 43/1 (1999): 59–81.

Dai, Xiudian, 'A New Mode of Governance? Transnationalisation of European Regions and Cities in the Information Age', *Telematics and Informatics*, 20/3 (2003): 193–213.

Denhardt, Robert B., 'The Future of Public Administration', *Public Administration and Management*, 4/2 (1999): 279–92.

Department of Economic and Social Affairs (United Nations), *World Public Sector Report: Globalization and the State 2001* (New York: United Nations, 2001).

Deutsch, Karl W., *The Analysis of International Relations*. Edited by Robert A. Dahl, Foundations of Modern Political Science Series (Engelwood Cliffs, NJ: Prentice–Hall Inc., 1968).

Dordick, Herbert S., and Georgette Wang, *The Information Society: A Retrospective View* (London: Sage Publications, 1993).

Drake, William J. (ed.), *The New Information Infrastructure: Strategies for US Policy* (New York: Twentieth Century Fund Press, 1995).

Drucker, Peter F., *Post–Capitalist Society* (New York: HarperCollins Publishers, 1994).

Drucker, Peter F., 'Really Reinventing Government', *The Atlantic Monthly*, February 1995, pp. 49–58.

Dudley, Leonard, 'Communications and Economic Growth', *European Economic Review*, 43/3 (1999): 595–619.

Dutton, William (ed.), *Society on the Line – Information Politics in the Digital Age* (Oxford: Oxford University Press, 1999).

European Commission, 'Innovation in a Knowledge–Driven Economy' (Brussels: European Commission, 2000).

Everard, Jerry, *Virtual States: The Internet and the Boundaries of the Nation State*. Edited by Michael Talalay and Chris Farrands, Technology and the Global Political Economy (London: Routledge, 2000).

Ferdinand, Peter (ed.), *The Internet, Democracy and Democratization* (London: Frank Cass, 2000).

Fleissner, Peter, and Wolfgang Hofkirchner, 'The Making of the Information Society: Driving Forces, 'Leitbilder' and the Imperative for Survival', *Biosystems*, 46/1–2 (1998): 201–07.

Fountain, Jane E., *Building the Virtual State: Information Technology and Institutional Change* (Washington DC: Brookings Institution, 2001).

Freeman, Chris, 'Social Inequality, Technology and Economic Growth', in Sally Wyatt, Flis Henwood, Nod Miller and Peter Senker (ed.), *Technology and in/ Equality: Questioning the Information Society* (London: Routledge, 2000), pp. 149–71.

Freeman, Chris, and Francisco Louçã, *As Time Goes by – From the Industrial Revolutions to the Information Revolution* (New York: Oxford University Press, 2002).

Goff, Patricia M., 'Invisible Borders: Economic Liberalisation and National Identity', *International Studies Quarterly*, 44/4 (2000): 533–62.

Graham, Andrew, 'The Assessment: Economics of the Internet', *Oxford Review of Economic Policy*, 17/2 (2001): 145–58.

Graham, Gordon, *The Internet: A Philosophical Inquiry* (London: Routledge, 1999).

Hertz, Noreena, *The Silent Takeover: Global Capitalism and the Death of Democracy* (London: William Heinemann, 2001).

Hirst, Paul, 'Democracy and Governance', in Jon Pierre (ed.), *Debating Governance: Authority, Steering, and Democracy* Oxford: (Oxford University Press, 2000), pp. 13–35.

Hirst, Paul, and Grahame Thompson, *Globalization in Question: The International Economy and the Possibilities of Governance* (Cambridge: Polity Press, 1996).

Hodgson, Geoffrey D., 'Socio–Economic Consequences of the Advance of Complexity and Knowledge', Paper presented at the 21st Century Dynamics: Towards the creative society. OECD Forum for the future, 6–7 December 1999.

Hoff, Jens, Ivan Horrocks, and Pieter Tops (eds.), *Democratic Governance and New Technology: Technologically Mediated Innovations in Political Practice in Western Europe*, Routledge/ ECPR Series in European Political Science (London: Routledge, 2000).

Hubert, Agnes, and Benedicte Caremier, *Democracy and the Information Society in Europe* (London: Kogan Page, 2000).

Huggins, Richard, 'The Transformation of Political Audience?' in Barrie Axford and Richard Huggins (ed.), *New Media and Politics* (London: Sage Publications, 2001), pp. 127–50.

Hulsink, Willem, and Andrew Davies, 'The Emergence of National Champions in Global Telecommunications', *Telematics and Informatics*, 14/4 (1997): 349–56.

Johnson, David R., and David Post, 'The New 'Civic Virtue' of the Internet', *First Monday*, 3/1 (1998).

Johnston, David L., 'Open Networks, Electronic Commerce and the Global Information Infrastructure', *Computer Standards & Interfaces*, 20/2–3 (1998): 95–99.

Kavanagh, Dennis, and David Richards, 'Departmentalism and Joined–up Government: Back to the Future?' *Parliamentary Affairs*, 54/1 (2001): 1–18.

Kettl, Donald F., 'The Transformation of Governance: Globalization, Devolution, and the Role of Government', *Public Administration Review*, 60/6 (2000): 488–97.

Kobrin, Stephen J., 'Back to the Future: Neomedievalism and the Postmodern Digital World Economy', *Journal of International Affairs*, 51/2 (1998): 361–83.

Kooiman, Jan, 'Findings, Speculations and Recommendations', in Jan Kooiman (ed.), *Modern Governance: New Government – Society Interactions* (London: Sage Publications, 1993), pp. 249–62.

Kooiman, Jan, 'Governance and Governability: Using Complexity, Dynamics and Diversity', in Jan Kooiman (ed.), *Modern Governance: New Government – Society Interactions* (London: Sage Publications, 1993), pp. 35–48.

Krauss, Clifford. '8 Countries Join in an Effort to Catch Computer Criminals', *New York Times*, 11 December 1997, p. 12.

Kubicek, Herbert, William Dutton, and Robin Williams (eds.), *The Social Shaping of Information Superhighways: European and American Roads to the Information Society* (New York: St Martin's Press, 1997).

Laudon, Kenneth C., *Communications Technology and Democratic Participation*, Praeger Special Studies (New York: Praeger, 1977).

Lebessis, Notis, and John Paterson, 'Evolutions in Governance: What Lessons for the Commission?' (Brussels: Forwards Studies Unit, European Commission, 1999).'

Loader, Brian D. (ed.), *The Governance of Cyberspace* (London: Routledge, 1997).

Lukasik, Stephen J., 'Protecting the Global Information Commons', *Telecommunications Policy*, 24/6–7 (2000): 519–31.

Macgregor Wise, John, *Exploring Technology and Social Space* (London: Sage Publications, 1997).

Macpherson, Michael, 'Citizen Politics and the Renewal of Democracy', <http://www.snafu.de/~mjm/CP/cp2.html>, accessed 1 January 2007.

Magaziner, Ira C., 'The Framework for Global Electronic Commerce: A Policy Perspective', *Journal of Common Market Studies*, 51/2 (1998): 527–38.

Malerba, Franco. 'Policies for Development and Employment in the Information Society', Paper presented at the XVI European Carrefour of Science and Culture, 15–16 October 1998.

Mansell, Robin, 'Communication by Design?' in Robin Mansell and Roger Silverstone (ed.), *Communication by Design: The Politics of Information and Communication Technologies* (Oxford: Oxford University Press, 1996), pp. 15–43.

Mansell, Robin (ed.), *Inside the Communication Revolution – Evolving Patterns of Social and Technical Interaction* (Oxford: Oxford University Press, 2002).

Mansell, Robin, and Uta Wehn, 'Innovative 'Knowledge Societies' – Consequences of ICT Strategies', in Robin Mansell and Uta Wehn (ed.), *Knowledge Societies – Information Technology for Sustainable Development* (Oxford: Oxford University Press, 1998), pp. 241–53.

Mathews, Jessica T., 'Power Shift', *Foreign Affairs*, 76/1 (1997): 50–66.

May, Christopher, *The Information Society: A Sceptical View* (Cambridge: Polity Press, 2002).

Mayntz, Renate, 'Governing Failures and the Problem of Governability: Some Comments on a Political Paradigm', in Jan Kooiman (ed.), *Modern Governance: New Government – Society Interactions* (London: Sage Publications, 1993), pp. 9–20.

McMahon, Peter, *Global Control: Information Technology and Globalization since 1845* (Cheltenham: Edward Elgar, 2002).

Melody, William H, 'Toward a Framework for Designing Information Society Policies', *Telecommunications Policy*, 20/4 (1996): 243–59.

Moore, Nick, 'Confucius or Capitalism? Policies for an Information Society', in Brian D. Loader (ed.), *Cyberspace Divide: Equality, Agency and Policy in the Information Society* (London: Routledge, 1998), pp. 149–60.

Mowlana, Hamid, *Global Information and World Communication: New Frontiers in International Relations*. 2nd ed. (London: Sage Publications, 1997).

Mulgan, Geoff, *Connexity: How to Live in a Connected World* (London: Chatto & Windus, 1997).

National Performance Review, Government Information Technology Services Board, and Al Gore. 'Access America: Reengineering through Information Technology' (Washington: GPO, 1997).

Navet, Georges, 'Gouvernance: Un Concept Ambigu', *International Law FORUM de droit international*, 4/3 (2002): 128–33.

Noam, Eli M., 'Principles for the Communications Act of 2034: The Superstructure of Infrastructure', *Federal Communications Law Journal*, 47/2 (1994).

Norman, Peter, 'Concern at German Internet Verdict.' *Financial Times*, 29 May 1998, p. 3.

Norris, Pippa (ed.), *Critical Citizens – Global Support for Democratic Government* (Oxford: Oxford University Press, 1999).

OECD, 'Impact of the Emerging Information Society on the Policy Development Process and Democratic Quality' (Paris: OECD, 1998).

OECD, 'Is There a New Economy? First Report on the OECD Growth Project' (Paris: OECD, 2000).

OECD, 'Issues and Developments in Public Management: Survey 1996–1997' (Paris: OECD, 1997).

OECD, 'The E–Government Imperative: Main Findings' (Paris: OECD, 2003).

Pollitt, Christopher, 'Joined–up Government: A Survey', *Political Studies Review*, 1/1 (2003): 34–49.

Pool, Ithiel De Sola, *Technologies of Freedom: On Free Speech in an Electronic Age* (Cambridge: Harvard Belknap, 1983).

Poster, Mark, 'Cyberdemocracy: Internet and the Public Sphere', <http://www.humanities.uci.edu/mposter/writings/democ.html>, accessed 1 January 2007.

Powell, Walter W., 'Neither Market nor Hierarchy: Network Forms of Organisation', in Grahame Thompson, Jennifer Frances, Rosalind Levacic and Jeremy Mitchell (ed.), *Markets, Hierarchies and Networks: The Coordination of Social Life* (London: Sage Publications, 1991), pp. 265–76.

Poynter, Gavin, and Alvaro De Miranda, 'Inequality, Work and Technology in the Services Sector', in Sally Wyatt, Flis Henwood, Nod Miller and Peter Senker (ed.), *Technology and in/Equality: Questioning the Information Society* (London: Routledge, 2000), pp. 172–96.

Pratchett, Lawrence, 'New Technologies and the Modernization of Local Government: An Analysis of Biases and Constraints', *Public Administration*, 77/4 (1999): 731–50.

Press, L, 'The Role of Computer Networks in Development', *Communications of the ACM*, 39/2 (1996): 23–9.

Price, Monroe E., *Media and Sovereignty: The Global Information Revolution and Its Challenge to State Power* (Cambridge: MIT Press, 2002).

Reinicke, Wolfgang H., *Global Public Policy: Governing without Government?* (Washington: The Brookings Institution, 1998).

Rheingold, Howard, 'The Virtual Community: Homesteading on the Electronic Frontier', <http://www.rheingold.com/vc/book/>, accessed 1 January 2007.

Rhodes, Rod A. W., *Understanding Governance: Policy Networks, Governance, Reflexivity and Accountability*. Edited by Rod A. W. Rhodes, Public and Policy Management (Buckingham: Open University Press, 1997).

Robins, Kevin, 'Cyberspace and the World We Live In', in Jon Dovey (ed.), *Fractal Dreams: New Media in Social Context* (London: Lawrence and Wishart, 1996), pp. 1–30.

Ronit, Karsten, 'Institutions of Private Authority in Global Governance: Linking Territorial Forms of Self–Regulation', *Administration & Society*, 33/5 (2001): 555–78.

Roper, Juliet, 'Government, Corporate or Social Power? The Internet as a Tool in the Struggle for Dominance in Public Policy', *Journal of Public Affairs*, 2/3 (2002): 113–24.

Rosenau, James N., *Along the Domestic–Foreign Frontier* (Cambridge: Cambridge University Press, 1997).

Rothkopf, David J., 'Cyberpolitik: The Changing Nature of Power in the Information Age', *Journal of International Affairs*, 51/2 (1998): 325–59.

Ruggie, John Gerard, 'International Responses to Technology: Concepts and Trends', *International Organization*, 29/3 (1975): 557–83.

Ruggie, John Gerard, 'Territoriality and Beyond: Problematizing Modernity in International Relations', *International Organization*, 47/1 (1993): 139–74.

Sassen, Saskia, 'Digital Networks and the State: Some Governance Questions', *Theory, Culture & Society*, 17/4 (2000): 19–33.

Sassen, Saskia, *Globalization and Its Discontents: Essays on the New Mobility of People and Money* (New York: The New Press, 1998).

Sbragia, Alberta M., 'The Dilemma of Governance with Government' (New York: School of Law, NYU, 2002).

Standage, Tom, *The Victorian Internet: The Remarkable Story of the Telegraph and the Nineteenth Century's Online Pioneers* (London: Phoenix, 1999).

Steinfeld, Charles, and Pamela Whitten, 'Community Level Socio–Economic Impacts of Electronic Commerce', *Journal of Computer Mediated Communication*, 5/2 (1999): 1–15.

Stolfi, F., and G. Sussman, 'Telecommunications and Transnationalism: The Polarization of Social Space', *The Information Society*, 17/1 (2001): 49–62.

Strange, Susan, *The Retreat of the State: The Diffusion of Power in the World Economy* (Cambridge: Cambridge University Press, 1996).

Targett, Simon, and Christopher Price, 'Internet Plan for Schools Unveiled', *Financial Times*, 8 October 1997, p. 9.

Tat–Kei Ho, Alfred, 'Reinventing Local Governments and the E–Government Initiative', *Public Administration Review*, 62/4 (2002): 434–44.

Thomas, Graham, and Sally Wyatt, 'Access Is Not the Only Problem: Using and Controlling the Internet', in Sally Wyatt, Flis Henwood, Nod Miller and Peter Senker (ed.), *Technology and in/Equality: Questioning the Information Society* (London: Routledge, 2000), pp. 21–45.

Thompson, Grahame. 'Networks of Complexity? Network Theory, International Economic Networks and the Development of ICTs', Paper presented at the EAEPE 2002: Complexity and the Economy, Aix–en–Provence, 7–10 November 2002.

Venturelli, Shalini, 'Inventing E–Regulation in the US, EU and East Asia: Conflicting Social Visions of the Information Society', *Telematics and Informatics*, 19/2 (2002): 69–90.

Wallace, Helen, 'The Institutional Setting: Five Variations on a Theme', in Helen Wallace and William Wallace (ed.), *Policy Making in the European Union* (Oxford: Oxford University Press, 2000), pp. 1–37.

Webster, Frank, *Theories of the Information Society* (London: Routledge, 1995).

Wendt, Alexander, *Social Theory of International Politics* (Cambridge: Cambridge University Press, 1999).

Zacher, Mark W., 'Capitalism, Technology, and Liberalization: The International Telecommunications Regime, 1865–1998', in James N. Rosenau and J.P. Singh (ed.), *Information Technologies and Global Politics: The Changing Scope of Power and Governance* (Albany: State University of New York Press, 2002), pp. 189–210.

Zacher, Mark W., 'The Decaying Pillars of the Westphalian Temple: Implications for International Order and Governance', in James N. Rosenau and Ernst–Otto Czempiel (ed.), *Governance without Government: Order and Change in World Politics* (Cambridge: Cambridge University Press, 1992), pp. 58–101.

Zeitlyn, David, Jane Bex, and Matthew David, 'Access Denied: The Politics of New Communications Media', *Telematics and Informatics*, 15/3 (1998): 219–30.

Zysman, John, and Stephen Weber. 'Governance and Politics of the Internet Economy: Historical Transformation or Ordinary Politics with a New Vocabulary?', *BRIE Working Paper*, 22, (Berkeley, CA, 2001).

Chapter 2

Digital Democracy and Its Application to the International Arena – From 'Deliberation' to 'Decision'

Alexander Siedschlag

Introduction

Not only is the information revolution transforming the international system as such. It also challenges our concepts of democracy, government, and governance. By enabling a transnational cyberspace, the information revolution blurs the distinction between the domestic and the international dimensions of classical categories in political science, such as decision-making and legitimacy. At the same time, democracy practised digitally need not remain confined to state-type political systems. Consequently, normative categories of domestic democratic discourse, such as deliberation, provide the potential to assess the intrinsic quality of debate in the international and transnational realm as well. However, despite the prevalence of communicative action, not all communication necessarily fosters action, however committed it may be to the best public argument, that is, however deliberative it may be. Investigating the linkage between deliberation in terms of communication and decision-making in terms of action is therefore a valuable contribution to assessing the impact of the information revolution on inter- and transnational relations. In aiming for such a contribution, this article starts by clarifying the concept of digital democracy on the theoretical and domestic scales. It continues by identifying trajectories that can lead us from cyber-deliberation, that is, arguing through internet-based communication, to real-world decision-making.

The article concludes by expanding the argument to the inter- and transnational realms. Apart from the discussion about computer-mediated change in community and domestic political affairs, there is a pending debate on the general effects of internet-related communication on international politics in the broad sense of the term. However, research coming from the academic field of international politics on internet-induced political change is not closely linked to the state of knowledge regarding the relationship between the internet and politics. Rather, it commonly departs from concepts specific to sub-disciplines, such as neorealist power analysis or post-international turbulence analysis.[1]

---

1   Cf. Juliann Emmons Allison (ed.), *Technology, Development, and Democracy. International Conflict and Cooperation in the Information Age* (Albany, 2002).

Nye and Owens, for instance, simply equated the increasing role of global information technology in general with an increase in individual capabilities at the level of the nation-state: 'Knowledge, more than ever before, is power. The one country that can best lead the information revolution will be more powerful than any other.'[2] Rosenau and Johnson, in contrast, expected the rise of border-crossing internet-based communication to empower 'sovereignty-free actors'.[3] They deemed information technology to be 'central to the emergence of the multicentric world [...] and, therefore, to the rise of multicentric actors that focus on new performance criteria such as human rights and protection of the natural environment.'[4] Thus, international politics perspectives on the role of digital communication and information exchange on a post-national scale leave us with a gap between two extremes, neither of which permits us to fit the results of general internet-and-politics research into the puzzle in a satisfactory way.

Conversely, this article begins with a discussion of selected elements of the state of the art in internet-and-politics research, seeking to expand the related concepts to the international scale while investigating possible transition points from deliberation to decision-making. It first introduces selected perspectives on online communities that have a real-world impact. Because our main assumptions about the impact of digital deliberation on decision-making will strongly depend on the chosen analytical concept of internet-based or internet-related democracy, this article then argues for 'digital democracy' as the reference model to choose – and will do so for the remainder of this explanation.

Digital democracy is a special case of internet-related democracy that offers terminological advantages, as will be argued below in detail. At the same time, digital democracy represents an overarching paradigm that opens up a comprehensive perspective on politics by virtual channels. However, the concept of digital democracy assumes that internet-based communication in the public sphere will not primarily lead to a new digital culture and bring forth a virtual structure of the political sphere, but will, at least selectively, follow the lines marked by the given structure and political culture of the respective political system under consideration.[5] By virtue of these points, the model of digital democracy can help us better reflect the results of empirical research theoretically. This includes Franda's comparative

---

2   Joseph S. Nye and William A. Owens, 'America's Information Edge', *Foreign Affairs* 75 (1996): 20.

3   James N. Rosenau and David Johnson, 'Information Technologies and Turbulence in World Politics', in Juliann Emmons Allison (ed.), *Technology, Development, and Democracy. International Conflict and Cooperation in the Information Age* (Albany, 2002), p. 74.

4   Ibid.

5   Cynthia J. Alexander and Leslie A. Pal (eds.), *Digital Democracy: Policy and Politics in the Wired World* (Toronto et al., 1998); Janet Caldow, 'The Virtual Ballot Box: A Survey of Digital Democracy in Europe. IBM Corporation, Institute for Electronic Government' (1999), <http://www.politik–digital.de/archiv/forschung/ibm_studie.pdf>; Barry N. Hague and Brian D. Loader (eds.), *Digital Democracy. Discourse and Decision Making in the Information Age* (London/New York, 1999).

study on models of political and societal internet use,[6] as well as the results of studies testing plebiscitary and cyber-political procedures. Noveck's work, which shows how the practical relevance of internet-related democracy depends on regional culture, history and values, is of exemplary value here.[7] Digital democracy, therefore, both as an analytical concept and as a political blueprint, contains a normative caveat: Do not proclaim a universal vision of internet and democracy, but develop general principles for translating digital deliberation into real-world decision-making – principles that leave room for the institutional variations to be taken into account in different political culture(s).

After identifying related management needs for politically relevant digital deliberation, this article discusses the problem of the culture-dependency of online communication. It then goes on to identify specific interfaces through which digital deliberative discourse may affect real-world political decision-making. This is the basis on which to assess possibilities of extending the digital-democracy model to the international level as well as to the problem of governing increasingly transnationalizing societies.

A State-of-the Art Selection of Conceptual Perspectives on Internet-related Government and Governance

Internet-and-politics research has largely bidden farewell to its founding idea of realizing Barber's 'strong democracy'[8] by virtual means: to create a new momentum for late-20th century democracy by defining it not just as a political order, but as a (re)public(an) lifestyle, rooted in a digitally mediated active pluralism throughout the 'net-empowered'[9] people. Today, research rather suggests that (re)public(an) internet use such as online deliberation does not directly impact political decision-making. Moreover, a consensus is emerging that the internet has neither become a political sphere *sui generis*, nor has it established fundamentally new, active-society centred criteria for assessing the deliberative and/or decision-making quality of politics.[10] Thus, at first sight, there remains little scope for new, digitally founded forms of governance. In fact, if we expand our scope beyond the OECD world, we are even confronted with a widespread public fear of the internet as a Western project of dominance and penetration, if not cultural threat.[11]

---

6   Marcus F. Franda, *Launching into Cyberspace: Internet Development and Politics in Five World Regions* (Boulder/London, 2002).

7   Cf. Todd Davies and Beth Noveck (eds.), *Online Deliberation: Design, Research, and Practice* (Chicago, 2006).

8   Benjamin R. Barber, *Strong Democracy. Participatory Politics for a New Age* (Berkeley, et al., 1984).

9   Lawrence K. Grossmann, *The Electronic Republic. Reshaping Democracy in the Information Age* (New York et al., 1995).

10   As originally assumed by Howard Rheingold, *The Virtual Community. Homesteading on the Electronic Frontier* (Reading et al., 1993), and taken up e.g. by Kevin A. Hill and John E. Hughes, *Cyberpolitics: Citizen Activism in the Age of the Internet* (Lanham et al., 1998).

11   See Franda, *Launching into Cyberspace*.

In contrast, Castells, writing in 1998, believed that a transnational network society already existed that did not discriminate against different cultures and that would open up new opportunities both for deliberation and decision-making.[12] Castells made his point mainly with reference to NGOs and their virtual networks for mobilization of protest. However, Castells did not suggest any answer to the question of whether, and if so, how, the internet contributes to an interactive society and to the transition from mobilization to deliberation as well as from deliberation to decision-making. In the final analysis, Castells did not seem to believe that internet-based communication and mobilization has the potential for affecting the conventional patterns and repertories of real-world decision-making. This is because he treated the internet as a symbolic environment of social and political reality, and moreover as a symbolic environment that does not constitute a shared context for its agents, but is strongly dependent on interpretations and, in its potential social power, inseparably linked to the real world and its social and power structures as well as to offline decision-making mechanisms.

However, we benefit from the use of working definitions of *real-world influencing online communities*, including important hints concerning criteria for identifying virtual community-building where the concomitant deliberative endeavours have a chance to impact real-world decision-making. An example is Preece's set of criteria:[13]

- A common goal, providing a specific reason for belonging to the respective community (this means that agenda-setting is a precondition for – not an achievement of – any virtual community).
- Institutionalization of the community independently of individuals.
- An internal social differentiation into specific roles to be taken by the members.
- Common 'policies', that is a set of social rules directed to achieving the community's aims.
- A 'folklore', that is, commonly accepted social norms and the consciousness of a common history.

In addition, Lazar and Preece have directly addressed the concept of 'governance'; however, they restrict their use of the term to denote the management of virtual communities themselves.[14] According to their results, a virtual community cannot constitute a socially relevant actor unless it meets some structural-functional prerequisites, for example, that the roles of founding fathers, community leaders, and moderators must be filled.

---

12 Manuel Castells, *The Rise of the Network Society.* Reprint (Malden, 1998).

13 Jennifer Preece, *Online Communities: Designing Usability, Supporting Sociability* (New York, 2000).

14 Jonathan Lazar and Jennifer Preece, 'Social Considerations in Online Communities: Usability, Sociability, and Success Factors', in Herre van Oostendorp (ed.), *Cognition in a Digital World* (Mahwah /London, 2003), pp. 137–38.

Just as digital governance does not emanate from a technical infrastructure, but requires a certain degree of virtual social organization, it is also politically 'neutral', as Rosenau and Johnson have pointed out: Information technologies

> can serve to tyrannize publics as well as to liberate them. They can facilitate the dynamics of globalization as well as those of violent nationalism. They can mislead policymakers as well as enlighten them. In short, whether the consequences of information technologies are beneficial or deleterious depends on the uses to which they are put by citizens and their leaders.[15]

Following Rosenau and Johnson, I dismiss the view that the information revolution – or a country's 'IT posture' – as such enables new governmental mechanisms and empowers new political actors.[16] Some schools of thought offer us interesting perspectives of modes of community-building that are based on online communication and online deliberation and have the potential to impact real-world decision-making. Nevertheless, elaborating on the impact of digital deliberation on democratic decision-making depends strongly on the analytical concept of the relationship between internet and democracy that we choose.

To start out from the respective concepts of e-government, e-governance, e-democracy, cyber-democracy, or digital democracy means choosing different frames of reference for analysis and different models for governing (in) the information age. This variety illustrates that there is no single model of internet-adapting democracy. Digital democracy as advocated in this article does attempt to provide an overarching framework, but it still needs to take account of and respect other models.

The range of models also underlines the truth that the 'digitality' or 'virtuality' of political processes as such does not imply any new standards for evaluating republican practice. Rather, the theoretical and practical requirements for 'good' internet-related or internet-based government and governance depend on the model that our judgement is based on. The five models already mentioned represent the most important trains of analysis and design of internet-bases democracy and are compared in Table 2.1: e-government, e-governance, e-democracy, cyber-democracy, and digital democracy. It is important to bear in mind that according to all five models, we need to anticipate, and provide for managing, certain negative by-effects when we take the step from online deliberation to real-world decision-making.[17]

---

15 Rosenau and Johnson, 'Information Technologies and Turbulence in World Politics', pp. 55ff.

16 This view was, along with others, disseminated by Richard O. Hundley, Robert H. Anderson, Tora K. Bikson and C. Richard Neu, *The Global Course of the Information Revolution. Recurring Themes and Regional Variations* (Santa Monica, 2003), esp. pp. 36ff.

17 Alexander Siedschlag, Arne Rogg and Carolin Welzel, *Digitale Demokratie. Willlensbildung und Partizipation per Internet* (Opladen, 2002), pp. 10–14.

Table 2.1   Main models of internet-related democracy

	e-government	e-governance	e-democracy	cyber-democracy	digital democracy
political function of the internet	increasing the efficiency of public administration	networked problem-solving in virtual communities, increase in efficiency	increased responsiveness of the leaders by occasional online consultations	grass-root democratic reorganization of the political system in the internet	depending on existing structures, aiming at mending present deficits
notion of democracy	enabling state/consumer democracy	network state/network democracy	elitist democracy	grass-root democracy	neo-republican democracy
notion of internet-based public	irrelevant	segmented into problem-bound forums	elite-provided channels for civic participation	new-style, non-power-corrupted public	separate, self-organizing audiences that amend offline public discourse
predominant form of communication	G2C	G2C and C2G	G2C, complemented by pre-given C2G channels	G2C, complemented by C2G	G2C, C2G and C2C
necessary services of the state	range of online-services	installation of IT-infrastructure and reform of administration	implementation of online consultations and elections	none: self-organization by online activists	promotion of deliberative forums and media competence
typical civic activities	online tax return or car registration	online discussion of communal problems	participation in online consultations and elections	net activism, participation in virtual communities	political information and online deliberation
objectives	minimal administrative burdens for the citizens, high efficiency of the administration	effective, non-central problem solving along with increased participation	improved basis of legitimacy of the political system	self-governing virtual grass-root communities	increased deliberation in the political discourse; increased participation
expectable negative consequences, management needs	neglect of existing potentials, insufficient civic participation	neglect of existing potentials	electronic populism, fragmentation of the virtual public into partial publics	erosion of democratic institutions; protest attitudes and activism	over-saturation of the citizens (e.g. due to limited capacities to receive and process information)

E-Government

E-government is a socio-technological model that advocates a 'consumer democracy'[18] in order to minimize public administration-related constraints on civic freedom. It does not make immediate theoretical reference to deliberation or public speech. However, it is the assumption of this model that increased efficiency of public administration processes and procedures will underpin the legitimacy of the state in a globalizing world. However, naturally, e-government is not geared towards deliberative decision-making, but towards the effective implementation of politically agreed administrative processes. In the final analysis, e-government implies disaggregating the political public: establishing web-based administrative mechanisms that allow problems to be solved as closely as possible to their locus of origin, that is, at a communal level. A negative by-effect that needs managing is an over-reliance on the enabling role of the state, leading to a neglect of existing civic potentials, since the predominant form of communication in e-government is government-to-citizen, or 'G2C'.

E-Governance

E-government only becomes a political concept in the strict sense of the word when extended towards *e-governance*.[19] E-governance draws on the general discussion about post-modern statehood and political management in a trans-nationalized world. It is a concept that centres on the nexus of deliberation and decision at the communal level, and that advocates networked problem-solving, organized in mixed online and offline problem-centred forums. E-governance as a practical model aims at basing deliberation about problem-solving in self-organizing communities and organizing problem-solving on the basis of criteria for efficiency. As these criteria transcend the framework of the state, e-governance seems particularly worth examining for potential use in transnational relations. However, from a theoretical point of view, we have to expect e-governance, like e-government, to subdivide the community of internet users into isolated problem-bound partial publics, and runs the risk of neglecting existing real-world potentials for cooperative problem-solving.

Nevertheless, institutions such as the OECD seem to advocate an amendment of e-government by e-governance in order to avoid merely technical approaches to problem-solving in communal and political affairs that do not respond to the citizens' needs. Such a model would combine government-to-citizen and citizen-to-government, or 'C2G', communication. In this sense, taking the debate about

---

18 Jens Hoff, Ivan Horrocks and Pieter Tops, 'Introduction: New Technology and the "Crises" of Democracy', in Jens Hoff, Ivan Horrocks and Pieter Tops (eds.), *Democratic Governance and New Technology. Technologically Mediated Innovations in Political Practice in Western Europe* (London/New York, 2000), p. 7.

19 E.g. Perri 6, *E–Governance. Styles of Political Judgement in the Information Age Polity* (Basingstoke et al., 2004); Max von Bismarck, Daniel Dettling and Tino Schuppan, 'E–Governance in der Wissensgesellschaft – neue Dimensionen der politischen Willensbildung', in Alexander Siedschlag and Alexander Bilgeri (eds.), *Kursbuch Internet und Politik*, vol. 2/2002 (Opladen, 2003), pp. 23–38.

political decision-making down to the level of local, problem-centred action may in fact increase democratic accountability in a network state within a globalizing world:

> Building trust between governments and citizens is fundamental to good governance. ICT can help build trust by enabling citizen engagement in the policy process, promoting open and accountable government and helping to prevent corruption.[20]

E-Democracy

E-Democracy goes a step further, providing the public with electronic channels for deliberation and participation.[21] However, as the state retains its exclusive role in defining and opening (and closing) those channels, e-democracy represents an elitist model of internet-based political deliberation and decision-making support. Usually, this involves attempts by the state's elites to improve the political system's legitimacy through pilot e-voting and case-by-case online consultations. Thus, the model focuses on G2C-communication amended by governmentally administered C2G-channels. E-democracy remains within the traditional notion of the state insofar as it depends on the state for the implementation of online consultation and deliberation. E-democracy's case-by-case approach means that it shares one expectable negative consequence with e-governance: the internet-based fragmentation of the political public into partial publics. However, a generic side effect of e-democracy is electronic populism: the attempt to make use of public deliberation not for better-informed decision-making, but for purposes of political customer relationship management. That is, the purpose is to secure votes, not to achieve responsive and accountable public policy. In this sense, internet use may in fact contribute to maintaining an inappropriate supremacy of the state.

Cyber-democracy

In a sense, cyber-democracy seems to strive to over-compensate for e-democracy's negative sides. This model insists on the need to use cyberspace to reorganize the political system in a grass-roots democratic style, by forging a digital democratic marketplace and creating a forum for a new political public that is not corrupted by power.[22] Citizen-to-citizen or 'C2C' communication is the catchphrase here. The cyber-democratic model sees no need for the state to provide deliberation and decision-making services, but follows a vision of civic self-organization structured by online activists who act as enablers for self-governing virtual grass-roots

---

20 OECD, Policy Brief 'The e–government imperative: main findings' (2003), http://www.oecd.org/dataoecd/60/60/2502539.pdf, p. 2.

21 Graeme Browning, *Electronic Democracy. Using the Internet to Influence American Politics.* 2nd ed. (Witton, 2002); Jens Hoff, Ivan Horrocks and Pieter Tops (eds.), *Democratic Governance and New Technology. Technologically Mediated Innovations in Political Practice in Western Europe* (London/New York, 2000).

22 Hill and Hughes, *Cyberpolitics;* David Holmes (ed.), *Virtual Politics. Identity & Community in Cyberspace* (London et al., 1997).

communities. Early proponents of cyber-democracy followed Grossman's vision of 'net empowerment':[23] A type of democratic structuring of cyberspace that would allow citizens to make immediate use of internet-provided communication opportunities in order to self-reliantly devise and realize solutions for public problems.[24] On these foundations, cyber-democracy expects responsible de-territorialized communities to emerge and a virtually networked civic-culture to develop, ideally on a world-wide scale. However, self-organized virtual communities are not devoid of self-interest, and as they consciously abdicate from any balance-of-power function that might be comparable to the institutional design of the offline political system, they risk disintegrating into activist groups and depreciating any form of formal organization of the political. At the same time, however, it has to be acknowledged, following Castells, that the cyber-democratic practices of the World Wildlife Fund, Greenpeace, and others have contributed to providing structuring elements of democratic processes beyond the nation-state.

Extending the Scope: Digital Democracy, Deliberation, and Communication Culture

As this overview has shown, all of these models have their merits and shortfalls, which are not always easy to weigh. Therefore, it seems promising to look at the emerging concept of *digital democracy*.[25] Representing both an analytical and a political model, digital democracy's perspective is twofold: First, it looks at the wide range of internet-based C2G, G2C, and C2C communication, yet without neglecting deliberative potentials of offline public speech. In so far as digital democracy sees itself depending on pre-existing offline structures and discourse communities in the political realm, it can be said to represent a neo-republican model of internet-based democracy that aims to address the deficits of current offline-style modern democracy.

Second, digital democracy as an analytical concept and as a cyber-political programme investigates interfaces between (internet-communication centred) deliberation and (real-world rooted) decision-making, for it maintains that deliberation as such will evoke neither procedural nor structural change in domestic or in international political decision-making. Thus, digital democracy places much emphasis on the step from deliberation to decision: For example, how, or, respectively, to what extent can internet-based communication lead to changes in, additions to, or substitutes for conventional patterns and repertories of decision-making in the political and in the societal arena? After confronting questions of this type, we can start developing models for assessing the role of online deliberation and a deliberative digital culture in governing increasingly transnationalized political communities.

---

23 Such as Grossman, *The Electronic Republic.*

24 Cf. Rheingold, *The Virtual Community.*

25 Cf. Alexander and Pal, *Digital Democracy*; Hague and Loader, *Digital Democracy*; Siedschlag, Rogg and Welzel, *Digitale Demokratie.*

Digital democracy entails a *pluralistic concept of governance* that, on the basis of existing decision-making systems and procedures, lets citizens develop their own spaces for designing solutions to common problems. Digital democracy is therefore not a full-fledged electronic consumer democracy model. Rather, to reiterate this crucial point, it assumes that the existing institutional order of a given public sphere as well as the respective political culture are the foundations on which digital modes of deliberation and governance can be built.[26]

Combining traditional and digital paths and modes of democracy, digital democracy as a political programme aims primarily at reinvigorating *civil society* – defined as the interface between the institutions of democracy and the general public. In an ideal digital democracy, political decisions would not be prepared, taken, legitimized, and implemented by an elite, but would result from a broad, issue-centred discussion at various levels. This approach thus borrows from the Habermasian concept of *deliberative democracy:* Politics gain legitimacy through the *discursive* nature of the processes of formation of opinion and of determination in a society.[27]

When we specifically refer to the end of the era of 'a tournament of distinctive knights'[28] with a view to international politics, this also means to deny the predominant role of the nation-state as an information broker: It is the people that, in the digital age, can secure real-time access to the international scene. This also means that the public needs to avail itself of digital media competence and a framework for navigating and assessing the new kind of information space. In a digital democracy however, media competence means more than technical knowledge: It empowers each individual to process information and place it into an overarching context – as well as to derive conclusions for individual political attitude and behaviour.

In terms of making the step from deliberation to decision-making, this brings us to the field of digital deliberation and *culture*. So far, especially with reference to the international system, *culture and communication* have mainly been analyzed with respect to the following question: How does the expansion of communication influence cultural change?[29] However, especially when investigating deliberation as a pillar of digital democracy and a reference point for reasoning about extending digital democracy to public spheres beyond the nation-state, we should also take

---

26 Caldow, 'The Virtual Ballot Box'; Siedschlag, Rogg and Welzel, *Digitale Demokratie.*

27 Jürgen Habermas, 'Popular Sovereignty as Procedure', in James Bohman and William Rehg (eds.), *Deliberative Democracy: Essays on Reason and Politics* (Cambridge, 1997), pp. 35–66.

28 Nicholas J. Rengger, 'No longer "A Tournament of Distinctive Knights"? Systemic Transition and the Priority of International Order', in Mike Bowker and Richard Brown (eds.), *From Cold War to Collapse* (Cambridge, 1993), pp. 145–74.

29 Cf. Robert Axelrod, 'The Dissemination of Culture: A Model with Local Convergence and Global Polarization', *Journal of Conflict Resolution*, 41 (1997): 203–26; see also the overview provided by Michael J. Greig, 'The End of Geography? Globalization, Communications, and Culture in the International System', *Journal of Conflict Resolution*, 46/2 (2002): 225–43.

into account the inverse relation: to what degree does a given culture *allow* for communication- and deliberation-induced political change?

Geertz has offered a classic definition of 'culture' as 'a historically transmitted pattern of meanings embodied in symbols, a system of inherited conceptions expressed in symbolic form by means of which men communicate, perpetuate, and develop their knowledge about and attitudes towards life.'[30] This definition, along with the tenets of cultural theory,[31] leads us to expect that any discourse within in a cultural community will primarily be *self-referential* rather than deliberative, i.e., not open to arguments and cognition, but necessarily confined to the cultural context.

Culture thus involves the self-referentiality of arguments and interpretation, risking cognitive and argumentative closure. This risk of closure brings about the risk of fragmentation of the online public into hermetic partial publics. Strictly speaking, this should render discourse between members of different cultural communities as improbable as an exchange of views on different concepts of identity and values. On these grounds, for instance, we cannot expect the internet to contribute to the evolution of a global norm of governance.

However, some authors propose ways to circumvent cultural communicative closure of this kind. Fishkin and Schiller, for example, have defined deliberation to include internet-based *agenda-setting* for political decision-making so as to avoid self-referential discursive closure.[32] However, Fishkin and Schiller obviously did not appreciate Preece's proposition that virtual social and political organization requires agenda-setting rather as a precondition for impacting real-world decision-making.[33] Fishkin and Schiller were also quick to link the concept of (virtual) civil society-rooted agenda-setting to the view that factions would take hold of cyberspace to exclude various publics from claiming a say in political agenda setting. Fishkin advocated 'deliberative polling' as a method of setting up 'deliberative micro-cosmoses' that are expected to guarantee a horizontally widespread discussion of governance issues without a pre-structuring of the discourse setting by political entrepreneurs.[34] The leading concept, then, is not to link public deliberation to political decision-making, but to improve civic skills for public debate.[35]

30 Clifford Geertz, *The Interpretation of Cultures* (New York, 1973), p. 89.

31 Roger M. Keesing, Theories of Culture, *Annual Review of Anthropology*, 3 (1974): 73–97; Robert Wuthnow, *Cultural Analysis. The Work of Peter L. Berger, Mary Douglas, Michel Foucault and Jürgen Habermas* (Boston et al., 1984); Michael Thompson, Richard J. Ellis and Aaron Wildavsky, *Cultural Theory* (Boulder et al., 1990).

32 James S. Fishkin, 'Toward Deliberative Democracy: Experimenting with an Ideal', in Stephen L. Elkin and Karol E. Sołtan (eds.), *Citizen Competence and Democratic Institutions* (University Park, PA, 1999), pp. 279–90; Herbert I. Schiller, *Information Inequality. The Deepening Social Crisis in America* (New York, 1996).

33 Preece, *Online Communities.*

34 Fishkin, 'Toward Deliberative Democracy', p. 290. For a newer account, see Shanto Iyengar, Robert C. Luskin and James S. Fishkin, 'Facilitating Informed Public Opinion: Evidence from Face–to–face and Online Deliberative Polls' (2003), <http://cdd.stanford.edu/research/papers/2003/facilitating.pdf>.

35 Stephen L. Elkin and Karol E. Sołtan (eds.), *Citizen Competence and Democratic Institutions* (University Park, 1999).

Indeed, regardless of the level of application (domestic, transnational, or global governance), digital democracy requires improving the reflexive as well as the lateral component of digitally mastered 'strong democracy'.[36] The *reflexive* component refers to the ability of citizens to deal with their own claims self-critically. The *lateral* component refers to a mutual discursive interaction of the citizens (citizen-to-citizen communication, or C2C), without the discourse being confined to citizen-to-government (C2G) communication. Laterality is important because a premature focus on citizen-to-government communication easily promotes activism on the side of the government.[37] Thus, much of the debate converges on the view that increased internet-based deliberation will not boil down to institutional substitution, but will bring forth 'institutional amplification'.[38] Institutional amplification refers to new chances for responsive governance through real-time information based politics, opening up new perspectives for multi-level governance.

Culture-oriented online-communication research (that is, research on *cyber-culture*) has its own concepts of linking deliberation and decision-making.[39] Extreme positions are represented by Turkle and Porter, who assume that social interaction in cyberspace produces purely virtual identities that are strictly distinct from the principles of social organization in the offline world.[40] Within cyber-cultural communities, Suler identifies a large potential for deliberation.[41] Appreciating the strong practices of identification with the respective cyber-culture, as described by Dery, for example,[42] we should assume the mode of online community-building that is sharply centred on the principles of inclusion and exclusion, as mentioned above, to favour the emergence of clusters of deliberation: The in-group has good foundations for discursive interaction, whereas between groups, socio-cognitive barriers to discourse tend to dominate.[43] These findings correspond to the axiom of self-referentiality in cultural theory in general.

---

36 Benjamin R. Barber, 'The Discourse of Civility', in Stephen L. Elkin/Karol E. Sołtan (eds.), *Citizen Competence and Democratic Institutions* (University Park, 1999), pp. 42–44.

37 C. Lawrence Evans and Walter J. Oleszek, 'The "Wired Congress": The Internet, Institutional Change, and Legislative Work', in James A. Thurber and Colton C. Campbell (eds.), *Congress and the Internet* (Upper Saddle River, 2003), p. 118.

38 E.g. Philip E. Agre, 'Real–Time Politics: The Internet and the Political Process', *The Information Society*, 18 (2002): 311–31.

39 For a comprehensive discussion, see David Silver, 'Looking Backwards, Looking Forwards: Cyberculture Studies 1990–2000', in David Gauntlett (ed.), *web.studies. Rewiring Media Studies for the Digital Age* (London, 2000), pp. 31–42.

40 David Porter (ed.), *Internet Culture* (New York/London, 1997); Sherry Turkle, *Life on the Screen: Identity in the Age of the Internet* (New York, 1995).

41 John Suler, 'E–Mail Communication and Relationships' (1998), <http://www.rider.edu/users/suler/psycyber/emailrel.html>.

42 Mark Dery, *Escape Velocity. Cyberculture at the End of the Century* (New York, 1996).

43 Nicola Döring, *Sozialpsychologie des Internet. Die Bedeutung des Internet für Kommunikationsprozesse, Identitäten, soziale Beziehungen und Gruppen.* 2nd ed. (Göttingen et al., 2003), p. 181.

Table 2.2   Online-offline interfaces

	form of coupling of online and offline public	*function of online-offline coupling*
crisis of legitimacy	extension of the range of institutional and civil-society communication	improved chance of legitimacy due to more transparency, responsiveness and mediation of knowledge; construction of an 'operational public'; communicative power-building in civil society
relaying	establishment of online-offline coupling by strategic actions of institutional actors	internet-based continuation of real-life politics
social psychological transfer	identification with virtual communities leads online-deliberators to position themselves in the offline-world according to their online political attitudes, or that of their online reference group	creation of online-offline transcending political group identities

Modelling Transitions from Digital Deliberation to Real-world Decision-making

In view of the variety of applicable models, how can we still comprehensively conceive of the step from (virtual) deliberation to (real-world) action that impacts collective decision-making? Two trains of thought can integrate many of the views discussed and allow us to make a connection to international-politics theorizing.

The first concept represents an *actor-based paradigm*. Related approaches follow a functional-structural frame of reference and explore *online-offline interfaces* and then investigate how certain types of actors may make use of these intersections to transport discourses, linguistic definitions of reality, etc. from online to offline or the other way round. Table 2.2 provides an overview of three contributions that appear to be especially suited for linking up with theoretical reasoning from the discipline of international politics.

The *crisis of legitimacy model*[44] with its emphasis on a communication-based involved public and on communicative power-building could be worth complementing with linguistic constructivist reasoning as presented by Kubálková, Onuf, and Kowert.[45] The *relay model*,[46] focusing on strategic communicative action within

---

44 Stefan Marschall, 'Netzöffentlichkeit und institutionelle Politik', in Christian Hartmann and Christoph Hüttig (eds.), *Netzdiskurs. Das Internet und der Strukturwandel von Kommunikation und Öffentlichkeit* (Rehburg–Loccum, 1998), pp. 157–70.

45 Vendulka Kubálková, Nicholas Onuf and Paul Kowert (eds.), *International Relations in a Constructed World* (Armonk et al., 1998).

46 Christoph Bieber, *Politische Projekte im Internet. Online–Kommunikation und politische Öffentlichkeit* (Frankfurt/M. et al., 1999), pp. 186–200.

institutional frameworks so as to gain new opportunities to foster existing opinions
and interests, could be extended by certain neorealist models such as Grieco's 'voice
opportunity'.[47] However, this model comes down to strategic rather that discursive
deliberation. The model *of social psychological transfer*,[48] which highlights identity
structures as independent variables and centres on decision-making communities,
appears worth linking to Wendt's social theory of international politics, or systemic
constructivism.[49] While less effective than strategic deliberation the relay-model
way, transfer-oriented linkages between digital deliberation and real-world decision-
making better correspond to the norm of public discourse.

The second train of thought represents a *system-based paradigm*[50] that centres
on the relationship between media culture and action. Relevant findings include the
following:

- New profiles of traditional institutions (such as e-parliamentarianism,
  envisioning parliaments as information mediators between the societal and
  the governmental sphere) can change the *interface* between *'agents'* and
  'structures'.[51] This is an especially interesting argument with a view to
  extending digital democracy-related thinking to the international arena, for
  example understanding e-parliamentarianism transnationally, as a means
  of exerting parliamentary control over less deliberation-governed areas of
  international integration and cooperation. A current e-parliamentarianism
  initiative extends to democratic control of international military cooperation
  and use of force; an initiative more pertinent to the subject of this paper comes
  from UNDP and aims at promoting regional democratization in West and
  Central Africa.[52]
- Societies gain new concepts for *experiencing their environment*[53] – for
  example, through transnational digital networking. However, we cannot expect
  this networking to result in a shared culture of transnational governance, for
  we know that we need given identities and cultures that allow us to make

47 Joseph M. Grieco, 'State Interests and Institutional Rule Trajectories: A Neorealist
Interpretation of the Maastricht Treaty and the European Economic and Monetary Union',
in Benjamin Frankel (ed.), *Realism. Restatement and Renewal* (London, 1996), pp. 261–301
(esp. pp. 287–88).

48 Döring, *Sozialpsychologie des Internet*, pp. 198–99.

49 Alexander Wendt, *Social Theory of International Politics* (Cambridge et al., 1999).

50 Theoretical foundations for this way to proceed from internet–based deliberation
to real–world decision–making can be derived, following Luhmann's system theory, from
Frank Marcinkowski, *Publizistik als autopoietisches System. Politik und Massenmedien. Eine
systemtheoretische Analyse* (Opladen, 1993).

51 Gunnar Grendstad and Per Selle, 'Cultural Theory and the New Institutionalism',
Journal of Theoretical Politics, 7/1 (1995): 6; Thompson, Ellis and Wildavsky, *Cultural
Theory*, esp. pp. 21–23.

52 Pierre Dandjinou, 'E–Parliament as a tool for fostering parliamentarian networks'
(2001), <http://www.undp.org/surf–wa/nepad/parliamentarians/docsen/eparliamenten.htm>.

53 Geertz, *The Interpretation of Cultures*; Keesing, 'Theories of Culture', pp. 75–76.

experiences and to attribute sense to our environment.[54] Thus, internet-mediated experience will rather push the trend in online communication towards further differentiation of the general public into partial publics in which communication processes follow an inherent logic and do not open up a common discursive public space.

- Within those *partial publics*, however, internet-based communication can lead to changes in the symbolically mediated management of knowledge, which can result in a new *collective attitude* towards 'reality' along with new *repertories of action*.[55] This attitudinal change then will also affect offline discourse and decision-making. In fact, Price and Cappella found in the case of the US that regular participation in policy-related chats is a predictor for increase in the participants' general social trust and thus may contribute to civic-culture change carrying the potential to transcend national boundaries.[56]
- At the same time, internet-based communication must be expected to reinforce *in-group/out-group differentiations*.[57] The condition of anonymity is found to be a major cause of this effect. In deliberation about conflict-laden issues, the digital setting of discourse thus risks radicalizing the positions of social groups.

These theoretical considerations suggest that there is a need to actively bring together internet-based self-organized governance and its communicative foundations into a 'connectable' discursive perspective that does not result in self-organizing closure, but is amenable to 'others'. Thus, also from this perspective, a good governance of the online-offline interfaces identified above appears crucial. This well corresponds to Clift's conclusion that online deliberation requires management and is not quite discursive by itself:

First, you need 'e-deliberators'. You need citizens with experience and comfort with online political conversation. I call them e-citizens. Without the social expectation that Internet should be used for democratic purposes, advanced e-government and democracy efforts will only exist primarily where internal champions lead the way or they exist as out of sight small experiments. We will not see the most compelling experiences and services spread more universally to democracies around the world without a focus on e-citizens.

---

54 Michael J. Greig, 'The End of Geography? Globalization, Communications, and Culture in the International System', *Journal of Conflict Resolution*, 46/2 (2002): 225–43.

55 Herbert Paschen, Bernd Wingert, Christopher Coenen and Gerhard Banse, *Kultur – Medien – Märkte. Medienentwicklung und kultureller Wandel* (Berlin, 2002), p. 89; Rainer Winter, *Die Kunst des Eigensinns. Cultural Studies als Kritik der Macht* (Weilerswist, 2001).

56 Vincent Price and Joseph N. Cappella, 'Online Deliberation and Its Influence: The Electronic Dialogue Project in Campaign 2000, IT & Society' (2002), <http://www.stanford.edu/group/siqss/itandsociety/v01i01/Vol01–1–A20–Price–Cappella.pdf>.

57 Caja Thimm (ed.), *Soziales im Netz. Sprache, Beziehungen und Kommunikationskulturen im Internet* (Opladen/Wiesbaden, 2000).

Second, you need well-resourced hosts who can create the structure necessary to facilitate a valuable, meaningful experience for those who take the time required to participate.[58]

One, only seemingly lapidary, precondition for any influence of a digital discourse on real-world decision-making must not be overlooked: The discourse needs to yield results. This requires a 'procedural consolidation' of the online discourse; the presented policy options and strategies must rest on a variety of perspectives and stocks of knowledge and are subject to a cycle of revision requiring them to prove their practicability in the light of iterated testing.[59] Given that online discourses imply asynchronous active participation of many unknown persons, Hohberg and Luehrs find it mandatory that online discourses be directed by a supporting methodical framework that consolidates the flow of the discussion and directs it towards commonly acceptable results.[60] One the one hand, this can imply procedural problems because, given the 'unknown participant', we cannot foresee the range of positions and arguments. On the other hand, this very condition can provide a chance to break up solidified lines of argumentation and conflict and introduce new aspects to the agenda.

Following the digital democracy model, this argument can be taken further: Digital discourse of a quality that makes its deliberative results eligible for real-world decision-making must, to a considerable extent, be based on digital real-world style procedures of articulation, selection, aggregation, and integration of interests.

This is again an argument in favour of *discursive clearing authorities* in internet-based processes of deliberation. Such discursive clearing authorities, exemplified by expert moderators of issue-specific forums, also enable us to meet a second need of real-world capable digital deliberation: Endeavouring to facilitate online discourse as well as the real-world impact of online deliberation, we need a sustainable deliberative public able to include new politically relevant publics, thus avoiding a situation where we are left with culturally caused deliberative closure and the so-called reinforcement model (which assumes that internet communication only reflects and refines real-world structures and attitudes). Both a deliberative internet public and an online-offline transfer will depend on the management of the online-offline interfaces identified above, with discursive clearing authorities as the managers in charge.

This point gains further salience when one considers the *inverse interfaces* that *critical cyber-culture studies* have been exploring since the end of the 1990s: how political elites translate real-world decision-making challenges into cyberspace in order to create benign virtual contexts for mobilizing support for their aims and interests. Cyber-culture in this sense is constructed by elite actors who seek to

---

58 Steven Clift, 'E–Government and Democracy. Representation and Citizen Engagement in the Information Age' (2004), <http://www.publicus.net/articles/cliftegovdemocracy.pdf>, p. 31.

59 Birgit Hohberg and Rolf Luehrs, 'Offline, Online, Inline – Zur Strukturierung internetvermittelter Diskurse', in Oliver Märker and Matthias Trénel (eds.), *Online–Mediation. Neue Medien in der Konfliktvermittlung – mit Beispielen aus Politik und Wirtschaft* (Berlin, 2003), p. 334.

60 Ibid., p. 333.

promote their self-interest by means of digital democracy.[61] We thus would not be well advised to wait for self-organized governance structures for internet-related deliberation and arguing to evolve. Rather, what is needed is governance of the use of the internet's potentials for new forms of governance. Only this way can we handle the risk of digital deliberative spaces becoming a source of 'other-empowerment' rather than of self-empowerment. This resonates with Hutchings' caveat that transnational democratic procedures in general have the potential to extinguish effective self-governance at local or national levels.[62]

Towards Digital Democracy on a Transnational Scale?

If it is correct that digital deliberation is a root promoter of new forms of governance to about the same extent as it is dependent on an existing pre-structuring of its field of application, the risks and challenges identified above, such as

- dependency on pre-existing social organization
- need for a communication culture
- inherent constraints that such a culture poses on deliberation
- self-referentiality, cognitive closure of discourse and partial publics
- need for online-offline interfaces
- need for governance of those interfaces, centred on discursive clearing authorities

must also be appreciated in considerations about an internet-empowered public sphere beyond the nation-state. Just as *global governance*[63] is not a strategy to abolish the nation-state, but rests on several pillars, one of which is reliance on nation-state capabilities and structuring forces, *deliberation* based on a digital democracy model transferred beyond the nation-state is not self-organized as such, but is itself in need of governance and discursive clearing. The concept of digital democracy advocated here therefore rests on the assumption that internet-mediated democracy and its discursive quality necessarily build (and depend) on existing structures. Moreover, as with global governance, a digital democracy perspective within and beyond the boundaries of the nation-state rests on the view that deliberation is a variable process involving a broad range of actors and institutions. The digital pillar is thus one among others within a framework of both formally and informally organized interactive procedures of weighting arguments and paving the ground for problem-responsive decision-making.

---

61 Cf. Wesley Cooper, 'Information Technology and Internet Culture', *The Journal of Virtual Environments*, 6/1 (2002), <http://www.brandeis.edu/pubs/HTML/V6/iculture.html>.

62 Kimberly Hutchings, *International Political Theory* (London, 1999), p. 166.

63 I follow the definition of the Commission on Global Governance: *Our Global Neighbourhood. The Report of the Commission on Global Governance* (Oxford/New York, 1995), p. 35 and the analytical model elaborated by Dirk Messner, *The Network Society* (London, 1997).

On this intellectual foundation, quite a few theoreticians and practitioners alike have suggested firstly not to globalise or trans-nationalise, but to 'localise' online deliberation. That is, to empower interested citizens to set up communal and regional 'public networks' engaging in digital discourse about local problems.[64] Behind this concept stands the assumption that the perception among citizens of a direct impact and a proximity to communal real-world decision-makers will best guarantee the qualitative standards that deliberative democracy requires. In this case, the online-offline link is established through recourse to pre-existent real-life communities. So, from a political-science point of view, public networks are complementary virtualisations of established structures of communal citizen engagement. However, from a critical point of view, making this model fruitful for transnational deliberation may risk boosting the digital divide to a world-wide scale, as Zinnbauer argues.[65] In less pessimistic terms, this argument underscores the point made above for a mediated, rather than self-organized, approach to online deliberation.

Just as digital democracy within the nation-state needs governance and also opens up new perspectives for governance, digital democracy transferred beyond the nation-state frame of reference can foster governance, but must itself be embedded in a framework of democratic internet governance. Correspondingly, the role of deliberative digital culture in governing increasingly trans-nationalising political communities can only be usefully defined on the basis of the existing social and political organization of the respective public space. Disillusioning though this prospect may seem, from a methodological point of view it implies remarkable systematic potential for the real-world decision-making impact of digital deliberation, because the model of *online-offline interfaces* becomes directly applicable.

Some of the few studies on the real-world impact of internet communication in a trans-nationalising world follow an approach comparative to that of Featherstone, which is highly critical of the concept of one single, world-wide culture, including communication culture.[66] Featherstone's argument was that globalization as such, and the globalization of communication opportunities in particular, are accompanied by the dissolution of social attachments, which implies an unclear range of identity and value choices, a decoupling of culture and communication from (local) historicity, and the overstretch of culturally bound meaning in alien contexts. However, following authors like Münch, it is interesting to note that this lays the ground for a specific role of internet-based transnational and international communication in the field of conflict management.[67] This is because we can then expect the global society of the 21st century to be based on an identity that develops from a primordial identity (defined by territory and origin) via a medial identity (defined by communication)

64 Steven Clift, 'E–Democracy, E–Governance and Public Net–Work' (2003), <http://www.mail–archive.com/do–wire@lists.umn.edu/msg00046.html>.

65 Dieter Zinnbauer, 'Internet, civil society and global governance: the neglected political dimension of the digital divide', *Information & Security*, 7 (2001): 45–64.

66 Mike Featherstone, *Undoing Culture. Globalization, Postmodernism and Identity* (London et al.,1995).

67 Richard Münch, *Globale Dynamik, lokale Lebenswelten. Der schwierige Weg in die Weltgesellschaft* (Frankfurt/M. et al., 1998), pp. 314–22.

into a *virtual identity*, which is abstract, and detached from everyday life. For the same reason, it is also not immediately convertible into capital for social interaction – so that identity-related conflict potential would result much less frequently in manifest conflict processes. In this perspective, the governance impact of virtual identities – for example, resulting from and reinforced by digital discourse and deliberation – would finally not be to foster, but to mellow integration beyond the sphere of the nation-state.

Nevertheless, there are also models that assess internet communication as an important factor in constituting a *transnational public* that contributes to solidifying, for example, the enlarged and deepened integration within the European Union (EU). McGrew for instance has argued that within the EU, publics can no longer be defined on spatial (e.g. national) grounds and can only be defined on an issue- and policy-related basis.[68] The resulting various deterritorialised publics would be transnational partial publics, and they would represent the field in which European governance would have to gain legitimacy and public support.[69] Classics of transnationalism and integration such as Nye, departing from their initially cited view of the internet as a soft-power resource available to nation-states, go as far as to see the virtual identity factor as a foundational principle for coming integration processes divorced from national grounds: 'Interactivity at low cost allows for the development of new virtual communities. While still in their infancy, transnational virtual communities are likely to grow and more complex identities and loyalties to develop.'[70]

Conclusion

In conclusion, one must not forget that digital democracy, regardless of the scale on which we place it, is not only a tool for forging a post-national deliberative communication culture, but also depends on the existent communication culture. The *UN World Summit on the Information Society*[71] of 2003 explicitly acknowledged this caveat. However, the World Summit's Plan of Action was not rooted in a critical discussion of the consequences for digital deliberation on a world-wide scale. Rather, it followed the more timid of a digital consumer democracy, or e-democracy, based on the concept of an enabling state (or, in this case, an enabling community of states) – deciding on a case-by-case basis which internet-based opportunities to

---

68 Anthony McGrew, 'Democracy beyond Borders? Globalization and the Reconstruction of Democratic Theory and Practice', in Anthony G. McGrew (ed.), *The Transformation of Democracy? Globalization and Territorial Democracy* (Cambridge, 1997), pp. 231–66.

69 Cf. Hans–Jörg Trenz, *Zur Konstitution politischer Öffentlichkeit in der Europäischen Union. Zivilgesellschaftliche Subpolitik oder schaupolitische Inszenierung?* (Baden–Baden, 2002).

70 Joseph S. Nye Jr., 'Transnational Relations, Interdependence and Globalization', in Michael Brecher and Frank P. Harvey (eds.), *Realism and Institutionalism in International Studies* (Ann Arbor, 2002), p.166.

71 <http://www.itu.int/wsis>.

provide for civic deliberation.[72] No wonder, then, that the Summit's Plan of Action met with a harsh counter-action plan of the plenary of the representatives of the civil society, emphasizing the general demand for increased rights of information and participation for the public on a global scale.[73]

Whereas state actors have not fully appreciated the governance potentials of post-national digital discourse and deliberation, non-state actors have overestimated the self-organizing potentials of internet-based public discourse and failed to appreciate the need of governance of digital democracy as fresh means of governance. We must bridge a similar gap in theorizing, especially when advancing from domestic to trans- and international applications of the digital democracy model. Research on the digital democratic potentials of increasingly transnationalising societies for governance should therefore proceed on the cutting edge between the fields of 'political system', 'political culture', 'political communication', 'comparative politics' and 'international politics' – for neither decision-making and governance issues nor the concept of deliberation as such fundamentally alter their substance and requirements when transferred to a different level of analysis and practice of internet-based deliberation.

Bibliography

6, Perri, *E-Governance. Styles of Political Judgement in the Information Age Polity* (Basingstoke: Macmillan, 2004).

Agre, Philip E., 'Real-Time Politics: The Internet and the Political Process', *The Information Society*, 18 (2002): 311–31.

Alexander, Cynthia J. and Leslie A. Pal (eds.), *Digital Democracy: Policy and Politics in the Wired World* (Toronto et al.: Oxford University Press, 1998).

Allison, Juliann Emmons (ed.), *Technology, Development, and Democracy. International Conflict and Cooperation in the Information Age* (Albany: State University of New York Press, 2002).

Axelrod, Robert, 'The Dissemination of Culture: A Model with Local Convergence and Global Polarization', *Journal of Conflict Resolution*, 41 (1997): 203–26.

Barber, Benjamin R., *Strong Democracy. Participatory Politics for a New Age* (Berkeley et al.: University of California Press, 1984).

Barber, Benjamin R., 'The Discourse of Civility', in Stephen L. Elkin and Karol E. Soltan (eds.), *Citizen Competence and Democratic Institutions* (University Park: Pennsylvania State University Press, 1999), pp. 39–47.

Bieber, Christoph, *Politische Projekte im Internet. Online-Kommunikation und politische Öffentlichkeit* (Frankfurt/M. et al.: Campus, 1999).

---

72 World Summit on the Information Society, 'Plan of Action. Document WSIS–03/GENEVA/DOC/5–E. 12 December 2003' (2003), <http://www.itu.int/dms_pub/itu–s/md/03/wsis/doc/S03–WSIS–DOC–0005!!PDF–E.pdf>.

73 WSIS Civil Society Plenary, 'Civil Society Declaration to the World Summit on the Information Society. Shaping Information Societies for Human Needs' (2003), <http://www.worldsummit2003.de/download_en/WSIS–CS–Decl–08Dec2003–en.pdf>.

Bismarck, Max von, Daniel Dettling and Tino Schuppan, 'E-Governance in der Wissensgesellschaft – neue Dimensionen der politischen Willensbildung', in Alexander Siedschlag and Alexander Bilgeri (eds.), *Kursbuch Internet und Politik*, vol. 2 (Opladen: Leske + Budrich, 2003), pp. 23–38.

Browning, Graeme, *Electronic Democracy. Using the Internet to Influence American Politics.* 2nd ed. (Witton: Pemberton, 2002).

Caldow, Janet, 'The Virtual Ballot Box: A Survey of Digital Democracy in Europe. IBM Corporation, Institute for Electronic Government' (1999), <http://www. politik–digital.de/archiv/forschung/ibm_studie.pdf>, accessed 1 January 2007.

Castells, Manuel, *The Rise of the Network Society.* Reprint (Malden, MA: Blackwell, 1998).

Clift, Steven, 'E-Democracy, E-Governance and Public Net-Work' (2003), <http://www.mail-archive.com/do-wire@lists.umn.edu/msg00046.html>, accessed 1 January 2007.

Clift, Steven, 'E–Government and Democracy. Representation and Citizen Engagement in the Information Age' (2004), <http://www.publicus.net/articles/cliftegovdemocracy.pdf>, accessed 1 January 2007.

Commission on Global Governance, *Our Global Neighbourhood. The Report of the Commission on Global Governance* (Oxford/New York: Oxford University Press, 1995).

Cooper, Wesley, 'Information Technology and Internet Culture', *The Journal of Virtual Environments*, 6/1 (2002).

Dandjinou, Pierre, 'E-Parliament as a tool for fostering parliamentarian networks' (2001), http://www.undp.org/surf-wa/nepad/parliamentarians/docsen/eparliamenten. htm>, accessed 1 January 2007.

Davies, Todd and Beth Noveck (eds.), *Online Deliberation: Design, Research, and Practice* (Chicago: University of Chicago Press, 2006).

Dery, Mark, *Escape Velocity. Cyberculture at the End of the Century* (New York: Grove, 1996).

Döring, Nicola, *Sozialpsychologie des Internet. Die Bedeutung des Internet für Kommunikationsprozesse, Identitäten, soziale Beziehungen und Gruppen.* 2nd ed. (Göttingen et al.: Hogrefe, 2003).

Elkin, Stephen L. and Karol E. Sołtan (eds.), *Citizen Competence and Democratic Institutions* (University Park: Pennsylvania State University Press, 1999).

Evans, C. Lawrence and Walter J. Oleszek, 'The 'Wired Congress': The Internet, Institutional Change, and Legislative Work', in James A. Thurber and Colton C. Campbell (eds.), *Congress and the Internet* (Upper Saddle River, NJ: Prentice-Hall, 2003), pp. 99–122.

Featherstone, Mike, *Undoing Culture. Globalization, Postmodernism and Identity* (London: Sage, 1995).

Fishkin, James S., 'Toward Deliberative Democracy: Experimenting with an Ideal', in Stephen L. Elkin and Karol E. Sołtan (eds.), *Citizen Competence and Democratic Institutions* (University Park: Pennsylvania State University Press, 1999), pp. 279–90.

Franda, Marcus F., *Launching into Cyberspace: Internet Development and Politics in Five World Regions* (Boulder: Rienner, 2002).

Geertz, Clifford, *The Interpretation of Cultures* (New York: Basic Books, 1973).

Greig, Michael J., 'The End of Geography? Globalization, Communications, and Culture in the International System', *Journal of Conflict Resolution*, 46/2 (2002): 225–43.

Grendstad, Gunnar and Per Selle, 'Cultural Theory and the New Institutionalism', *Journal of Theoretical Politics*, 7/1 (1995): 5–27.

Grieco, Joseph M., 'State Interests and Institutional Rule Trajectories: A Neorealist Interpretation of the Maastricht Treaty and the European Economic and Monetary Union', in Benjamin Frankel (ed.), *Realism. Restatement and Renewal* (London: Cass, 1996), pp. 261–301.

Grossman, Lawrence K., *The Electronic Republic. Reshaping Democracy in the Information Age* (New York et al., Viking Penguin, 1995).

Hague, Barry N. and Brian D. Loader (eds.), *Digital Democracy. Discourse and Decision Making in the Information Age* (London/New York: Routledge, 1999).

Hill, Kevin A. and John E. Hughes, *Cyberpolitics: Citizen Activism in the Age of the Internet* (Lanham: Rowman and Littlefield, 1998).

Hoff, Jens, Ivan Horrocks and Pieter Tops (eds.), *Democratic Governance and New Technology. Technologically Mediated Innovations in Political Practice in Western Europe* (London/New York: Routledge, 2000).

Hoff, Jens, Ivan Horrocks and Pieter Tops, 'Introduction: New Technology and the 'Crises' of Democracy', in Jens Hoff, Ivan Horrocks and Pieter Tops (eds.), *Democratic Governance and New Technology. Technologically Mediated Innovations in Political Practice in Western Europe* (London/New York: Routledge, 2000), pp. 1–10.

Hohberg, Birgit and Rolf Luehrs, 'Offline, Online, Inline – Zur Strukturierung internetvermittelter Diskurse', in Oliver Märker and Matthias Trénel (eds.), *Online–Mediation. Neue Medien in der Konfliktvermittlung – mit Beispielen aus Politik und Wirtschaft* (Berlin: edition sigma, 2003), pp. 327–48.

Holmes, David (ed.), *Virtual Politics. Identity & Community in Cyberspace* (London: Sage, 1997).

Hundley, Richard O., Robert H. Anderson, Tora K. Bikson and C. Richard Neu, *The Global Course of the Information Revolution. Recurring Themes and Regional Variations* (Santa Monica: RAND, 2003).

Hutchings, Kimberly, *International Political Theory* (London: Sage, 1999).

Iyengar, Shanto, Robert C. Luskin and James S. Fishkin, 'Facilitating Informed Public Opinion: Evidence from Face–to–face and Online Deliberative Polls' (2003), <http://cdd.stanford.edu/research/papers/2003/facilitating.pdf>, accessed 1 January 2007.

Keesing, Roger M., 'Theories of Culture', *Annual Review of Anthropology*, 3 (1974): 73–97.

Kubálková, Vendulka, Nicholas Onuf and Paul Kowert (eds.), *International Relations in a Constructed World* (Armonk et al.: Sharpe, 1998).

Lazar, Jonathan and Jennifer Preece, 'Social Considerations in Online Communities: Usability, Sociability, and Success Factors', in Herre van Oostendorp (ed.), *Cognition in a Digital World* (Mahwah/London: Erlbaum, 2003), pp. 127–51.

Marcinkowski, Frank, *Publizistik als autopoietisches System. Politik und Massenmedien. Eine systemtheoretische Analyse* (Opladen: Westdeutscher Verlag, 1993).

Marschall, Stefan, 'Netzöffentlichkeit und institutionelle Politik', in Christian Hartmann and Christoph Hüttig (eds.), *Netzdiskurs. Das Internet und der Strukturwandel von Kommunikation und Öffentlichkeit* (Rehburg–Loccum: Evangelische Akademie Loccum, 1998), pp. 157–70.

McGrew, Anthony, 'Democracy beyond Borders? Globalization and the Reconstruction of Democratic Theory and Practice', in Anthony G. McGrew (ed.), *The Transformation of Democracy? Globalization and Territorial Democracy* (Cambridge: Polity, 1997), pp. 231–66.

Messner, Dirk, *The Network Society* (London: Cass, 1997).

Münch, Richard, *Globale Dynamik, lokale Lebenswelten. Der schwierige Weg in die Weltgesellschaf* (Frankfurt/M. et al.: Suhrkamp, 1998).

Nye, Joseph S. Jr., 'Transnational Relations, Interdependence and Globalization', in Michael Brecher and Frank P. Harvey (eds.), *Realism and Institutionalism in International Studies* (Ann Arbor: University of Michigan Press, 2002), pp. 160–73.

Nye, Joseph S. and William A. Owens, 'America's Information Edge', *Foreign Affairs*, 75/2 (1996): 20–36.

OECD, Policy Brief 'The e-government imperative: main findings' (2003), <http://www.oecd.org/dataoecd/60/60/2502539.pdf>, accessed 1 January 2007.

Paschen, Herbert, Bernd Wingert, Christopher Coenen and Gerhard Banse, *Kultur – Medien – Märkte. Medienentwicklung und kultureller Wandel* (Berlin: edition sigma, 2002).

Porter, David (ed.), *Internet Culture* (New York/London: Routledge, 1997).

Preece, Jennifer, *Online Communities: Designing Usability, Supporting Sociability* (New York: Wiley, 2000).

Price, Vincent and Joseph N. Cappella, 'Online Deliberation and Its Influence: The Electronic Dialogue Project in Campaign 2000, IT & Society' (2002), <http://www.stanford.edu/group/siqss/itandsociety/v01i01/Vol01-1-A20-Price-Cappella.pdf>.

Rengger, Nicholas J., 'No longer 'A Tournament of Distinctive Knights'? Systemic Transition and the Priority of International Order', in Mike Bowker and Richard Brown (eds.), *From Cold War to Collapse* (Cambridge: Cambridge University Press, 1993), pp. 145–74.

Rheingold, Howard, *The Virtual Community. Homesteading on the Electronic Frontier* (Reading: Addison-Wesley, 1993).

Rössler, Patrick (ed.), *Online-Kommunikation. Beiträge zur Nutzung und Wirkung* (Opladen: Westdeutscher Verlag, 1998).

Rosenau, James N. and David Johnson, 'Information Technologies and Turbulence in World Politics', in Juliann Emmons Allison (ed.), *Technology, Development, and Democracy. International Conflict and Cooperation in the Information Age* (Albany: State University of New York Press, 2002), pp. 55–78.

Schiller, Herbert I., *Information Inequality. The Deepening Social Crisis in America* (New York: Routledge, 1996).

Siedschlag, Alexander, Arne Rogg and Carolin Welzel, *Digitale Demokratie. Willlensbildung und Partizipation per Internet* (Opladen: Leske + Budrich, 2002).

Suler, John, 'E-Mail Communication and Relationships' (1998), <http://www.rider.edu/users/suler/psycyber/emailrel.html>, accessed 1 January 2007.

Thimm, Caja (ed.), *Soziales im Netz. Sprache, Beziehungen und Kommunikationskulturen im Internet* (Opladen/Wiesbaden: Westdeutscher Verlag, 2000).

Trenz, Hans–Jörg, *Zur Konstitution politischer Öffentlichkeit in der Europäischen Union. Zivilgesellschaftliche Subpolitik oder schaupolitische Inszenierung?* (Baden–Baden: Nomos, 2002).

Turkle, Sherry, *Life on the Screen: Identity in the Age of the Internet* (New York: Simon and Schuster, 1995).

Wendt, Alexander, *Social Theory of International Politics* (Cambridge: Cambridge University Press, 1999).

Winter, Rainer, *Die Kunst des Eigensinns. Cultural Studies als Kritik der Macht* (Weilerswist: Velbrück Wissenschaft, 2001).

World Summit on the Information Society, 'Plan of Action. Document WSIS-03/GENEVA/DOC/5-E. 12 December 2003' (2003), <http://www.itu.int/dms_pub/itu-s/md/03/wsis/doc/S03-WSIS-DOC-0005!!PDF-E.pdf>, accessed 1 January 2007.

WSIS Civil Society Plenary, 'Civil Society Declaration to the World Summit on the Information Society. Shaping Information Societies for Human Needs' (2003), <http://www.worldsummit2003.de/download_en/WSIS-CS-Decl-08Dec2003-en.pdf>, accessed 1 January 2007.

Wuthnow, Robert, *Cultural Analysis. The Work of Peter L. Berger, Mary Douglas, Michel Foucault and Jürgen Habermas* (Boston, MA et al.: Routledge, 1984).

Zinnbauer, Dieter, 'Internet, civil society and global governance: the neglected political dimension of the digital divide', *Information & Security*, 7 (2001): 45–64.

Chapter 3

The Information Revolution and the Rules of Jurisdiction in Public International Law

Mika Hayashi

Introduction

When the information revolution became apparent in the 1990s, two suggestions about the regulatory powers of states in cyberspace prevailed. Normatively, it was suggested that cyberspace was a space of new freedom where state regulations should not be as extensive as they were in real space.[1] As a matter of fact, it was suggested that the regulations of states could not function in the way they did in real space, because of the physical difference between the two.[2] The second suggestion had important implications for rules of jurisdiction in public international law. The most remarkable physical difference between cyberspace and real space is the borderless environment of the former, and the rules of jurisdiction in the latter have always been closely linked to the concept of territory. Therefore, they became the most difficult issue as a result of the information revolution.[3] The purpose of this

---

1 A good summary of this normative claim in 1990s is found in Michael Geist, 'Cyberlaw 2.0', *Boston College Law Review*, 44 (2003): 325–33.

2 Ibid., 323–25.

3 Joel P. Trachtman, 'Cyberspace, Sovereignty, Jurisdiction, and Modernism', *Indiana Journal of Global Legal Issues*, 5/2 (1998): 569. Apart from the rules of jurisdiction, issues of public international law that are frequently discussed in the context of the information revolution include the law of armed conflict (Louise Doswald-Beck, 'Some Thoughts on Computer Network Attack and the International Law of Armed Conflict', in Michael N. Schmitt and Brian T. O'Donnell (eds.), *Computer Network Attack and International Law* (Newport, 2002), pp. 163–85; James J. Busuttil, 'A Taste of Armageddon: The Law of Armed Conflict as Applied to Cyberwar', in Guy S. Goodwin-Gill and Stefan Talmon (eds.), *The Reality of International Law: Essays in Honour of Ian Brownlie* (Oxford, 1999), pp. 37–55; use of force (Jason Barkham, 'Information Warfare and International Law on the Use of Force', *New York University Journal of International Law and Policy*, 34 (2001): 57–113); coercion (Christopher C. Joyner and Catherine Lotrionte, 'Information Warfare as International Coercion: Elements of a Legal Framework', *European Journal of International Law*, 12/5 (2001): 825–65); governance (Bartram S. Brown, 'Developing Countries in the New Global Information Order', in Laurence Boisson de Chazournes and Vera Gowlland-Debbas (eds.), *The International Legal System in Quest of Equity and Universality: Liber Amicorum Georges Abi-Saab* (The Hague, 2001), pp. 411–26).

chapter is to verify whether or not rules of jurisdiction that were developed before the information revolution are still used in cyber-context today. If there are changes in these rules, then the distribution of states' regulatory powers in cyberspace is different from that in real space: the rules of jurisdiction are the rules of allocation of states' regulatory powers on the international plane. In this chapter, two categories of rules of jurisdiction will be examined, namely, rules found in general international law, and rules found in treaties.

The primary concern of rules of jurisdiction in the first category is to determine which state may regulate acts that are transnational in their composition or effects, and on what grounds they may do so. Cases where more than one state is interested in exercising jurisdiction were not unheard of even before the information revolution, since many acts in real space are also transnational. For example, in 1889, a German citizen who had cried '*Vive la France*' on the French side of the Franco-German border was later prosecuted in Germany for this transnational act, which was heard in the German territory.[4] There is, however, a quantitative difference between a single seditious cry in real space in 1889 and posting a message in the internet today. In cyberspace, the repercussions of such an act are felt in multiple territories simultaneously, and can easily involve a large number of internet users. Thus, the focus in the examination of the first category of rules of jurisdiction is on whether this quantitative change in cyberspace has produced any change in the rules themselves, or in the ways in which they are applied. It will be argued that the information revolution has not produced any new rules, though there may be changes in the practical functions of some of the established rules when they are applied to cyberspace.

In the second category of rules of jurisdiction in treaties, a different concern emerges. States that draw up multilateral treaties are interested in adopting rules of jurisdiction that help these common regulations achieve their goals best. With regard to the information revolution, states are increasingly interested in the prevention and repression of so-called cyber-crimes. Many of these cyber-crimes are again transnational in their composition and effects. Consequently, their prevention and repression can be significantly frustrated if the prosecution is strictly limited to cyber-crimes that occur entirely within the territory. Against this background, the Cybercrime Convention,[5] a multilateral treaty, adopted its own set of rules of jurisdiction. Therefore, the focus in the examination of the rules of the second category is on whether the rules adopted in the Cybercrime Convention show any innovation, compared to the prior multilateral treaties that deal with crimes in real space. It will be shown that there is no discernible new development that is particular to cyberspace in the second category.

The question of jurisdiction over online acts can arise both in a criminal context and in a civil context. As the outline above suggests, this chapter deals with criminal

---

4   See *Journal du droit international privé et de la jurisprudence comparée*, 17 (1890): 498–99.

5   Convention on Cybercrime, European Treaty Series No. 185 [hereinafter referred to as the Cybercrime Convention].

jurisdiction, a subject of public international law,[6] as opposed to civil jurisdiction.[7] The chapter is divided into two parts. The first part presents the rules of jurisdiction in two categories prior to the information revolution. In the second part, the developments in each category are analyzed in the context of cyberspace.

Rules of Jurisdiction Prior to the Information Revolution

Rules of Jurisdiction in General International Law

Territorial Principle and Its Extended Forms   States have jurisdiction over acts that occur in their territory, as a corollary of their territorial sovereignty. The weight of this territorial principle differs, however, depending on the different aspects of jurisdiction that are at issue. Regarding enforcement jurisdiction, the territorial principle is absolute. Even if State A wishes to apprehend suspects of a crime, once the suspects flee to State B, the authorities of State A cannot arrest them in State B and bring them back to State A without the consent of State B. Without it, an arrest or kidnapping would be an illegal exercise of enforcement jurisdiction. The territorial principle of enforcement jurisdiction is firmly supported by state practice: kidnappings of individuals by foreign state authorities instead of requesting their extradition are condemned as illegal.[8] In this sense, enforcement jurisdiction in one's territory is exclusive. In contrast, there are exceptions to the territorial principle in prescriptive jurisdiction, that is, jurisdiction to prescribe rules.[9] States have prescriptive jurisdiction over acts that occur in their territory. Unlike enforcement jurisdiction, however, the territorial principle of prescriptive jurisdiction is not absolute and admits exceptions.[10] Most of them are based on the idea that even

---

6   'Criminal jurisdiction' in this context refers not only to jurisdiction over criminal matters in a narrow sense. It refers to jurisdiction over all matters related to coercive measures by the state authorities that are implemented to secure compliance with the law. Andreas F. Lowenfeld, 'Public Law in the International Arena: Conflict of Laws, International Law, and Some Suggestions for Their Interaction', *Recueil des cours*, 163 (1979): pp. 311–445; Douglas E. Rosenthal and William M. Knighton, *National Laws and International Commerce: Problem of Extraterritoriality* (London, 1982).

7   For recent studies of civil jurisdiction and cyberspace, see e.g., Oren Bigos, 'Jurisdiction over Cross-Border Wrongs on the Internet', *International and Comparative Law Quarterly*, 54/3 (2005): 585–620.

8   For examples of state practice, see Antonio Cassese, *International Law* (Oxford, 2004), pp. 50–52.

9   For the distinction between enforcement jurisdiction and prescriptive jurisdiction, see D.W. Bowett, 'Jurisdiction: Changing Patterns of Authority over Activities and Resources', *British Yearbook of International Law*, 53 (1982): p. 1; Vaughan Lowe, 'Jurisdiction', in Malcolm D. Evans (ed.), *International Law* (Oxford, 2003), pp. 332f.

10 Since these exceptions to the strict territorial principle are the focus of this chapter, unless otherwise indicated, jurisdiction in this chapter refers to prescriptive jurisdiction. For the purposes of this chapter, the application of municipal law by municipal courts is considered as an actualization of the prescription, i.e., the exercise of prescriptive jurisdiction in concrete cases.

though the act in question may not occur in the territory in its entirety, there may be a legitimate and sufficient link between the state and the act in question that justifies the exercise of jurisdiction.[11]

One series of exceptions could be called the extended forms of the territorial principle.[12] Even when a part of the act occurs outside the territory of State A, the act may still be considered sufficiently important for State A by the regulators of State A. For example, acts may be commenced in State A but completed in State B. There may also be acts that are commenced outside State A but completed in the territory of State A. State A may have a legitimate interest in regulating some of these acts, depending on their nature and their repercussion on State A. To cope with such transnational conducts, municipal law often provides that the states have jurisdiction when one of the constituent elements of the crime takes place within their territory. When the state where the act began claims jurisdiction, the link between the state and the act is the occurrence of (the beginning of) this act in the territory, though the act continued in another state as well. A partial territorial link of this kind is generally accepted as a legitimate basis for a jurisdictional claim. It is called the subjective territorial principle, and is one of the extended forms of the territorial principle. Similarly, the state where an act was completed may claim jurisdiction over that act even if the act in question did not begin in its territory. Likewise, there is a partial territorial link in this case, and the justification for this type of claim is called the objective territorial principle. The well-known decision concerning the *S.S. Lotus* rendered by the Permanent Court of International Justice (hereinafter referred to as the P.C.I.J.)[13] is frequently cited as the authority for the objective territorial principle.[14] The case concerned the collision of two vessels, French and Turkish, on the high seas. Eight Turkish sailors and passengers aboard the Turkish vessel died as a result of this collision. When the *Lotus,* the French vessel, eventually came into a

---

11 One exception to these exceptions is universal jurisdiction: this type of jurisdiction is exercised over certain category of crimes, even when these crimes have no particular factual link with the state that prosecutes them. See Christian Tomuschat, *Human Rights: Between Idealism and Realism* (Oxford, 2003), p. 274.

12 There are also other types of exceptions. They are still based on the idea that the claim of jurisdiction must be based on some kind of link between the state and the act in question, but the link is not territorial in these exceptions. For instance, many states have legislation that allows them to exercise jurisdiction on the basis of the nationality of the offender (nationality principle), regardless of the location of the physical act. Some states also have legislation that allows them to do so on the basis of the nationality of the victim (passive nationality principle), again regardless of the location of the physical act. States can also enact laws to prosecute crimes that harm the vital interests of states, even if they occur abroad and are committed by foreigners (protective principle). A well-known example of such a crime is the forgery of national currency.

13 *S. S. Lotus* (France v. Turkey), PCIJ Reports, Series A. No. 10 (7 September 1927) [hereinafter referred to as the *S.S. Lotus* case].

14 Robert Jennings, 'Extraterritorial Jurisdiction and the United States Antitrust Laws', *British Yearbook of International Law*, 33 (1957): 159f.; Michael Akehurst, 'Jurisdiction in International Law', *British Yearbook of International Law*, 46 (1972–73): 152; Lowe, 'Jurisdiction', p. 338.

Turkish harbour after the collision, one of its officers was arrested, and the Criminal Court in Istanbul delivered its judgment, upholding the criminal responsibility of the French officer under the Turkish criminal law. France disagreed that Turkey had jurisdiction over the case, and the two states took the case to the P.C.I.J. The P.C.I.J. decided that Turkish authorities could claim jurisdiction to prosecute the offender. Using an analogy between vessels and territories, the P.C.I.J. explained that '[T]he courts of many countries [...] interpret criminal law in the sense that offences, the authors of which at the moment of commission are in the territory of another State, are nevertheless to be regarded as having been committed in the national territory, if one of the constituent elements of the offence, and more especially its effects, have taken place there.'[15] In this case, the death of the passengers aboard the Turkish vessel was interpreted to mean that one constituent element of the alleged offence did occur in the Turkish 'territory'.

With regard to the following discussion on developments since the information revolution, the significance of the example of the *S.S. Lotus* case is three-fold.[16] First, even in real space prior to the information revolution, acts were not always confined within a territory of one state.[17] In that sense, offences that are intra-territorial are not a new phenomenon in cyberspace. Second, in the *S.S. Lotus* case, it was the act, and not only its repercussions, that was characterized by the P.C.I.J. as being intra-territorial. Third, public international law has thus always recognized a partial territorial link of this kind to be a sufficient basis of jurisdiction as an application of the objective territorial principle.

Limits of Extraterritorial Jurisdiction   The rationale behind the territorial principle and its extended forms is plain. When there is a substantive difference between the regulations of the territorial state and the regulations that another state seeks to impose by exercising extraterritorial jurisdiction, the conduct of the latter may seriously collide with the local regulatory policies. It is inevitably an attempt to restrict the freedom of other states to act within their own territories.[18] Thus, in the physical world built upon the concept of territorial states, and in the legal order built upon the concept of territorial sovereignty, to permit the extraterritorial exercise of jurisdiction without requiring any link between the state claiming jurisdiction and the act in question would be a contradiction in itself. In the present legal order, which is constructed upon the logic of territorial sovereignty, extraterritorial jurisdiction has to remain an exception. In plain terms, when jurisdiction is exercised extraterritorially, there has to be sufficient justification, i.e., a link between the state and the act over which it wishes to exercise jurisdiction. The extended forms of the

---

15 *S. S. Lotus* case, see above, note 13, at p. 23.

16 While the *S.S Lotus* case retains its significance for the discussions of jurisdictional issues in general, its significance as a precedent in the law of the sea is minimum: analogy between vessels and territories is no longer used in the contemporary law of the sea; the provision on jurisdiction concerning vessel collisions in the U.N. Law of the Sea Convention did not follow the *S.S. Lotus* case, either.

17 Lowe, 'Jurisdiction', pp. 347f.

18 Michael Byers, *Custom, Power, and the Power of Rules: International Relations and Customary International Law* (Cambridge, 1999), p. 65.

territorial principle, such as the objective territorial principle, constitute sufficient justification, and are accepted in state practice.

The evolution of the controversy over the effects doctrine highlights this general concern about setting limits to extraterritorial jurisdiction. The effects doctrine is another extended form of the territorial principle. It was developed by the US courts in the application of the US anti-trust regulations. The US assertion went beyond what the objective territorial principle would permit, in that these courts tried to exercise jurisdiction over cartel arrangements and collusions which had not physically taken place within the US at all. The link that the US relied on in such instances was the 'effects' felt within the US as a result of acts abroad that were contrary to the US anti-trust regulations. The effects doctrine meant that '[a]ny state may impose liabilities, even upon persons not within its allegiance, for conduct outside its borders that has consequences within its borders which the state reprehends,'[19] or that the US anti-trust law 'applies to foreign conduct that was meant to produce and did in fact produce some substantial effects in the United States' even if these conducts were lawful in the state where they occurred.[20]

The effects doctrine remained a controversial proposition for a long time, except in the US.[21] Other states protested against the US exercise of jurisdiction based on the effects doctrine. They enacted blocking legislation, and ordered the private actors involved in their territory not to comply with US court orders.[22] The general concern was that the effects doctrine would do away with the limits of extraterritorial jurisdiction altogether: this justification based on effects alone would justify extraterritorial jurisdiction infinitely. The concern was eloquently expressed in the emphasis on the difference between the effects doctrine and the objective territorial principle. The objective territorial principle requires intra-territorial action, whereas according to the effects doctrine, a jurisdictional link between the act and the state that claims jurisdiction is constituted by the effects. The effects doctrine does not suggest in any way that a part of the conduct constituting the offence occurred within the territory.[23] The actions that produced these effects could have occurred abroad in their entirety according to the effects doctrine.[24] In short, the objective territorial principle imposes restrictions on the assertion of extraterritorial jurisdiction, whereas

---

19 *United States v. Aluminum Co. of America*, 148 F. 2d 416 (1945).

20 *Hartford Fire Insurance Co. v. California*, 113 S. Ct. 2891 (1993) [hereinafter referred to as the *Hartford Fire Insurance* case].

21 The US endorsement of the effects doctrine is clearly demonstrated not only in the relevant US jurisprudence, but also in the following documents. Restatement (Third) of Foreign Relations Law of the United States (1987); Anti-Trust Enforcement Guidelines for International Operations, issued by the Department of Justice and the Federal Trade Commission (1995).

22 For examples of blocking legislation, see A. V. Lowe, 'Blocking Extraterritorial Jurisdiction: The British Protection of Trading Interests Act, 1980', *American Journal of International Law*, 75/2 (1981): 257–82; Pierre-Marie Dupuy, *Droit international public* (Paris, 2004), p. 86.

23 Bowett, 'Jurisdiction', p. 7; Roger O'Keefe, 'Universal Jurisdiction: Clarifying the Basic Concept', *Journal of International Criminal Justice*, 2/3 (2004): 739 and footnote 16.

24 Lowe, 'Jurisdiction', p. 339.

the effects doctrine does not. Though this difference was sometimes not easy to establish in concrete cases, it was thought to be critically important. The general reactions to the 1989 *Wood Pulp* case[25] heard by the European Court of Justice again stressed this difference.[26] The case involved a cartel of manufacturers located outside the European market. The cartel agreement included price-fixing for customers in the Community, but the manufacturers involved had no base within the Community territory. Thus, they challenged the jurisdiction of the court, arguing that the alleged offence had taken place outside the Community. The court, however, avoided any discussion of the effects of this offence as a basis of jurisdiction. Instead, it 'concentrate[d] on the place of *implementation* of the agreement'[27] as something that actually occurred in the European market. In other words, the European Court of Justice used a 'fiction that there was some quasi-territorial basis for jurisdiction'.[28] It meant that the court preferred the objective territorial principle to the effects doctrine, and that the basis of jurisdiction in the *Wood Pulp* case was 'significantly narrower than the 'effects' doctrine in its most extreme form'.[29]

Though hostility towards the effects doctrine has decreased significantly since then, this lack of limits of extraterritorial jurisdiction in the effects doctrine remains an unanswered problem. The *Gencor* case[30] illustrates both a certain degree of acceptance of the effects doctrine by the EU[31] and the persistence of this problem. When Gencor and Lonrho, two South African mining firms, decided to merge, their decision was approved by the South African authorities. The European Commission, on the other hand, decided that this concentration was incompatible with the EC Merger Regulation. Article 1 of the Regulation stipulates that it 'shall apply to all concentrations with a Community dimension'. Gencor filed a suit in the European Court of Justice, and argued that the Community had no jurisdiction in the matter, since the activities in question were carried out in the territory outside

---

25 *Ahlstrom and Others v. Commission of European Communities* [1988] ECR 5193 [hereinafter referred to as the *Wood Pulp* case].

26 Antonio F. Bavasso, 'Boeing/McDonnell Douglas: Did the Commission Fly Too High', *European Competition Law Review*, 19/4 (1998): 244f.; Malcolm N. Shaw, *International Law* (Cambridge, 2003), pp. 618–20.

27 Stephen Weatherill and Paul Beaumont, *EU Law* (London, 1999), p. 812 [emphasis in the original].

28 Dieter G. F. Lange and John Byron Sandage, 'The Wood Pulp Decision and its Implications for the Scope of EC Competition Law', *Common Market Law Review*, 26 (1989): 157. See also Dupuy, p. 82.

29 Vaughan Lowe, 'International Law and the Effects Doctrine in the European Court of Justice', *Cambridge Law Journal*, 48 (1989): 11.

30 *Gencor Ltd v. Commission of the European Communities* (T102/96, Court of First Instance, 25 March 1999) [hereinafter referred to as the *Gencor* case].

31 Morten P. Broberg, 'The European Commission's Extraterritorial Powers in Merger Control: The Court of First Instance's Judgment in *Gencor v. Commission*', *International and Comparative Law Quarterly*, 49/1 (2000): 172f.; G. Porter Elliott, 'The Gencor Judgment: Collective Dominance, Remedies and Extraterritoriality under the Merger Regulation', *European Law Review*, 24/6 (1999): 641; Eleanor M. Fox, 'The Merger Regulation and its Territorial Reach', *European Competition Law Review*, 20/6 (1999): 335.

the Community. The court rejected this argument, and stated unequivocally that '[A]pplication of the Regulation is justified under public international law when it is foreseeable that a proposed concentration will have an immediate and substantial effect in the Community.'[32] Once again, according to the effects doctrine of the *Gencor* judgment, the link between the state and the act over which it purports to exercise jurisdiction can consist simply of the effects of the latter on the territory of the state. The judgment does not contain anything that indicates the limits of extraterritorial jurisdiction justified by the effects doctrine.[33] By way of contrast, the jurisdictional basis offered by the objective territorial principle is more verifiable, less prone to manipulations, and more importantly, is capable of demonstrating the limits of extraterritorial jurisdiction: when there is no intra-territorial act, the exercise of extraterritorial jurisdiction is not permitted. The effects doctrine lacks this assurance that the objective territorial principle can offer.

This recurrent difference between the objective territorial principle and the effects doctrine, and the concerns it reflects – the limits of extraterritorial jurisdiction – will be key issues in cyberspace again.

Treaty-Based Broad Extraterritorial Jurisdiction[34]

The second category of rules of jurisdiction examined in this chapter consists of those found in certain multilateral treaties. Rules of jurisdiction in the first category were meant to coordinate competing jurisdiction and alleviate tensions among them. In the second category, these rules are primarily expected to provide a different function. When states reach a consensus on preventing and prosecuting certain crimes and establish a treaty for that purpose, tensions among competing jurisdictions are no longer the main issue. Rather, the primary concern relates to possible loopholes of jurisdiction that may prevent effective prosecution. The inconvenience of the territorial principle of jurisdiction in these circumstances is evident. As a result, multilateral treaties regulating certain crimes on which there is a consensus share three characteristics. First, these treaties provide a network of jurisdiction based on broad jurisdictional bases. The combined bases are much broader than the territorial principle and its extensions. Second, establishing jurisdiction on these broad bases in these treaties is usually not optional or voluntary, but obligatory. Third, the rules of jurisdiction in these treaties are accompanied by a provision on extradition called *aut dedere, aut iudicare*: if the alleged offender is found in its territory, the state has to either prosecute him there, or extradite him to another state that will prosecute him. For the purpose of this chapter, the development of the first characteristic is relevant.

---

32 *Gencor* case, see above, note 30, at paragraph 90.

33 Alina Kaczorowska, 'International Competition Law in the Context of Global Capitalism', *European Competition Law Review*, 21/2 (2000): 122.

34 The expression is borrowed from the *Arrest Warrant of 11 April 2000* (Democratic Republic of the Congo v. Belgium), ICJ (14 February 2002), Joint Separate Opinion of Judges Higgins, Kooijmans and Buergenthal, at paragraph 40 [hereinafter referred to as the *Arrest Warrant* case, Joint Separate Opinion (Higgins et al.)].

The early examples are multilateral treaties for the safety of civil aviation, such as the 1970 Convention for the Suppression of Unlawful Seizure of Aircraft (hereinafter referred to as the Hague Convention) and the 1971 Convention for the Suppression of Unlawful Acts Against the Safety of Civil Aviation (hereinafter referred to as the Montreal Convention). In both treaties, the state whose aircraft is the place of the alleged offence must establish jurisdiction.[35] But in addition, regardless of the place of the alleged offence, the simple presence of the offender in the territory after the completion of the offence is also a compulsory basis of jurisdiction in both treaties.[36] Moreover, a state must establish jurisdiction if the aircraft in question has been leased, without a crew, to a person whose principal place of business is found in that state.[37] If this lessee has no such place of business, then the state in which he has his permanent residence establishes jurisdiction.[38] In sum, the links used as bases of jurisdiction are no longer territorial in the sense of the territorial principle, since these links are based on nothing more than the landing of the aircraft, the presence of the accused, and so on. In other words, the link between the offence and jurisdiction is no longer about intra-territorial conduct and constituent elements that are covered by the subjective territorial principle and the objective territorial principle. Therefore, jurisdiction established according to these provisions should be regarded as a basis for extraterritorial jurisdiction that goes beyond the logic of the territorial principle.[39] During the negotiation of the Hague Convention, some states expressed their reluctance to go beyond the logic of the territorial principle. In particular, there was a reluctance to assume jurisdiction on the basis of the mere presence of the alleged offender in its territory. However, the reluctant states finally agreed to the present formula in the Hague Convention, since they also recognized the gravity of the offence in question.[40]

Multilateral treaties for other types of crimes, for which there is equally a consensus of many states, likewise provide for broad jurisdictional bases. In other words, the bases of jurisdiction in these treaties are not limited to the territorial principle and its extensions. Very often they are grounded on a combination of the territorial principle, the nationality principle, the passive nationality principle and possibly other bases of jurisdiction. For example, the 1973 Convention on the Prevention and Punishment of Crimes Against Internationally Protected Persons provides that a contracting state must establish jurisdiction over crimes when they are committed in its territory or on board ships or aircraft registered in that state.[41] This is clearly based on the territorial principle and its variants. The same convention also provides that a contracting state must establish jurisdiction over a crime when it is committed by its nationals[42] or

---

35 Article 4(1)(a) of the Hague Convention; Article 5(1)(a) and (b) of the Montreal Convention.

36 Article 4(1)(b) of the Hague Convention; Article 5(1)(c) of the Montreal Convention.

37 Article 4(1)(c) of the Hague Convention; Article 5(1)(d) of the Montreal Convention.

38 Ibid.

39 Jean Combacau and Serge Sur, *Droit international public* (Paris, 2004), p. 354.

40 *Arrest Warrant* case, Joint Separate Opinion (Higgins et al.), see above, note 34, at paragraph 35.

41 Article 3(a).

42 Article 3(b).

when it is committed against an internationally protected person functioning on behalf of that state.[43] The former is based on the nationality principle, and the latter is a variant of the passive nationality principle. This convention is followed by the 1979 International Convention Against the Taking of Hostages (hereinafter referred to as the Hostage Convention). In the Hostage Convention, states are again obliged to establish jurisdiction on the territorial principle[44] and the nationality principle,[45] and may do so on the basis of the passive nationality principle as well.[46] States are also obliged to establish jurisdiction for cases where these states themselves are the 'targets' of the offences in question.[47] The same concern for effective apprehension and prosecution of the offender also led to the adoption of the 1984 Convention against Torture with broad, obligatory bases of jurisdiction.[48] Further examples of treaties with similar, broad bases of extraterritorial jurisdiction include the 1997 International Convention for the Suppression of Terrorist Bombings,[49] the 1999 International Convention for the Suppression of the Financing of Terrorism,[50] and the 2000 United Nations Convention against Transnational Organized Crime.[51]

In sum, in these multilateral treaties that deal with crimes in real space, as opposed to cyberspace, there is a clear tendency to accept wide-ranging bases for extraterritorial jurisdiction, mostly as an obligation. The common background to all the multilateral treaties cited is the consensus on crimes, and the need for cooperation in jurisdictional matters in order to secure the effective prevention and repression of these crimes. This pattern of treaty-based broad extraterritorial jurisdiction will be compared to the jurisdictional bases adopted in the Cybercrime Convention.

Developments in Cyber-Context

Developments Concerning the Rules in General International Law

Concerning the first category of rules of jurisdiction, i.e., rules in general international law, the information revolution has highlighted the problem of the limits of extraterritorial jurisdiction. Certain European states, such as France and Germany, penalize Nazi-related speech, including its publication in websites.[52] States outside

---

43 Article 3(c).

44 Article 5(1)(a).

45 Article 5(1)(a).

46 Article 5(1)(d).

47 Article 5(1)(c).

48 Article 5. See Tomuschat, pp. 273f.

49 Article 6.

50 Article 7.

51 Article 15.

52 The compatibility of legislation to this effect with freedom of expression protected by human rights treaties has been discussed in a number of judicial and quasi-judicial fora. As a broad tendency, Nazi-related speech is not considered as an expression that enjoys the protection of these treaties, established to protect certain values. Accordingly, legislation outlawing Nazi-related speech is not considered to be unlawful *per se*. For the jurisprudence of European Court of Human Rights, see *Lehideux et Isorni c. France* (No. 24662–94), *Arrêt*

Europe do not share the same history, and they do not possess similar legislation. To date, a number of municipal courts of France and Germany have faced cases involving the internet in which the alleged offender and his server were located abroad where Nazi-related speech or other types of hate speech were legal. The central question is whether or not this assertion of jurisdiction in such cases is consistent with the rules of jurisdiction established before the information revolution. Then there are sub-questions that follow. If the answer to the central question is negative, what are the new grounds on which jurisdiction is asserted? If the answer is positive, how do these cases circumvent the obvious difficulties in applying the established rules to the context of cyberspace? Is the application of the established rules of jurisdiction accompanied by any new patterns or issues that were not observed prior to the information revolution?

Affirmation of the Objective Territorial Principle The first observation for this category of rules is that the municipal courts seem to be willing to apply the established rules of jurisdiction in cases involving internet, even though they may not explicitly say so. In a case where the author of a website or the internet service provider with its server is located abroad, the typical justification for jurisdiction of the state where one can access the website is sought in the objective territorial principle.

The *Töben* case of the German Federal Court of Justice is such an example.[53] The accused was an Australian citizen. He expressed his revisionist views concerning the Nazi atrocities on the website of the Adelaide Institute, of which he was the director. The institute was located in Australia, and so was the server of its website. Because of these facts of the case, the jurisdictional provisions of the German Penal Code and how they applied to the internet publication abroad were discussed. Article 3 of the German Penal Code establishes jurisdiction on the territorial principle: 'German criminal law shall apply to acts which were committed domestically.'[54] This place of act is further specified by Article 9(1): 'An act is committed at every place the perpetrator acted, or in case of an omission, should have acted, or at which the result, which is an element of the offence, occurs or should occur according to the

du 23 septembre 1998, Recueil des arrêts et décisions 1998–VII, p. 2864. For the European Convention on Human Rights, see also *Arrêt du 7 décembre 2004, Cour de Cassation, Chambre Criminelle, No. 03–82832* in France. For the International Covenant on Civil and Political Rights, see *Faurisson v. France* (No. 550/1993), 8 November 1996 [1997], Report of the Human Rights Committee, vol. II, UN Doc. A/52/40. For a brief comparison between Article 10 of the European Convention on Human Rights and the First Amendment of the US Constitution, see Cherie Dawson, 'Creating Borders on the Internet: Free Speech, the United States, and International Jurisdiction', *Virginia Journal of International Law*, 44/2 (2003): 645f.

53 BGH, Urt. v. 12. 12. 2000 – 1 StR 184/00 (LG Mannheim), NJW 54(8), pp. 624–628 (2001) [hereinafter referred to as the *Töben* case]. See Uta Kohl, 'Eggs, Jurisdiction, and the Internet', *International and Comparative Law Quarterly*, 51/3 (2002): 577f.

54 The English version is taken from the translation by the German Federal Ministry of Justice, available at <http://www.iuscomp.org/gla/statutes/StGB.htm> (last visited on 7 February 2006).

understanding of the perpetrator.' In the lower court, though the court condemned the accused on other accounts, it could not establish jurisdiction concerning the application of Article 130(1)(ii) to the internet publication abroad. According to the court, the act was carried out solely in Australia, and it did not produce any result that belonged to the constituent elements of this offence in Germany, as required by Article 9 of the Penal Code.[55] The Federal Court, however, disagreed. Article 130(1) of the German Penal Code provides that '[W]hoever, in a manner that is capable of disturbing the public peace: (i) incites hatred against segments of the population or calls for violent or arbitrary measures against them; or (ii) assaults the human dignity of others by insulting, maliciously maligning, or defaming segments of the population, shall be punished with imprisonment from three months to five years.' In addition, Article 130(3) provides that '[W]hoever publicly or in a meeting approves of, denies or renders harmless an act committed under the rule of National Socialism of the type indicated in Article 220a subsection (i), in a manner capable of disturbing the public peace shall be punished with imprisonment for not more than five years or a fine.' Having examined these substantive rules extensively, as well as the relevant jurisdictional provisions of the Penal Code, the Federal Court concluded that in the present case, 'the result, which is an element of the offence, has occurred in Germany, thus the commission of the offence in the territory exists.'[56] Establishing jurisdiction this way at the receiving end of information on a website, which is uploaded and maintained abroad, is effectively an application of the objective territorial principle.

A similar justification of jurisdiction based on the objective territorial principle was employed by French courts in cases concerning Yahoo! Auction site, whose server was located in the US and maintained by a US company. The *First Yahoo! Auction* case[57] was brought to the *Tribunal de Grande Instance* in Paris by two French organizations dedicated to fighting anti-Semitism, *la Ligue contre le Racisme et l'Antisémitisme* and *l'Union des Etudiants Juifs de France*.[58] The defendants were Yahoo! Inc., a US corporation, and Yahoo! France, a French corporation. The complaint against them was based on the fact that internet users in France that logged on to the US Yahoo! Auction site had an access to the Nazi items on sale there. In France, '[E]xcept as needed for film-making, theatrical performances and historical expositions, it is a crime to wear or exhibit in public a uniform, insignia or emblem resembling the uniforms, insignias or emblems worn or exhibited' by

---

55 LG Mannheim, Urt. v. 10.11.1999.

56 *Töben* case, see above, note 53, at p. 627.

57 *Ordonnance de référé, rendue le 22 mai 2000, Tribunal de Grande Instance de Paris, No. RG: 00/05308, 00/05309.* «Référé » is a French judicial system for a summary procedure through which the plaintiff can petition a judge for redress. The decisions are meant to provide interlocutory measures and provisional remedies. Usually, only one judge hears the case. He can decide to grant the request of the plaintiff and take various measures, as well as impose *astreinte*, a fixed monetary penalty per day to force the defendant to comply with the decision. Both parties can appeal to the *Cour d'Appel* in case of dissatisfaction.

58 The lawsuit was an *action civile*, in which the party asks for a compensation of damage arising from a crime.

the Nazis according to Article R645-1 of the Penal Code.[59] So was displaying and selling the Nazi items in an auction site. The court decided that it had jurisdiction on the following basis: 'By permitting the display of these items and the eventual participation of the internet user in France in such exposition/sales, Yahoo! commits a wrong (*faute*) in the French territory.' The court observed that this had caused damage to the two organizations that filed the lawsuit, and that since the damage had been incurred in France, the court had jurisdiction to hear the case.[60] The same court reiterated in the subsequent phase of the same case that 'a simple displaying of such objects in France constitutes a violation of Article R. 645-1 of the Penal Code,' and reaffirmed that 'this displaying evidently causes damage in France.'[61] Though there is no reference to rules of jurisdiction in international law, the basis of jurisdiction in this case is also arguably the objective territorial principle.

The idea of the objective territorial principle was also used to justify jurisdiction in the *Second Yahoo! Auction* cases. The lawsuit was filed by another organization, *Association amicale des déportés d'Auschwitz et des camps de Haute Silésie,* later joined by other organizations.[62] The complaint was that the internet users in France were still able to access and view Nazi items on the auction site of Yahoo! Inc. in January 2001, in spite of the earlier orders from the *First Yahoo! Auction* case. This was claimed to be a violation of the French Penal Code, as well as the 1881 Press Liberty Law[63] and the 1982 Audiovisual Communication Law.[64] Both the *Tribunal*

---

59 The translation of the French Penal Code is available at <http://www.legifrance.gouv.fr>, but *Partie Réglementaire – Décrets en Conseil d'Etat* in which this article appears is not included (last visited on 7 February 2006).

60 The New Code of Civil Procedures in its Article 46 establishes jurisdiction of the courts in the place where the damage of the tort occurred. See Article 46, *Nouveau Code de Procédure Civile*.

61 See *Ordonnance de référé, rendue le 20 novembre 2000, Tribunal de Grande Instance de Paris, No RG: 00/05308.* In the *First Yahoo! Auction* case, after this decision was handed down in November 2000, Yahoo! Inc. decided not to pursue the matter in France, and instead, filed a suit in the US District Court for the Northern District of California. The court affirmed jurisdiction on 7 June 2001 (145 F. Supp. 2d 1168, N.D. Cal. 2001), and Yahoo! Inc. succeeded in obtaining a summary judgment on 7 November 2001 to the effect that the orders of the French court were not recognizable or enforceable in the US (169 F. Supp. 2d 1181, N.D. Cal. 2001). The reason for this judgment was the incompatibility of the French court orders with the First Amendment of the US Constitution. See Christine Duh, 'Yahoo! Inc. v. LICRA', *Berkeley Technology Law Journal*, 17 (2002): 359–78. Thereupon, the two French organizations that had sued Yahoo! Inc. in France appealed to the US Court of Appeals, California. The court decided on 23 August 2004 that it did not have jurisdiction, on the grounds that it lacked personal jurisdiction over the two French organizations (379 F.3d 1120, 9th Cir. 2004). A rehearing of this judgment was decided on 10 February 2005 (399 F.3d 1010, 9th Cir. 2005), and the decision on 12 January 2006 eventually turned down the request of Yahoo! Inc. The decision [hereinafter referred to as the *Yahoo! v. LICRA* case (2006)] is available at <http://www.ca9.uscourts.gov> (last visited on 14 February 2006).

62 This time, the lawsuit was filed in the criminal division of the court against the company, Yahoo! Inc., and its CEO at that time.

63 *Loi sur la liberté de la presse, loi du 29 juillet 1881.*

64 *Loi sur la communication audiovisuelle, loi n° 82–652 du 29 juillet 1982.*

de Grande Instance and the *Cour d'Appel* examined the jurisdictional issue, in 2002 and 2004, respectively, and both affirmed French jurisdiction.[65] One of the arguments advanced by Yahoo! Inc. and the defence team on both occasions consisted of denying jurisdiction of the French courts, by relying on the territorial principle of jurisdiction: According to their point of view, the auction service of Yahoo.com is organized and maintained in the US, and Yahoo! Inc. had not carried out any act in France.[66] The French courts did not accept this view. The *Tribunal de Grande Instance* first identified the objective territorial principle in the French Penal Code: 'French Criminal law is applicable to all offences committed within the territory of the French Republic. An offence is deemed to have been committed within the territory of the French Republic where one of its constituent elements was committed within that territory.'[67] In the absence of any particular agreements concerning jurisdiction over internet cases, the court deemed that it was free to determine its own principles of international criminal jurisdiction, in order to sanction certain offences 'which are entirely or partially committed abroad, and which may injure the national interests in the sense that, as in the present case, the messages or the content of the site are made accessible in the French territory through the internet.'[68] It concluded that the offence in question had not occurred exclusively abroad, as Yahoo! Inc. and the defence team argued, but had occurred equally in the French territory.[69] The *Cour d'Appel* entirely agreed, and furthermore observed that when a company carried out its activities in its country for the residents there, it was effectively offering its activities for internet users all over the world, including those in France.[70] Though the rules of jurisdiction of public international law are not explicitly referred to, it is clear that these courts used the basic idea of the objective territorial principle in establishing jurisdiction: the partial occurrence of an act or activities in the territory.

---

65 Both courts dealt with the preliminary questions and the substantive questions separately. One of the preliminary questions was jurisdiction, discussed in *Jugement du 26 février 2002, Tribunal de Grande Instance de Paris, 17ème Chambre, Chambre de la Presse, No. 0104305259* [hereinafter referred to as the *Second Yahoo! Auction* case (TGI)], and *Arrêt du 17 mars 2004, Cour d'Appel de Paris, 11ème Chambre des Appels Correctionnels, No. 03/01520* [hereinafter referred to as the *Second Yahoo! Auction* case (CA)]. As for the substantive questions, both courts acquitted the accused on the criminal charges, and dismissed the charges in *partie civile* as well (*Jugement du 11 février 2003, Tribunal de Grande Instance de Paris, 17ème Chambre, Chambre de la Presse, No. 0104305259*, confirmed by the *Cour d'Appel* on 5 April 2005, according to *Libération* (6 April 2005) and Daniel Arthur Laprès, 'Affaires Yahoo! (I et II) et Al Manar: l'approche universaliste confirmée deux fois', *Juriscom. net*, 17 May 2005 (2005): <http://www.juriscom.net> (last visited on 14 February 2006).

66 *Second Yahoo! Auction* cases (TGI) (CA), see above, note 65.

67 Article 113–2, French Penal Code, see above, note 59. How broad this basis of jurisdiction can be in the context of cyberspace is discussed in Pierre Sirinelli, 'L'adéquation entre le village virtuel et la création normative – Remise en cause du rôle de l'Etat?' in Katharina Boele-Woelki and Catherine Kessedjian (eds.), *Internet: Which Court Decides? Which Law Applies? Quel tribunal décide? Quel droit s'applique?* (The Hague, 1998), p. 11.

68 *Second Yahoo! Auction* case (TGI), see above, note 65.

69 *Second Yahoo! Auction* case (TGI), see above, note 65.

70 *Second Yahoo! Auction* case (CA), see above, note 65.

Affirmation of the Concept of Territory The concrete orders by the French courts vis-à-vis foreign companies also show an interesting loyalty to the foundation of the rules of jurisdiction established before the information revolution. They are loyal to the concept of territory. The exercise of jurisdiction in the *Yahoo! Auction* cases is frequently criticized for their lack of respect for territoriality: 'the French court was trying to bind the whole world.'[71] More generally, they are described as leading to 'a lowest common denominator world where the most restrictive rule of any country would govern all speech in the Internet.'[72] For the following reason, however, it is submitted that the criticism is not accurate. Many orders of French courts vis-à-vis foreign companies are marked by an effort to contain the repercussions of extraterritorial jurisdiction within the simulated territory of France in cyberspace.

For example, in the first decision of the *First Yahoo! Auction* case, Yahoo! Inc., the US corporation, was specifically ordered 'to take all necessary measures to dissuade and render impossible any access [from French territory] via Yahoo.com to the Nazi artifact auction service and to any other site or service that may be construed as constituting an apology for Nazism or a contesting of Nazi crimes.'[73] Faced with this order, Yahoo! Inc. argued that filtering of users from different states, in order to comply with the order, was technically difficult if not impossible. Consequently, a panel of experts conducted a feasibility study. It concluded that such filtering was technically possible: it was possible to block 70 per cent of the access from France to the sites in question.[74] According to this panel of experts, the blocking rate would be as high as 90 per cent if the website to be viewed required the internet users to declare their location. Given this assessment, the court reaffirmed its earlier order.[75]

Restraining the scope of the order in this way to access from France is an effort to avoid interfering with the activities of Yahoo! Inc. concerning the rest of the world.[76] The effort is indeed very consistent, at least in French jurisprudence. Since the *First Yahoo! Auction* case, the orders issued vis-à-vis internet companies abroad have

---

71 Ralf Michaels, 'Territorial Jurisdiction after Territoriality', in Piet Jan Slot and Mielle Bulterman (eds.), *Globalisation and Jurisdiction* (The Hague, 2004), p. 117.

72 Caitlin T. Murphy, 'International Law and the Internet: An Ill-Suited Match', *Hastings International and Comparative Law Review*, 25 (2002): 415f. See also Daniel Arthur Laprès, 'L'exorbitante affaire Yahoo', *Journal du droit international*, 129/4 (2002): 975–99.

73 *Ordonnance de référé, rendue le 22 mai 2000, Tribunal de Grande Instance de Paris, No. RG: 00/05308, 00/05309*. The translation of the order is taken from the *Yahoo! v. LICRA* case (2006), see above, note 61.

74 *Ordonnance de référé, rendue le 20 novembre 2000, Tribunal de Grande Instance de Paris, No RG: 00/05308*. Details of this expert opinion are presented in Murphy, 'International Law and Internet', pp. 418–20.

75 *Ordonnance de référé, rendue le 20 novembre 2000, Tribunal de Grande Instance de Paris, No RG: 00/05308*.

76 Horatia Muir Watt, '*Yahoo!* Cyber-Collision of Cultures: Who Regulates?' *Michigan Journal of International Law*, 24 (2003): 692; Mark S. Kende, 'Yahoo!: National Borders in Cyberspace and Their Impact on International Lawyers', *New Mexico Law Review*, 32 (2002): 8; Andreas Manolopoulos, 'Raising "Cyber-Borders": The Interaction Between Law and Technology', *International Journal of Law and Information Technology*, 11/1 (2003): 43f.

never required the complete removal of messages deemed to be illegal under French law from the website. Instead, they require these companies to take measures that block access to the website in question by internet users from France.[77] By restricting the order to access from France, the French courts in internet cases rely on the concept of territory even when they deal with cases involving cyberspace. Simulating territoriality in cyberspace in this way has been discussed under the term 'zoning'.[78] In fact, both companies and governments increasingly resort to international zoning of cyberspace.[79] The result is that today, technologies that can simulate territories in cyberspace are available at a relatively low cost.[80] By encouraging the simulation of territory, municipal courts in their consideration of jurisdictional issues decline to seek innovations in cyberspace. Instead, the foundation of the established rules of jurisdiction is upheld.

Diminished Significance of Distinction between the Objective Territorial Principle and the Effects Doctrine The previous examination showed a tendency in municipal courts to accept and use the established rules of jurisdiction – in particular, the objective territorial principle – in asserting jurisdiction in cases involving the internet. They also seemed willing to simulate borders in cyberspace, so that these established rules could function in the new environment. On a closer examination, however, there are new features, too. Above all, it is not as clear as it may seem at a first glance where these judicial decisions stand in terms of the objective territorial principle and the effects doctrine. In fact, a number of commentators of the *Yahoo! Auction* cases consider the reasoning in these cases to be a variant of the effects doctrine, rather than an example of the objective territorial principle.[81] Of course, if one pays attention to the language of reasoning in these cases, the occurrence of one or more constituent elements of the offence in the territory undeniably plays a decisive role in the justification of jurisdiction. This is the language of the objective territorial principle, not of the effects doctrine. The line between the two justifications in internet cases, however, is a very fine one. On one hand, one may accept the characterization of the situation by the French courts, which assessed Yahoo's services as an act of making information available on computer screens

---

77 For an example, see *Ordonnance de référé, rendue le 20 avril 2005, Tribunal de Grande Instance de Paris, No RG: 05/52674–05/53871* (one of the orders in the so-called *AAARGH* case).

78 Lawrence Lessig and Paul Resnick, 'Zoning Speech on the Internet: A Legal and Technical Model', *Michigan Law Review*, 98 (1999): 395–431, though the focus of their discussions is a zoning between states within the United States.

79 Geist, 'Cyberlaw 2.0', at 332f.; Jack L. Goldsmith, 'The Internet and the Abiding Significance of Territorial Sovereignty', *International Journal of Global Legal Studies*, 5/2 (1998): 487f.

80 Goldsmith, 'Unilateral Regulation of the Internet: A Modest Defence', *European Journal of International Law*, 11/1 (2000): 140f.

81 Kohl, 'Eggs, Jurisdiction, and the Internet', p. 577; Manolopoulos, 'Raising "Cyber-Borders"', p. 56f.; Julie L. Henn, 'Targeting Transnational Internet Content Regulation', *Boston University International Law Journal*, 21 (2003): 173. See also Murphy, 'International Law and Internet', p. 413.

in French territory. On the other hand, it is also possible to characterize the same situation as an effect of the uploading and maintenance of a website abroad that is accessible to internet users in French territory. Nothing in the facts of the *Yahoo! Auction* cases shows convincingly that the former is a more accurate characterization of the situation than the latter. This explains why some commentators prefer to see the reasoning in these cases as a disguised effects doctrine.

More importantly, the general implication of this fine line between the two characterizations is that whichever characterization a municipal court chooses to rely on, the extent of extraterritorial jurisdiction justified will be the same. Prior to the information revolution, the two justifications, the objective territorial principle and the effects doctrine, were thought to place very different limits on extraterritorial jurisdiction in certain cases. This is no longer true in cases involving the internet, where the extent of extraterritorial jurisdiction justified by the objective territorial principle seems to be as limitless as the one justified by the effects doctrine. In cyberspace, the objective territorial principle loses its inherent virtue of setting limits to extraterritorial jurisdiction.[82]

As explained previously, the cause for this diminished significance of the distinction between the two justifications in cyberspace is that the act of letting a message or information be seen in another territory, and the effect, namely that it is seen in another territory, are hard to distinguish. One could try to distinguish them by examining the intention of those who create or maintain a website: an act is an intended action, whereas the effects of this act can be unintended. This may be a way to re-establish the limiting function of the objective territorial principle, and employ it as a justification that is meaningfully different from the effects doctrine. In the *Yahoo! Auction* cases, however, the consideration of intention did not lead to the limitation of jurisdiction. In the first decision of the *First Yahoo! Auction* case, the unintentional character of the act in question was explicitly recognized by the court, but it did not prevent the court from affirming jurisdiction. In the later phase of the same case, as well as in the *Second Yahoo! Auction* cases, the courts characterized the act of letting a message or information be seen in France as intentional. The way they argued this connection indicates that in cyberspace, the fact of making information available on the internet is always considered to be accompanied by an intention of a world-wide display.[83]

Since the objective territorial principle no longer has the function of setting limits to extraterritorial jurisdiction in any significant way in the context of cyberspace, limiting techniques of municipal courts become an important element in practice. In fact, in the application of the effects doctrine by the municipal courts prior to

---

82 See Shōtaro Hamamoto, 'Yafū! Ōkushon Jiken [Yahoo! Auction Cases]' in Yoshirō Matsui (ed.), *Hanrei Kokusaiho [Cases of International Law]* (Tokyo, 2006, in Japanese), p. 96.

83 Uta Kohl, 'The Rule of Law, Jurisdiction and the Internet', *International Journal of Law and Information Technology*, 12/3 (2004): 373–75. Though the *Töben* case does not discuss clearly whether the author of the website intended to display the information in Germany, Kohl (2004) presents it as another example where the intention was assumed automatically.

the information revolution, several limiting techniques were employed to keep extraterritorial jurisdiction in check. In the application of the effects doctrine by the US courts in 1970s, these courts took into account the interests of the states concerned, balanced the US interests against these interests, and tried to assess the reasonableness of exercising jurisdiction in the given cases.[84] The technique was characterized as a balancing test, or a principle of reasonableness.[85] Though this balancing test could be criticized on various grounds,[86] it did give the US courts a chance to consider implications of the extraterritorial exercise of jurisdiction, including its impact on the territorial state.[87] A number of commentators of internet cases also support the approach of balancing or reasonableness.[88] In the *Yahoo! Auction* cases and the *Töben* case, such an approach would have led the courts of France and Germany, respectively, to examine whether the US or Australia possesses a system of values and priorities different from those of France and Germany that would be severely impaired by the application of French or German law.[89] However, neither a balancing test as a matter of comity nor the principle of reasonableness as a legal obligation were discussed in any of these cases. On the contrary, in the *Second Yahoo! Auction* cases, the *Tribunal de Grande Instance* seems to dismiss the idea of balancing or reasonableness when it states that the legality of the conduct in the US did not matter: France had jurisdiction over the alleged offence, 'even if the alleged offence is not criminalized by the penal legislation of the country of origin of the author of the alleged facts, or of the country where the host of the contested site is geographically located.'[90] The *Cour d'Appel* even expressed the concern that the use of such limiting techniques of jurisdiction would promote a kind of tax-haven phenomenon of hate speech in cyberspace.[91]

In sum, though the municipal courts in internet cases do affirm the objective territorial principle established before the information revolution, the principle seems to lose its distinctive virtue of setting limits to extraterritorial jurisdiction in

---

84 *Timberlane Lumber Co. v. Bank of America*, 549 F.2d 597 (1976); *Mannington Mills v. Congoleum Corporation*, 595 F.2d 1287 (1979).

85 See also Restatement (Third) of Foreign Relations Law of the United States (1987), in which this was not a matter of comity, but of a legal principle of reasonableness.

86 Rosenthal and Knighton, pp. 26–8; Bowett, 'Jurisdiction', pp. 21f.

87 However, many authors consider that the *Hartford Fire Insurance* case indicates the abandonment of the reasonableness/balancing approach. Harold Hongju Koh, 'International Business Transactions in United States Courts', *Recueil des cours*, 261 (1996): 71–75; Phillip R. Trimble, 'The Supreme Court and International Law: The Demise of Restatement Section 403', *American Journal of International Law*, 89/1 (1995): 53–7.

88 Elizabeth Longworth, 'The Possibilities for a Legal Framework for Cyberspace', in Teresa Fuentes-Camacho (ed.), *The International Dimensions of Cyberspace Law* (Paris, 2000), pp. 33f.; Ellen S. Podgor, 'International Computer Fraud: A Paradigm for Limiting National Jurisdiction', *U.C. Davis Law Review*, 35 (2002): 315f.

89 See Andreas F. Lowenfeld, 'Conflict, Balancing of Interests, and the Exercise of Jurisdiction to Prescribe: Reflections on the Insurance Antitrust Case', *American Journal of International Law*, 89/1 (1995): 51.

90 *Second Yahoo! Auction* case (TGI), see above, note 65.

91 *Second Yahoo! Auction* case (CA), see above, note 65.

internet cases. In cyberspace, the objective territorial principle is indistinguishable from the effects doctrine, because the former also seems to justify extraterritorial jurisdiction infinitely. At the same time, this diminished significance of difference between the two justifications of jurisdiction is not sufficiently recognized. This may explain partially why the limiting techniques developed in the application of the effects doctrine before the information revolution are not readily considered in the application of the objective territorial principle in internet cases.

Treaty-Based Developments: Cybercrime Convention   The Cybercrime Convention was adopted by the Council of Europe in 2001 and came into force in July 2004, though the number of contracting states is still limited.[92] The convention is meant to be a universal instrument regulating cyber-crimes, and signatories include non-European states such as the US, Canada, Japan, and South Africa. It is based on the consensus that certain acts in cyberspace should be regulated uniformly as crimes.[93] The Cybercrime Convention provides the categories of conducts to be regulated, though it does not provide the details. Given the variety of existing national legislation, it is sensible to leave the details to the national legislation. As in the treaties related to crimes in real space that were discussed previously, one of the major issues in the Cybercrime Convention is jurisdiction.[94] The territorial principle alone is not sufficient for the purpose of this convention, because cyber-crimes are frequently transnational in complex ways.[95] Even the combined rules of jurisdiction of general international law are insufficient in themselves, because they do not oblige states to establish jurisdiction. Against this background, the states that join the Cybercrime Convention are under an obligation to establish jurisdiction according to the broad bases laid out in the relevant provisions of the convention. In other words, they must ensure that their domestic legislation criminalizes several categories of conduct in the convention, and make certain that the domestic procedures allow the prosecution of such crimes.

---

92 As of June 2006, there are 15 contracting states and 28 signatory states <http://conventions.coe.int>. For the overview of the convention, see Mike Keyser, 'The Council of Europe Convention on Cybercrime', *Journal of Transnational Law and* Policy, 12 (2003): 287–326; Ryan M.F. Baron, 'Comment: A Critique of the International Cybercrime Treaty', *CommLaw Conspectus*, 10 (2002): 263–78.

93 Marc D. Goodman and Susan W. Brenner, 'The Emerging Consensus on Criminal Conduct in Cyberspace', *International Journal of Law and Information Technology*, 10/2 (2002): 139–223. There is also a protocol specifically regulating hate speech. Protocol on the Criminalization of Acts of a Racist and Xenophobic Nature Committed Through Computer Systems, European Treaty Series No. 189. It was adopted in 2002 and came into effect in March 2006. As of June 2006, the protocol has 7 contracting states, and there are 24 other signatory states <http://conventions.coe.int>. See also Jane Baily, 'Private Regulation and Public Policy: Toward Effective Restriction of Internet Hate Propaganda', *McGill Law Journal*, 49 (2004): 78–80.

94 Richard W. Downing, 'Shoring Up the Weakest Link: What Lawmakers Around the World Need to Consider in Developing Comprehensive Laws to Combat Cybercrime', *Columbia Journal of Transnational Law*, 43/3 (2005): 719.

95 Ian Walden, 'Crime and Security in Cyberspace', *Cambridge Review of International Affairs*, 18/1 (2005): 56.

In the light of the prior development of jurisdictional patterns in multilateral treaties, the rules of jurisdiction adopted in the Cybercrime Convention are almost conservative. Nothing in the rules of jurisdiction in this convention suggests that cyber-crimes are more transnational or more challenging than other types of crimes. Article 22 of the convention sketches out the network of jurisdiction it purports to establish.[96] The combination of bases of jurisdiction found in this article is the same as the one employed in previous treaties. According to Article 22(1)(a) of the Cybercrime Convention, each state is under an obligation to regulate crimes that are committed in its territory.[97] According to the Explanatory Report provided by the Council of Europe,[98] under this provision, 'for example, a Party would assert territorial jurisdiction if both the person attacking a computer system and the victim system are located within its territory, and where the computer system attacked is within its territory, even if the attacker is not.'[99] Establishing jurisdiction in the latter circumstance includes a typical application of the objective territorial principle. Articles 22(1)(b) and (c) are also familiar variants of jurisdictional bases in previous treaties. They require the state to establish criminal jurisdiction over offences committed aboard ships flying its flag or aircraft registered under its laws. According to the Explanatory Report, a state also has jurisdiction over crimes committed aboard its own ship passing through the territorial waters of another state or in its

---

96 '1 Each Party shall adopt such legislative and other measures as may be necessary to establish jurisdiction over any offence established in accordance with Articles 2 through 11 of this Convention, when the offence is committed:

    a in its territory; or

    b on board a ship flying the flag of that Party; or

    c on board an aircraft registered under the laws of that Party; or

    d by one of its nationals, if the offence is punishable under criminal law where it was committed or if the offence is committed outside the territorial jurisdiction of any State.

    2 Each Party may reserve the right not to apply or to apply only in specific cases or conditions the jurisdiction rules laid down in paragraphs 1.b through 1.d of this article or any part thereof.

    3 Each Party shall adopt such measures as may be necessary to establish jurisdiction over the offences referred to in Article 24, paragraph 1, of this Convention, in cases where an alleged offender is present in its territory and it does not extradite him or her to another Party, solely on the basis of his or her nationality, after a request for extradition.

    4 This Convention does not exclude any criminal jurisdiction exercised by a Party in accordance with its domestic law.

    5 When more than one Party claims jurisdiction over an alleged offence established in accordance with this Convention, the Parties involved shall, where appropriate, consult with a view to determining the most appropriate jurisdiction for prosecution.'

97 Article 22(1)(a), see above, note 96.

98 Council of Europe, Explanatory Report (8 Nov. 2001), paragraph 233 [hereinafter referred to as the Explanatory Report]. For the status of this Explanatory Report with regard to the Convention, see Miriam F. Miquelon-Weismann, 'The Convention on Cybercrime: A Harmonized Implementation of International Penal Law: What Prospects for Procedural Due Process?' *John Marshall Journal of Computer and Information Law*, 23/2 (2005): 330.

99 Explanatory Report, see above, note 98, at paragraph 233.

own aircraft in the airspace of another state. This may prove to be useful, since the territorial state in which the crime takes place in these cases may not be interested in investigating these crimes, or 'may face significant practical impediments to the exercise of its jurisdiction'.[100] Article 22(1)(d) is a provision based on the nationality principle. States that join the convention are required to establish jurisdiction over crimes committed by their nationals, even when they are abroad. This obligation is subject to the condition that when the crime takes place in the territory of another state, the conduct is also an offence under the law of that state.[101]

Establishing a network of jurisdiction in this way means that 'there will be occasions in which more than one Party has jurisdiction over some or all of the participants in the crime. For example, many virus attacks, frauds and copyright violations committed through use of the Internet target victims located in many states.'[102] Despite this recognition, the Cybercrime Convention does not provide any hierarchy among overlapping jurisdictions. Instead, states are required by the Cybercrime Convention to consult one another where appropriate.[103] Case-by-case negotiation to decide whose jurisdiction prevails can be an important obstacle for investigations of cyber-crime, for which the swiftness is critical. Besides, the convention does not specify any next step when these consultations fail to produce any result. Several commentators criticize this lack of guidelines for settling issues of overlapping jurisdiction.[104] That feature, however, was evidently not impressive enough to change the established pattern of jurisdiction in treaties prior to the information revolution.In sum, while the Cybercrime Convention is definitely one response to the information revolution, its jurisdictional rules show no departure from the patterns employed by multilateral treaties in the past. On the contrary, the pattern of broad jurisdictional bases developed by these treaties is fully capitalized on in the Cybercrime Convention.

Conclusion

The purpose of this chapter has been to establish whether or not rules of jurisdiction developed prior to the information revolution were still used in cyber-context. In order to answer this question, two categories of rules of jurisdiction were examined: rules of jurisdiction in general international law and rules of jurisdiction adopted in multilateral treaties.

---

100   Ibid.

101   So far, France is the only state that made reservations on jurisdictional matters. Reservations by France, contained in the instrument of approval, deposited on 10 January 2006.

102   Explanatory Report, see above, note 98, at paragraph 239.

103   Article 22(5), see above, note 96.

104   Shannon L. Hopkins, 'Cybercrime Convention: A Positive Beginning to a Long Road Ahead', *Journal of High Technology Law*, 2 (2003): 117f.; Susan W. Brenner and Bert-Jaap Koops, 'Approaches to Cybercrime Jurisdiction', *Journal of High Technology Law*, 4 (2004): 42f.

Concerning the rules in the first category, though the examination does not provide a clear-cut answer, it is fair to conclude that the changes observed are not in the rules themselves. In dealing with jurisdictional issues in the context of cyberspace, municipal courts do not look for a new rule of jurisdiction. Instead, they rely on the established rules, in particular, the objective territorial principle, which was developed prior to the information revolution. The change seems to be in the function of the objective territorial principle. In the context of cyberspace, it no longer sets limits to extraterritorial jurisdiction in the way it did in cases before the information revolution. In spite of this functional change in the rule, or perhaps being unaware of this functional change, the municipal courts do not hesitate to apply the objective territorial principle in internet-related cases. In addition, the concept of territory is faithfully simulated and applied to cyberspace in these cases. The concept of territory has of course been a foundation for the rules of jurisdiction in real space. Thus, the finding for the first category of rules of jurisdiction is that the information revolution so far has not changed them. As to the rules in the second category, the result is more straightforward. The jurisdictional pattern adopted in the Cybercrime Convention does not depart at all from the pattern developed in multilateral treaties before the information revolution. Though the lack of hierarchy among a variety of jurisdictional bases in this convention is criticized, the criticism is also valid for the jurisdictional clauses of previous multilateral treaties. The finding for this second category is that cyberspace has not led to any innovation in jurisdictional rules in treaties. On the contrary, they are still fully used in the unchanged form.

The above findings are consistent with the observations in many other chapters of this book. The changes regarding the states' regulatory powers as a result of the information revolution are not as visible as has been predicted or advocated. In the concrete example of public international law, the rules of their allocation have not dramatically changed in cyberspace, either in general international law or in treaties dealing with cyberspace. On the contrary, states appear to make efforts to regulate cyberspace using the same rules that allocated their regulatory powers in real space. The most striking example in this regard is the Cybercrime Convention. This conscious and explicit effort of regulation demonstrates that cyberspace is not inherently inimical to states' regulations, or at least, not so in the minds of states that joined this convention. States purport to exercise their regulatory powers in cyberspace, and cooperate, through this convention, just as they did for other matters in real space before the information revolution.

Bibliography

Akehurst, Michael, 'Jurisdiction in International Law', *British Yearbook of International Law*, 46 (1972–73): 145–257.

Baily, Jane, 'Private Regulation and Public Policy: Toward Effective Restriction of Internet Hate Propaganda', *McGill Law Journal*, 49 (2004): 59–103.

Barkham, Jason, 'Information Warfare and International Law on the Use of Force', *New York University Journal of International Law and Policy*, 34 (2001): 57–113.

Baron, Ryan M.F., 'Comment: A Critique of the International Cybercrime Treaty', *CommLaw Conspectus*, 10 (2002): 263–78.

Bavasso, Antonio F., 'Boeing/McDonnell Douglas: Did the Commission Fly Too High', *European Competition Law Review*, 19/4 (1998): 243–8.

Bigos, Oren, 'Jurisdiction over Cross-Border Wrongs on the Internet', *International and Comparative Law Quarterly*, 54/3 (2005): 585–620.

Bowett, D.W., 'Jurisdiction: Changing Patterns of Authority over Activities and Resources', *British Yearbook of International Law*, 53 (1982): 1–26.

Brenner, Susan W. and Koops, Bert-Jaap, 'Approaches to Cybercrime Jurisdiction', *Journal of High Technology Law*, 4 (2004): 1–46.

Broberg, Morten P., 'The European Commission's Extraterritorial Powers in Merger Control: The Court of First Instance's Judgment in *Gencor* v. *Commission*', *International and Comparative Law Quarterly*, 49/1 (2000): 172–82.

Brown, Bartram S., 'Developing Countries in the New Global Information Order', in L. Boisson de Chazournes and V. Gowlland-Debbas (eds.), *The International Legal System in Quest of Equity and Universality: Liber Amicorum Georges Abi-Saab* (The Hague: Martinus Nijhoff, 2001), pp. 411–26.

Busuttil, James J., 'A Taste of Armageddon: The Law of Armed Conflict as Applied to Cyberwar', in G. S. Goodwin-Gill and S. Talmon (eds.), *The Reality of International Law: Essays in Honour of Ian Brownlie* (Oxford: Clarendon Press, 1999), pp. 37–55.

Byers, Michael, *Custom, Power, and the Power of Rules: International Relations and Customary International Law* (Cambridge: Cambridge University Press, 1999).

Cassese, Antonio, *International Law*, 2nd ed. (Oxford: Oxford University Press, 2004).

Combacau, Jean and Sur, Serge, *Droit international public*, 6th ed. (Paris: Montchrestien, 2004).

Dawson, Cherie, 'Creating Borders on the Internet: Free Speech, the United States, and International Jurisdiction', *Virginia Journal of International Law*, 44/2 (2003): 637–63.

Doswald-Beck, Louise, 'Some Thoughts on Computer Network Attack and the International Law of Armed Conflict', in M. N. Schmitt and B. T. O'Donnell (eds.), *Computer Network Attack and International Law*, vol. 76 (Newport: Naval War College, 2002), pp. 163–85.

Downing, Richard W., 'Shoring Up the Weakest Link: What Lawmakers Around the World Need to Consider in Developing Comprehensive Laws to Combat Cybercrime', *Columbia Journal of Transnational Law*, 43/3 (2005): 705–62.

Duh, Christine, 'Yahoo! Inc. v. LICRA', *Berkeley Technology Law Journal*, 17 (2002): 359–78.

Dupuy, Pierre–Marie, *Droit international public*, 7th ed. (Paris: Dalloz, 2004).

Elliott, G. Porter, 'The Gencor Judgment: Collective Dominance, Remedies and Extraterritoriality under the Merger Regulation', *European Law Review*, 24/6 (1999): 638–52.

Fox, Eleanor M., 'The Merger Regulation and its Territorial Reach', *European Competition Law Review*, 20/6 (1999): 334–36.

Geist, Michael, 'Cyberlaw 2.0', *Boston College Law Review*, 44 (2003): 323–58.

Goldsmith, 'Unilateral Regulation of the Internet: A Modest Defence', *European Journal of International Law*, 11/1 (2000): 135–48.

Goldsmith, Jack L., 'The Internet and the Abiding Significance of Territorial Sovereignty', *International Journal of Global Legal Studies*, 5/2 (1998): 475–91.

Goodman, Marc D. and Brenner, Susan W., 'The Emerging Consensus on Criminal Conduct in Cyberspace', *International Journal of Law and Information Technology*, 10/2 (2002): 139–223.

Hamamoto, Shōtaro, 'Yafū! Ōkushon Jiken [Yahoo! Auction Cases]' in Y. Matsui (ed.), *Hanrei Kokusaiho [Cases of International Law]*, 2nd ed. (Tokyo: Toshindo, 2006, in Japanese), pp. 94–97.

Henn, Julie L., 'Targeting Transnational Internet Content Regulation', *Boston University International Law Journal*, 21 (2003): 157–77.

Hopkins, Shannon L., 'Cybercrime Convention: A Positive Beginning to a Long Road Ahead', *Journal of High Technology Law*, 2 (2003): 101–21.

Jennings, Robert, 'Extraterritorial Jurisdiction and the United States Antitrust Laws', *British Yearbook of International Law*, 33 (1957): 146–75.

Joyner, Christopher C. and Lotrionte, Catherine, 'Information Warfare as International Coercion: Elements of a Legal Framework', *European Journal of International Law*, 12/5 (2001): 825–65.

Kaczorowska, Alina, 'International Competition Law in the Context of Global Capitalism', *European Competition Law Review*, 21/2 (2000): 117–27.

Kende, Mark S., 'Yahoo!: National Borders in Cyberspace and Their Impact on International Lawyers', *New Mexico Law Review*, 32 (2002): 1–10.

Keyser, Mike, 'The Council of Europe Convention on Cybercrime', *Journal of Transnational Law and Policy*, 12 (2003): 287–326.

Koh, Harold Hongju, 'International Business Transactions in United States Courts', *Recueil des cours*, 261 (1996): 9–242.

Kohl, Uta, 'Eggs, Jurisdiction, and the Internet', *International and Comparative Law Quarterly*, 51/3 (2002): 555–82.

Kohl, Uta, 'The Rule of Law, Jurisdiction and the Internet', *International Journal of Law and Information Technology*, 12/3 (2004): 365–76.

Lange, Dieter G. F. and Sandage, John Byron, 'The Wood Pulp Decision and its Implications for the Scope of EC Competition Law', *Common Market Law Review*, 26 (1989): 137–65.

Laprès, Daniel Arthur, 'L'exorbitante affaire Yahoo', *Journal du droit international*, 129/4 (2002): 975–99.

Laprès, Daniel Arthur, 'Affaires Yahoo! (I et II) et Al Manar : l'approche universaliste confirmée deux fois', *Juriscom.net*, 17 mai 2005.

Lessig, Lawrence, and Resnick, Paul, 'Zoning Speech on the Internet: A Legal and Technical Model', *Michigan Law Review*, 98 (1999): 395–431.

Longworth, Elizabeth, 'The Possibilities for a Legal Framework for Cyberspace', in T. Fuentes-Camacho (ed.), *The International Dimensions of Cyberspace Law* (Paris: UNESCO, 2000), pp. 9–69.

Lowe, A. V., 'Blocking Extraterritorial Jurisdiction: The British Protection of Trading Interests Act, 1980', *American Journal of International Law*, 75/2 (1981): 257–82.

Lowe, Vaughan, 'International Law and the Effects Doctrine in the European Court of Justice', *Cambridge Law Journal*, 48 (1989): 9–11.

Lowe, Vaughan, 'Jurisdiction', in M. D. Evans (ed.), *International Law* (Oxford: Oxford University Press, 2003), pp. 329–55.

Lowenfeld, Andreas F., 'Public Law in the International Arena: Conflict of Laws, International Law, and Some Suggestions for Their Interaction', *Recueil des cours*, 163 (1979): 311–445.

Lowenfeld, Andreas F., 'Conflict, Balancing of Interests, and the Exercise of Jurisdiction to Prescribe: Reflections on the Insurance Antitrust Case', *American Journal of International Law*, 89/1 (1995): 42–53.

Manolopoulos, Andreas, 'Raising 'Cyber-Borders': The Interaction Between Law and Technology', *International Journal of Law and Information Technology*, 11/1 (2003): 40–58.

Michaels, Ralf, 'Territorial Jurisdiction after Territoriality', in P. J. Slot and M. Bulterman (eds.), *Globalisation and Jurisdiction* (The Hague: Kluwer Law International, 2004), pp. 105–30.

Miquelon-Weismann, Miriam F., 'The Convention on Cybercrime: A Harmonized Implementation of International Penal Law: What Prospects for Procedural Due Process?' *John Marshall Journal of Computer and Information Law*, 23/2 (2005): 329–61.

Murphy, Caitlin T., 'International Law and the Internet: An Ill-Suited Match', *Hastings International and Comparative Law Review*, 25 (2002): 405–27.

O'Keefe, Roger, 'Universal Jurisdiction: Clarifying the Basic Concept', *Journal of International Criminal Justice*, 2/3 (2004): 735–60.

Podgor, Ellen S., 'International Computer Fraud: A Paradigm for Limiting National Jurisdiction', *U.C. Davis Law Review*, 35 (2002): 267–317.

Rosenthal, Douglas E. and Knighton, William M., *National Laws and International Commerce: Problem of Extraterritoriality* (London: Routledge, 1982).

Shaw, Malcolm N., *International Law*, 5th ed. (Cambridge: Cambridge University Press, 2003).

Sirinelli, Pierre, 'L'adéquation entre le village virtuel et la création normative – Remise en cause du rôle de l'Etat ?' in K. Boele-Woelki and C. Kessedjian (eds.), *Internet: Which Court Decides? Which Law Applies? Quel tribunal décide? Quel droit s'applique?* (The Hague: Kluwer Law International, 1998), pp. 1–22.

Tomuschat, Christian, *Human Rights: Between Idealism and Realism* (Oxford: Oxford University Press, 2003).

Trachtman, Joel P., 'Cyberspace, Sovereignty, Jurisdiction, and Modernism', *Indiana Journal of Global Legal Issues*, 5/2 (1998): 561–81.

Trimble, Phillip R., 'The Supreme Court and International Law: The Demise of Restatement Section 403', *American Journal of International Law*, 89/1 (1995): 53–57.

Walden, Ian, 'Crime and Security in Cyberspace', *Cambridge Review of International Affairs*, 18/1 (2005): 51–68.

Watt, Horatia Muir, '*Yahoo!* Cyber–Collision of Cultures: Who Regulates?' *Michigan Journal of International Law*, 24 (2003): 673–96.

Weatherill, Stephen and Beaumont, Paul, *EU Law* (London: Penguin Books, 1999).

Chapter 4

Between Transnational Take-off and National Landing: Jurisdictional Dynamics in the Domain Name Area

Dirk Lehmkuhl

Introduction

While describing patterns of economic globalisation is relatively easy, coming to grips with its consequences is far more difficult. There is a broadly shared consensus that globalisation can be referred to as the proliferation of cross-border economic transactions including the distribution and exchange of tangible and intangible goods.[1] In contrast to this widely accepted description of economic globalisation, often ambivalent conclusions are drawn about the effects of globalisation on governance capacities, that is the capacity to set, monitor, and enforce rules in internationalised environments. As stated in the introduction of the volume, premature obituaries for the state are at odds with empirical observations that see states maintaining or recapturing the capacity to guard their internal and external sovereignty. As a consequence, controversial statements in both observation and interpretation mirror this ambivalence in coping with the effects of internationalised patterns of exchange.

Just as globalization inherently exerts stimuli that can be both complementary and contradictory in nature, its effects on patterns of governance are frequently described in dichotomies that are part of the same picture: convergence and divergence, universalism and particularism, centralization and decentralization, transnationalisation and nationalization or even localisation.[2] In a similar vein, theoretical statements are often locked in a stalemate between opposing viewpoints:

---

1 Michael Zürn, 'From Interdependence to Globalization', in Walter Carlsnaes, Thomas Risse, and Beth Simmons (eds.), *Handbook of International Relations* (London/Thousand Oaks/New Delhi, 2002), pp. 235–53.

2 James N. Rosenau, 'Distant Proximities: The Dynamics and Dialectics of Globalization', in B. Hettne (ed.), *International Political Economy: Understanding Global Disorder* (London, 1995), pp. 46–65; James N. Rosenau, *Along the Domestic–Foreign Frontier: Exploring Governance in a Turbulent World* (Cambridge, 1997); Boaventura de Sousa Santos, *Toward a New Common Sense. Law, Science and Politics in Paradigmatic Transition* (New York, 1995); Saskia Sassen, 'The State and Globalization', in Rodney B. Hall and Thomas J. Bierstecker (eds.), *The Emergence of Private Authority in Global Governance* (Cambridge, 2002), pp. 91–112.

Some see the danger of a 'hollowed-out' state, while others dismiss fears that the state could become powerless as fanciful.[3] While the former describe constellations in which international organisations and actors at the international level gain importance at the expense of national institutions,[4] the latter group emphasises the transformative capacity of national institutions and units.[5]

This contribution proposes that it is more fruitful to acknowledge the respective analytical potential of these divergent viewpoints than to discuss them as opposites. To this end, the present discussion is based on the observation that 'international economic integration – itself differentiated and uneven – is producing a new fabric of global governance that displays many variations and shadings.'[6] Nevertheless, variations exist not only in the governance fabric of different fields and sectors, but also within single areas. This variation can be demonstrated in instances where institutionalised governance becomes more detached from national influences, while states simultaneously try to subject these arrangements and their outcomes to the control of national institutions again. The assumption is that these patterns of *transnational take-off* and *national landing* can be observed at the same time but that the way in which national institutions subject outcomes of transnational regulations to national review varies. As such, the detaching-re-controlling pattern is an example for the emergence of overlapping regulatory activities that seem to be a characteristic feature of contemporary governance in internationalized environments.

To explain the link between the national and the transnational levels of governance, this paper breaks down the concept of 'governance' into the three aspects of setting, sanctioning and enforcing rules. This distinction not only allows for a nuanced description of constellations characterised by a dispersion of governance capacities across different locations including states, international organisations, subnational units, and non-state actors. Disaggregating governance is also a promising approach to capture the dynamics resulting from the contest between different locations claiming authority in one or more of these dimensions. As governance capacities in internationalised environments are not allocated according to a master plan, conflicting claims of jurisdictional competence are often seen as a major problem – both in practice and in theory.[7]

---

3   Reich, Robert B., *The Work of Nations: Preparing ourselves for the 21st-Century Capitalism* (New York, 1991); Weiss, Linda, *The Myth of the Powerless State. Governing the Economy in a Global Era* (Cambridge, 1998).

4   David Held, Anthony McGrew, David Goldblatt, and Jonathan Perraton, *Global Transformations. Politics, Economics and Culture* (Stanford, 1999); Susan Strange, *The Retreat of the State. The Diffusion of Power in the World Economy* (Cambridge, 1996).

5   Linda Weiss, *States in the Global Economy. Bringing Domestic Institutions Back In* (Cambridge, 2003).

6   Miles Kahler, and David Lake, 'Globalization and Governance', in Miles Kahler and David Lake (eds.), *Governance in A Global Economy. Political Authority in Transition* (Princeton/Oxford, 2003), pp. 412–38.

7   Lisbeth Hooghe and Garry Marks, 'Unravelling the Central State, but How? Types of Multi-level Governance', *American Political Science Review*, 97/2 (2003): 233–43; Bruce H. Kobayashi and Larry E. Ribstein, 'Multi-Jurisdictional Regulation of the Internet', in Vinton G. Cerf, Adam Thierer and Clyde W.J. Crews (eds.), *Who Rules the Net? Internet Governance*

With these considerations in mind, the next section develops a framework that integrates political scientists and legal approaches to cope with the phenomenon of complementary and competing claims for governance authority in descriptive, analytical, and normative terms. The main analytical instrument, that is the distinction between prescriptive, judicial, and enforcement jurisdiction, will be used to describe and analyse the conflict between trademark provisions and the Internet's domain name system. While trade names are usually issued according to national principles, the Internet's architecture ignores national and territorial principles, and the domain names system requires a universal rule. The third part of this paper contextualises the tension between trademarks and the domain name system and, furthermore, presents the Uniform Dispute Resolution Policy as the institutionalised arrangement to govern the interface between these two. The fourth section demonstrates that after three years of operation, the Uniform Dispute Resolution Policy is generally acknowledged as a successful model of transnational dispute resolution. However, this generally positive assessment is clouded by problems such as a bias towards holders of well-known trademarks. The fifth part directs attention to the cures that are offered to address the problems of the governance arrangement. It focuses on the 'national landing' of the transnational governance solution. The final part of this paper emphasises the general implications of this state of affairs? for our understanding of the link between national and transnational governance.

Global Governance, Authority, and Jurisdiction

'But across the centuries, it has been nation-states – especially the leading great powers – that have made the critical choices to construct the world economy.'[8] Within the neorealist paradigm of the study of international relations, states in general and the most powerful ones in particular are not only the central actors in the international state system. Based on their military power, they not only guarantee order and stability in the international system, but also make and enforce rules for the global political economy. Even without referring explicitly to the neorealist paradigm, a state-centric approach to international governance posits a continuation of the power of nation-states to control the outcomes of international governance.

This insistence on the historical and continued power of states' institutions and rules to regulate the world economy faces significant resistance for a number of reasons. From a historical perspective, one can emphasise that new forms of trade already breached the boundaries of the established political orders before the evolution of modern nation-states.[9] This expansion of private economic activities was accompanied by a diffusion of privately developed rules and principles of trade

and Jurisdiction (Washington, D.C., 2003), pp. 159–215; Joel P. Trachtmann, 'Externalities and Extraterritoriality: The law and economics of prescriptive jurisdiction', in Jagdeep S. Bhandari and Alan O. Sykes (eds.), *Economic Dimensions in International Law. Comparative and Empirical Perspectives* (Cambridge, 1997), pp. 642–83.

8   Joseph Grieco and G. John Ikenberry, *State Power and World Markets. The International Political Economy* (New York/London, 2003), p. 2.

9   John B. Condliffe, *The Commerce of Nations* (London, 1951).

that are at the heart of economic exchange until this day.[10] A more contemporary critique refers to the state-centrism in accounts of international affairs and claims that the actors in world politics cannot simply be conceived of as states.[11] Rather, it is claimed that the international system's horizontal (relations between states), vertical (hierarchical), and functional dimensions are shifting all at once. This shift implies that the 'salient ingredients' of power – object, control mode, and assets – are also subject to transformation.[12]

A major impact of this transformation of the international system is a *pluralizing of global governance*. While in the traditional military realm, in particular, states remain central actors (while new threats to security also involve non-state actors to a significant degree), both economic and social aspects of the anatomy of international affairs have become more complex with a decentralised, networked, and vibrant diversity of actors, including international organisations, a multiplicity of transnational corporations and transnational business associations, national stakeholders, global NGOs, and local and community organizations.[13] Alongside this transformation, well-established concepts such as power have lost their explanatory potential for the analysis of politics in international relations.

Although attempts have been made to apply and adapt the power concept to this pluralised constellation,[14] more frequently, the notion of *authority* has been used in accounts of the changing nature of global governance. Rather than framing the transformation of international politics as a 'power shift',[15] the concept of authority is seen to be more apposite for coping analytically with a plurilateral world characterised by a variety of locations of governance capacities with cross-cutting and intersecting links, as it indicates the need to move the state out of the centre of analysis. Due to structural changes in the economy[16] and the technical revolution in information

10 Harold J. Berman, *Law and Revolution, The Formation of the Western Legal Tradition* (Cambridge, 1983), pp. 339ff.; Michael Mann, 'A History of Power from the Beginning to AD 1760', in Michael Mann (ed.), *The Sources of Social Power* (2 vols., Cambridge, 1986), vol. 1, p. 504.

11 Robert O. Keohane and Joseph S. Nye, 'Introduction', in Joseph S. Nye, and John D. Donahue (eds.), *Governance in a Globalizing World* (Washington. D.C., 2000), p. 22.

12 Stanley Hoffmann, 'Notes on the Elusiveness of Modern Power', *International Journal*, 30 (1975): 183–206.

13 Joseph S. Nye, *The Paradox of American Power. Why the World's Only Superpower Can't Get It Alone* (Oxford, 2002).

14 Bas Arts, *Non-State Actors in Global Governance: Three Faces of Power*. Preprints of the Max-Planck-Project Group on Common Goods, Bonn, <http://www.mpp-rdg.mpg.de/pdf_dat/2003_4.pdf>, last accessed 1 January 2007; Theodor Cohn, Stephen McBride, and John Wiseman (eds.), *Power in the Global Era. Grounding Globalization* (Houndsmill, 2002); Henri Goverde, Philip G. Cerny, Mark Haugaard, and Howard H. Lentner (eds.), *Power in Contemporary Politics* (London, 2000).

15 Jessica Mathews, 'Power Shift', *Foreign Affairs*, 76/1 (1997): 50–66.

16 Susan Strange, *States and Markets: An Introduction to International Political Economy* (London, 1998); Strange, *The Retreat of the State. The Diffusion of Power in the World Economy*.

and communication,[17] private authority in international affairs has been described as being related to increased coordination between corporations,[18] as a move from influence towards 'epistemic authority' by private market actors challenging states' prerogatives[19] or, in an even broader understanding, as the emergence of market, moral, and illicit authority related to firms, civil society, and organised violence.[20] Given the 'profound transformation in the institutions, structures, and processes that sustain economic, political, and social life today,' Rosenau states that 'authority is clearly among the conceptual tools that need clarification and specification if analysis is to move meaningful beyond globalization and address how micro-macro interactions contribute to the changing dynamics of fragmengration'.[21]

One problem related to the clarification of the concept of authority refers the limitations of traditional theorising about order beyond the national level to conduct of states. Originating in the national realm, the intrinsic link between authority and the state has impeded thinking about private authority, that is, conduct induced, monitored, or even enforced by private actors. Put differently, 'most political and legal theorists focus on the actions and obligatory status of public authority. The obligatory character of private authority raises rather different considerations that pose obstacles to conceptualizing private action as authoritative'.[22] The conventional assumption that according to 'liberal and democratic theory, only the public sphere is empowered and entitled to prescribe behaviour for others, for only public authorities are accountable through political institutions' ranks very prominently amongst these obstacles.[23]

Even a brief account of actual constellations in international politics reveals that preserving the prescriptive and legitimate authority of states or, in an advanced form, of states and international organisations, fails to take into consideration two real developments: Just as rating agencies are an integral part of the architecture of international financial markets, providers of private commercial arbitration services have established themselves in cross-border economic relations, and a group of big banks has successfully managed to establish principles to prevent money

---

17 Nye, *The Paradox of American Power. Why the World's Only Superpower Can't Get It Alone*.

18 Claire A. Cutler, Virginia Haufler, and Tony Porter, 'The Contours and Significance of Private Authority and International Affairs', in A.C. Cutler, V. Haufler, and T. Porter (eds.), *Private Authority and International Affairs* (Albany, 1999), pp. 333–76.

19 Timothy J. Sinclair, 'Bond-Rating Agencies and Coordination in the Global Political Economy', in A.C. Cutler, V. Haufler, and T. Porter (eds.), *Private Authority in International Affairs* (Albany, 1999), pp. 159ff.

20 Rodney Bruce Hall and Thomas J. Biersteker (eds.), *The Emergence of Private Authority in Global Governance* (Cambridge, 2002).

21 James N. Rosenau, *Distant Proximities: Dynamics beyond Globalization* (Princeton, 2003).

22 Cutler, Haufler, Porter, 'The Contours and Significance of Private Authority and International Affairs', p. 365.

23 Ibid., p. 18.

laundering.[24] Also, so-called hybrid forms of governance incorporate states and private actors in new relationships.[25] As these new forms of governance represent neither the retreat of the state in the face of private actors, nor a simple reassertion of state authority, nor yet traditional multilateral institutions,[26] they pose particular problems for traditional theories of international relations. Moreover, private authority is not restricted to markets or to private addressees, but also can affect the conduct of states, since, for instance, the naming, blaming, and shaming policies of non-governmental organisations influence state behaviour in the areas of human rights, the environment, and public procurement.[27]

These considerations have a number of implications for the study of the impact of globalization on patterns of governance. The concept of authority allows us to take off the state-centric blinders and to account for the plurality of participants in contemporary world politics. Second, given that the overall distribution of authority across all sites and locations of governance has not been undertaken according to a master plan, but has rather developed and is still developing incrementally, overlapping and competing authorities will be the rule rather than the exception. As a consequence, questions arise as to the relationships between different spheres of authority.[28] And third, an important feature in our study of authority in international affairs must relate to the outcomes and the question of the normative implications of governance arrangements involving private authority.[29]

24 Timothy J. Sinclair, 'Passing Judgment: Credit Rating Processes as Regulatory Mechanisms of Governance in the Emerging World Order', *Review of International Political Economy*, 1/1 (1994): 133–59; A. Claire Cutler, *Private Power and Global Authority: Transnational Merchant Law and the Global Political Economy* (Cambridge, 2003), pp. 153–68. Walter Mattli, 'Private Justice in a Global Economy. From Litigation to Arbitration', *International Organization*, 55/4 (2001): 919–48; Mark Pieth and Gemma Aiolfi, 'The Private Sector becomes active: The Wolfsberg Process', *Journal of Financial Crime*, 10/4 (2003): 359–69.

25 Henry Farrell, 'Hybrid Institutions and the Law', *Zeitschrift für Rechtssoziologie*, 23/1 (2002): 18–34. Christoph Knill, and Dirk Lehmkuhl, 'Private Actors and the State: Internationalization and Changing Patterns of Governance', *Governance: An International Journal of Policy, Administration and Institutions*, 15/1 (2002): 41–63.

26 Henry Farrell, 'Constructing the International Foundations of E-Commerce – The EU-US Safe Harbor Arrangement and Transnational Relations', *International Organization*, 57/2 (2003): 277–306.

27 Thomas Risse, Stephen Ropp, and Kathryn Sikkin (eds.), *The Power of Human Rights. International Norms and Domestic Change* (Cambridge, 1999); Ann M. Florini, *The Third Force. The Rise of Civil Society* (Tokyo/Washington D.C., 2000); Frederik Galtung, 'A Global Network to Curb Corruption: The Experience of Transparency International', in A.M. Florini (ed.), *The Third Force. The Rise of Civil Society* (Tokyo/Washington D.C., 2000), pp. 17–48.

28 Yuval Shany, *The Competing Jurisdictions of International Courts and Tribunals* (Oxford, 2003).

29 Robert O. Keohane, and Joseph S. Nye, 'Redefining Accountability for Global Governance', in M. Kahler, and D.A. Lake (eds.), *Governance in a Global Economy. Political Authority in Transition* (Princeton, 2003), pp. 412–38.

This being understood, the stage is set to approach the concept of authority in global governance analytically and normatively. The analytical dimension refers to the origin, the operation, and the acceptance of the authoritative action by both the addressees and – of particular interest in the context of this contribution – of national institutions.[30] The normative dimension refers to the outcomes of governance arrangements, that is, to whether they are explainable, sanctionable, and accepted as legitimate by the addressees.

Approaches to studying the authoritative allocation of values (Easton) have taken different perspectives. For the study of political authority in transition, I rely on an interpretation of the concept of political authority as the 'right to make laws and regulations, to judge and to punish for failing to conform to certain standards, or to order some redress for the victims of such violations, as well as a right to command'.[31] The advantage of this definition is its affinity to an approach that conceives global governance as an ongoing contest of different locations to assert jurisdiction.

Jurisdiction in legal terms refers to three areas in which a legal or regulatory body can assert authority: jurisdiction to *prescribe*, i.e., to apply a community's norms to a dispute; jurisdiction to *adjudicate*, i.e., to subject persons or things to legal process; and (3) jurisdiction to *enforce*, i.e., to induce or compel compliance with a determination reached.[32] This definition of jurisdiction offers some important opportunities for the analysis of phenomena of global governance.

First, it is a broad enough definition that goes well enough beyond the immediate legal appearance and has the potential to make jurisdiction the locus for debates about community definition, sovereignty, and legitimacy. By so doing, the concept allows for more than merely asking for the most efficient way of regulating problems that have cross-border implications or reach, and also encompasses the underlying normative assumption in the distribution of competences. Second, it is specific enough to channel an analytical approach to global governance. Its three dimensions represent an approach that divides the analysis into categories that are at the same time linked and may be separated.

Third, while scholars of international relations generally assume that the state, as a multifaceted and multipurpose organisation, provides all aspects of governance, the disaggregating of governance authority is not confined to the assumption of one centre or location, but enables us to conceive different dimensions of jurisdiction being distributed across different levels of organisations and across various institutions. Put differently, jurisdiction with its dimensions of prescription, adjudication, and enforcement includes not only the possibility of a distribution of facets of authority across the subnational, national, and international levels –as seen in federalist political systems or in the European Union – but also accounts for the authority of private actors or institutions asserting and exercising their specific share

---

30 Steven Lukes, 'Perspectives on Authority', in Joseph Raz (ed.), *Authority* (Oxford, 1990), pp. 203–17.

31 Joseph Raz, 'Introduction: Conceptualizing Multiple', in Joseph Raz (ed.), *Authority* (Oxford, 1990), pp. 1–19.

32 Paul Schiff Bermann, 'The Globalization of Jurisdiction', *University of Pennylvania Law Review*, 151/2 (2002): 311–529.

of jurisdiction in a particular area – as shown by many studies on private authority in international affairs.[33]

This explicit account for multiple sites that might assert jurisdiction has a particular appeal when it comes to the regulation of Internet-related activities. In this respect, we are frequently confronted with situations in which the location of a specific action or transaction is not the same as that of the state that asserts jurisdiction over this action.[34] Take for example the question of taxation in e-commerce or consumer protection standards – in both cases, one might argue for or against the principles of origin or destination, respectively. Another example refers to the question of content control of online services. The famous Yahoo! Case, in which both a French and a Californian court claimed jurisdiction over the question of whether or not Internet service providers can be held responsible for the content on the websites of their clients. As both courts pursued their national approach to the question and applied their respective national provisions, their judgements were remarkably dissimilar.[35]

These examples indicate that one of the major analytical issues in the governance of the Internet relates to jurisdictional questions. While some argue that the Internet (or cyberspace) cannot be governed by territorially based governments and, instead, call for the development of a truly deterritorialised (i.e., denationalised) jurisdiction of cyberspace,[36] others deny the exceptionality of cyberspace transactions by grounding cyberspace in real-state law.[37] Furthermore, it is argued that state regulation is not only possible, but is even desirable, as competition between jurisdictions may yield more efficient regulations.[38] Reality mirrors this debate and the importance of jurisdictional questions in a twofold way. Within the last few years, national legislators, courts at different levels, and sub-national administrative units have

---

33 In a similar vein, Trachtman asserts that the prescriptive jurisdiction of individual states faces four loci of power: other states, sub–national units, transnational institutions, and private markets (Joel P. Trachtman, 'Externalities and Extraterritoriality: The law and economics of prescriptive jurisdiction', pp. 642ff).

34 Jonathan Zittran, 'Be Careful What You Ask For: Reconciling A Global Internet and Local Law', in Vincent G. Cerf, Adam Thierer and Clyde W.J. Crews (eds.), *Who Rules the Internet? Governance and Jurisdiction* (Washington, D.C., 2003), pp. 13–30; Michael Geist, '"Targeting" for International Jurisdiction', in Vincent G. Cerf, Adam Thierer and Clyde W.J. Crews (eds.), *Who Rules the Internet? Governance and Jurisdiction* (Washington D.C., 2003), pp. 91–118.

35 Benoit Frydman and Isabelle Rorive, 'Regulating Internet Content through Intermediaries', *Zeitschrift für Rechtssoziologie*, 23/1 (2002): 41–59; John Hughes, 'The Internet and the Persistence of Law', *Boston College Law Review*, 43/2 (2003): 359–96.

36 David R. Johnson and David G. Post, 'Law and Borders – The Rise of Law in Cyberspace', *Stanford Law Review*, 48 (1996): 1367–402; David G. Post, 'Against "Against Cyberanarchy"', in A. Thierer and C.W.J. Crews (eds.), *Who Rules the Internet? Governance and Jurisdiction* (Washington, D.C., 2003), pp. 71–90.

37 Jack L. Goldsmith, 'Against Cyberanarchy', in A. Thierer and C.W.J. Crews (eds.), *Who Rules the Internet? Governance and Jurisdiction* (Washington D.C., 2003), pp. 31–70. Id., 'Against Cyberanarchy', *The University of Chicago Law Review*, 65/4 (1998): 1199–250.

38 Bruce H. Kobayashi and Larry E. Ribstein, 'Multi-Jurisdictional Regulation of the Internet', pp. 159–215.

declared their jurisdiction over specific persons or subject matters.[39] At the same time, solutions beyond the national level have been established to regulate specific Internet-related activities explicitly without recourse to any national provision. Frequently, these solutions take the shape of the aforementioned hybrid forms of governance involving public and private actors.

For the purposes of the present discussion, the focus will remain on one particular problem, namely the analysis of jurisdictional problems with special attention being paid to the conditions under which different assertions of authority operate, how they relate to each other, and what provides them with legitimacy. Equipped with the concept of jurisdiction to prescribe, adjudicate, and enforce, this contribution addresses these issues with a particular focus on the way in which national and transnational claims for authority are related to each other. The analytical question relates to the degree to which private transnational claims for jurisdiction operate in isolation/separately from national assertions of jurisdiction. The assumption is that patterns of transnational take-off and national landing can be observed simultaneously, but that we should expect variation in the way that national institutions exert their jurisdictional claim to prescribe, to enforce, and to adjudicate.

The empirical case that will illustrate the usefulness of the concept relates to the resolution of conflicts at the interface between trademark regulation and the domain name system as one of the pillars of the Internet's architecture. The three following chapters will discuss the problem and its solution, problems with the solution, and, finally, alternative solutions.

The Problem and Its Transnational Solution

The commercialization of the Internet has transformed Internet-related policies and politics significantly. A good example is the Internet's domain name system. Domain names that had mainly been user-friendly addresses have turned more and more into tradable commodities and brand names. Since the mid 1990s, a growing number of firms have realized the economic importance of domain names, but for many this realization came only after they discovered that their preferred names had already been registered by others. These others were not always firms with an equally 'legitimate' claim to a domain, but also included 'pirates' or 'cybersquatters' who had grabbed a well known domain name in order to make money by selling it to the trademark owner at an inflated price.[40]

At the heart of these conflicts at the interface between domain names and trademarks is the profound tension between the principle of territoriality in

---

39 Marcus Franda, Governing the Internet. The Emergence of International Regime (Boulder/London, 2001), pp. 146ff.

40 Elisabeth G. Thornburg, 'Going Private: Technology, Due Process, and Internet Dispute Resolution', *U.C. Davis Law Review*, 34/1 (2000): 11–220. Two related problems are the so-called 'reverse domain name hijacking", that is the bad faith attempt of a trademark owner to deprive a registered domain name holder of a domain name, and typo-squatting that occurs when a registrants uses a name similar name to a trademark holder's in order to attract attention in cases of misspellings.

trademark law and the ubiquity of Internet domain names. Traditionally, trademarks are issued by national governments, and trademark law is organized predominantly on national, geographic, and sectoral principles. These principles, however, are badly matched with the Internet's architecture, which ignores both national borders and sectors. Thus, the Internet enforces a much greater degree of uniqueness that is at odds with territory-based, national approaches to protecting trademark rights, as the jurisdiction of domain names must necessarily go beyond that of traditional trademark provisions.

The problems related to national efforts to tackle the issue, that is the lack of agreement on the ability of national courts to deal with domain name registrants located in foreign jurisdictions, as well as the time-consuming and expensive procedure in national courts, made a payoff more likely.[41] Since the mid-1990s, various transnational initiatives have been started, including Network Solutions, Inc. (NSI), the company then responsible for the registration of second-tier domain names in the most important dotcom, dotorg, and dotnet top-level domains; the Internet Assigned Numbers Authority (IANA), which was responsible for the administration of the Internet, and the Internet Society as a non-governmental international organization for global cooperation and coordination with respect to the Internet.[42]

All these initiatives were superseded by an intervention of the National Telecommunications and Information Agency, which belongs to the US Department of Commerce, in early 1998 that documented the Internet's increasing political salience. In its 'Statement of Policy on the Management of Internet Names and Addresses' (also known as the 'White Paper'), the US government not only announced the establishment of a private, non-profit organization to which the control of the domain name system should be transferred (this plan was realized with the establishment of the Internet Corporation of Assigned Names and Numbers, ICANN, in October 1998).[43] The White Paper also proclaimed that the 'U.S. Government will

---

41 Laurence R. Helfer, and Graeme B. Dinwoodie, 'Designing Non-National Systems: The Case of the Uniform Domain Name Dispute Resolution Policy', *William and Mary Law Review*, 48 (2001): 141–273; Annette Kur, 'UDRP' (9 January 2002), Max-Planck-Institute for Foreign and International Patent, Copyright and Competition Law, Munich in cooperation with the Institute for Market Law and Intellectual Property at the University of Stockholm and the Institute for Information Law at the Technical University of Karlsruhe 2002. Available from <http://www.intellecprop.mpg.de/Online-Publikationen/UDRP–e.htm>, accessed 12 January 2002.

42 Helfer, Dinwoodie, 'Designing Non–National Systems: The Case of the Uniform Domain Name Dispute Resolution Policy'; Jonathan Weinberg, 'ICANN and the Problem of Legitimacy', *Duke Law Journal*, 50 (2000): 200ff; Raymund Werle and Volker Leib, 'The Internet Society and its Struggle for Recognition and Influence', in Carsten Ronit and Volker Schneider (eds.), *Private Organizations in Global Politics* (London/New York, 2000), pp. 102–22.

43 See, e.g., Marc Holitscher, *Internet Governance: Die Reform des Domain Namen Systems und die Entstehung der Internet Corporation for Assigned Names and Numbers. Eine Fallstudie zur Rolle privater Akteure jenseits des Nationalstaates* (Zürich, 2002); Milton Müller, 'Dancing the Quango: ICANN and the Privatization of International Governance', <http://istweb.syr.edu/~mueller/onlinepubs.htm>, accessed 1 January 2007; Milton Müller,

seek international support to call upon the World Intellectual Property Organization (WIPO) to initiate a balanced and transparent process'[44] that should suggest the format for a uniform dispute resolution system. However, given the complexity and controversial character of the issues at stake, the White Paper urged to limit the jurisdiction of any new dispute settlement body to cases of 'cybersquatting and cyberpiracy', leaving it to national courts to solve cases of 'legitimate competing rights'.[45]

Following the publication of the White Paper, WIPO carried out process of consultation, generally known as the 'first domain name process' or 'WIPO I process', between July 1998 and April 1999.[46] The most important recommendations of the final report referred to the establishment of a uniform dispute resolution policy and procedure for resolving disputes over alleged bad faith and deliberate misuse of trademarks in domain names. WIPO handed its recommendation to ICANN as the organization that had been granted authority to regulate the domain name system since October 1998. Between May and October 1999, ICANN reviewed the recommendations internally and externally, and, finally, ICANN's Uniform Domain Name Dispute Resolution Policy and the Rules for Uniform Domain Name Dispute Resolution went into effect in December 1999.

In sum, the process through which the rules governing conflicts at the interface between domain names and trademarks emerged had some particular features. UDRP provisions were neither developed by an international treaty nor unilaterally by a powerful state. Rather, WIPO as an international organization engaged, on behalf of a single government, in an international deliberation involving a range of public and private entities and actors. Final approval of the WIPO recommendation, again, occurred not by an act of international agreement, but by the declaration of ICANN, a non-profit organization under Californian law bestowed with prescriptive, adjudicative, and enforcement jurisdiction for the Internet domain name system by the US government. As ICANN was under significant pressure to set up its own organisational statutes in the early days of its existence, the nature of WIPO's recommendations was more prescriptive than advisory.[47]

'Success by default: A New Profile of Domain Name Trademark Disputes under ICANN's UDRP, <http://istweb.syr.edu/~mueller/onlinepubs.htm>, accessed 1 January 2007.

44 White Paper 1998, p. 747.

45 Ibid., p. 88.

46 'The Management of Internet Names and Addresses: Intellectual Property Issues'. Final Report of the WIPO Internet Domain Name Process, April 30, 1999, p. 135. Available from <http://www.wipo.int/amc/en/index.html>, accessed 1 January 2007.

47 Helfer, Dinwoodie, 'Designing Non–National Systems: The Case of the Uniform Domain Name Dispute Resolution Policy'; A. Michael Froomkin, 'A Commentary on WIPO's *The Management of Internet Names and Addresses: Intellectual Property Issues*', *University of Miami School of Law*, available from <www.law.miami.edu>, accessed 1 January 2007; A. Michael Froomkin, 'ICANN's 'Uniform Dispute Resolution Policy" – Causes and (partial) Cures', *Brooklyn Law Review*, 67/3 (2002): 605–718; Michael Geist, 'Fair.com?: An Examination of the Allegations of Systemic Unfairness in the ICANN UDRP', *UDRPinfo. com*, available from <http://www.udrpinfo.com/resc/fair.pdf>, accessed 1 January 2007; Michael Geist, 'Fundamentally Fair.com? An Update on Bias Allegations and the ICANN

The Problems With the Solution

The Procedure

Given all its limitations, the Uniform Domain Name Dispute Resolution Policy (UDRP) covers only a narrow segment of the countless intellectual property disputes that are currently of importance in cyberspace. It provides a quick and relatively inexpensive forum for parties to challenge domain name holders' rights to a name. Under UDRP rules,[48] someone who believes that his rights were violated by a particular domain name registration (complainant) initiates the dispute and chooses the dispute service provider. He can do so if the domain name is identical or confusingly similar to a trademark or service mark that the complainant holds the rights to; if the domain name holder has no rights or legitimate interests in respect of the domain name; or if the domain name has been registered and is being used in bad faith.

Once the provider verifies that the complaint is in accordance with the UDRP provisions, the company informs the domain name holder (respondent) within three days. Within twenty days of the commencement of the proceedings, the respondent must address the complaints and deliver a defence. If he fails to respond, a decision is made based on the complaint. Otherwise, upon receiving the response, the dispute resolution provider has five days to set up a one- or three-person panel, which must issue a decision within two weeks. If the decision is in favour of the complainant, ICANN rules require a cancellation of the domain name or a transfer to the complainant. No monetary remedies are awarded.

To allow competition amongst different providers, an evaluation of applicants led ICANN to approve four dispute resolution service providers by May 2000: the National Arbitration Forum (NAF), the World Intellectual Property Organization, CPR Institute for Dispute Resolution, and eResolution. Since December 2001, however, there have been two changes. On the one hand, eResolution has folded its operations due to a lack of cases by the end of November 2001 and, on the other hand, on 3 December 2001 ICANN announced the accreditation of the Asian Domain Name Dispute Resolution Centre as a new provider that was expected to begin accepting disputes on 28 February 2002 through offices in its centres in Beijing and Hong Kong.

The dispute resolution service providers play an important role in the settlement of domain name versus trademark conflicts. These service providers have to ensure that the cases are handled according to the administrative aspects of the UDRP procedures, and they must provide a list of at least 20 qualified and neutral panellists.

The Performance and its Problems

A first glance at the plain data gives not only the impression that there is a need for a global uniform procedure of resolving conflicts at the interface between domain

---

UDRP', available from <www.lawbytes.ca>; Milton Müller, 'Dancing the Quango: ICANN and the Privatization of International Governance'; Milton Müller, 'Success by default: A New Profile of Domain Name Trademark Disputes under ICANN's UDRP'.

48 <http://www.icann.org/udrp/>, accessed 1 January 2007.

names and trademarks, but also that ICANN's UDRP is a success story. By the end of October 2003, the approved dispute resolution providers had resolved roughly 8.250 cases involving about 13.780 domain names, and hundreds more were still pending.[49] A closer look at the data, however, indicates that concerns remain about issues such as due process or fairness.

A first interesting finding in this respect derives from a correlation of the distribution of cases between the different service providers and the likelihood of a transfer or cancellation of a domain name. A study based on the analyses of all 3.094 UDRP cases decided as of July 2001 (and an update on the basis of 4.332 ICANN UDRP cases as of 18 February 2002)[50] confirmed earlier findings,[51] according to which the number of cases is not evenly distributed amongst dispute resolution providers: WIPO takes the lion's share of 58 per cent (59.2 per cent), followed by NAF with 34 per cent (34.5 per cent), while eResolution and CPR have a share of 7 per cent (5.6 per cent) and 1 per cent respectively.[52] Intriguingly, there is a significant correlation between the market share of a dispute resolution service provider and the tendency to take away domain names from respondents: the statistical data as of July 2001 (and 2002) show that complainants win 84 per cent (83 per cent) of the cases with WIPO and 85 per cent (86 per cent) with the NAF, but only 63 per cent (64 per cent) of the cases with eResolution.[53]

These data indicate that the choice of forum affects the probability of an outcome beneficial to a complainant. The right of a complainant to choose an arbitration provider remains, and the statistical data show that the choice of the complainant is not driven by alternative considerations such as price differences or geographical location of the dispute resolution provider.[54] Rather, it seems plausible that the choice of forum is driven by the likelihood of achieving a favourable decision, which in turn would provide an incentive for dispute service providers to favour complainants.

Given these empirical data, both the tendency among complainants to 'shop' for the forum must favourable to them and panellists' bias in favour of trademark owners have been cause for complaints. In addition, the quality of panel decisions,[55]

---

49 Ibid.

50 Geist, 'Fair.com?: An Examination of the Allegations of Systemic Unfairness in the ICANN UDRP'; Geist, 'Fundamentally Fair.com? An Update on Bias Allegations and the ICANN UDRP'.

51 Milton Müller, 'Rough Justice. An analysis of ICANN's Uniform Dispute Resolution Policy?', <http://dcc.syr.edu/miscarticles/roughjustice.pdf>, accessed 1 January 2007.

52 Geist, 'Fair.com?: An Examination of the Allegations of Systemic Unfairness in the ICANN UDRP', p. 6; Geist, 'Fundamentally Fair.com? An Update on Bias Allegations and the ICANN UDRP', pp. 5f.

53 Ibid.

54 Geist, 'Fair.com?: An Examination of the Allegations of Systemic Unfairness in the ICANN UDRP'; Müller, 'Rough Justice. An analysis of ICANN's Uniform Dispute Resolution Policy?'.

55 Geist, 'Fair.com?: An Examination of the Allegations of Systemic Unfairness in the ICANN UDRP'.

the time restrictions of the procedure,[56] the ambiguous provisions on the burden of proof,[57]and finally, the extension of UDRP's jurisdiction, especially by WIPO panellists,[58] have been criticized.[59]

The last aspect is particularly intriguing for the present context. In contrast to traditional commercial arbitration, UDRP provisions require written and published awards. From the outset, the intention has been to make UDRP decision-making part of a process of norm creation. The goal of a 'trademark-domain name jurisprudence'[60] that is based on written and published decisions also refers to adjudication more generally. *Precedents* have achieved very high prominence for the overall system of trademark-related domain name dispute settlement. More recent data shows that the majority of arbitrators cite other cases and refer to precedents as justifications for their arguments. 'This is significant because the *precedents being established via the UDRP may evolve into a global trademark law for cyberspace. [...]* Two of the most widely cited cases, WIPO D2000-0210, and WIPO D2000-0235, involve disputes over untrademarked personal names, showing how precedent is creating new rights'.[61] To paraphrase this observation in the language of the present contribution, panel decisions have not only adjudicative, but also prescriptive authority.

The Alternative Solution: The National Landing

The criticism of the transnational UDRP led to reactions on several levels. For instance, ICANN as the organisation responsible for the regulation of the domain

---

56 Müller, 'Dancing the Quango: ICANN and the Privatization of International Governance', p.12; Müller, 'Success by default: A New Profile of Domain Name Trademarks Dispute under ICANN's UDRP'.

57 Annette Kur, 'UDRP'.

58 Froomkin, 'ICANN's 'Uniform Dispute Resolution Policy" – Causes and Partial Cures'; Ian Stewart, 'The Best Laid Plans: How Unrestrained Arbitration Decisions Have Corrupted the Uniform Domain Name Dispute Resolution Policy', *Federal Communication Law Journal*, 53 (2001): 509–32; Beth G. Thornburg, 'Fast, Cheap & Out of Control: Lessons from the ICANN Dispute Resolution Process', *Journal of Small & Emerging Business Law*, 7 (2001).

59 Not surprisingly, however, some of the allegations have been countered by the International Trademark Association (<http://www.inta.org/downloads/tap_udrp_2paper2002. pdf>, accessed 1 January 2007); see also Geist's response to his critics (<http://aix1.uottawa. ca/ per cent7Egeist/geistintaresp.pdf>, accessed 1 January 2007). In addition, an empirical study by a German Max–Planck Institute came to the conclusion that despite some irritations, 'the UDRP is functioning well as a matter of principle' (Kur, 'UDRP', p. 57).

60 Laurence R. Helfer, and Graeme B. Dinwoodie, ,Designing Non–National Systems: The Case of the Uniform Domain Name Dispute Resolution Policy', p. 82.

61 Cf. Müller, 'Dancing the Quango: ICANN and the Privatization of International Governance', p. 19, or Müller, 'Success by Default: A New Profile of Domain Name Trademark Dispute under ICANN's UDRP', p. 19; Hooghe, and Marks, 'Unravelling the Central State, but How? Types of Multi-level Governance'; Martin Shapiro and Alec Stone Sweet, *On Law, Politics, and Judicialization* (Oxford, 2002), chapter 2.

name system commissioned a review by its staff,[62] and the EU Commission ordered a report of the UDRP practice. While these studies were in the nature of evaluations, two other reactions are much more consequential, as they represent alternative claims to the prescriptive and adjudicative jurisdiction of the transitional UDRP. One refers to national provisions touching on or explicitly regulating cybersquatting, and the other is the judicial review of UDRP awards before national courts. Both avenues of jurisdictional contest will be addressed in the following.

National Provision Claiming Jurisdiction

The discontent with national approaches to tackle domain name vs. trademark disputes not only led to the development of the UDRP in the first place, but also contributed to its general acceptance. Nevertheless, neither national legislators nor courts stood aside to watch the transnational dispute resolution passively. Rather, national provisions on trade names, competition, and anti-trust or dilution have been applied throughout.

Most of the decisions involve country-code Top-Level Domains, an area of significant importance for domestic business. Over time, court decisions have developed into a relatively predictable jurisprudence for the domestic part of the new legal frontier of the domain names system.[63] At the same time, there are relatively few cases in which courts in Austria, Germany, and France have been active in cases involving generic top-level domains.[64] If they have done so and if they have applied domestic laws, cases did not involve parties from foreign countries. Interestingly, decisions developed in the realm of country-code TLDs and cases involving generic TLDs influence each other, as courts try to contribute to the development of a consistent trademark-vs.-domain name jurisprudence when applying national provisions.

The US is the only country that, in addition to combating cyberpiracy with existing legislation, has enacted new legislation explicitly targeting trademark infringements in the domain-name area. The Anti-Cybersquatting Consumer Protection Act (ACPA) of 1999,[65] a set of amendments to the Trademark Act of 1946 (Lanham Act), has been introduced to 'protect consumers and promote electronic commerce by amending certain trademark infringement, dilution, and counterfeiting laws.' So doing, it creates a new cause of action for trademark owners against cybersquatters

---

62 Staff Manager's Issues Report on UDRP Review (1 August 2003), <http://www.icann. org/gnso/issue-reports/udrp-review-report-01aug03.htm>, accessed 1 January 2007.

63 Roland Karl, 'Die Verletzung von Serien- und Wort-Bild-Marken durch Domain-Namen', *Österreichische Juristen–Zeitung ÖJZ*, 58/4 (2003): 128–38.

64 For exceptions, such as 'autovermietung.com', 'herstellerkatalog.com', or 'Veltins. com', see www.domain–recht.de/magazin/article.php?id=24 [7/31/2003]. For a similar case in Austria, see Der Standard, 19 December 2000, 'Zweifelhafter'Gewinn' im Internet'; Lebensmittel Zeitung, 17 August 2001; OLG Hamm, 4 U 32/01.

65 Pub. L. No. 106–113, title III, 113 Stat. 1501A–545 (1999) (codified at 15 U.S.C. §§ 1114, 1116, 1117, 1125, 1127, 1129 (1994 & Supp. 1999)).

and provides protection against the unauthorized registration of personal names as domain names.[66]

Thus, the ACPA confronts the transnational jurisdiction of the UDRP explicitly with its national jurisdiction.[67] One instrument in particular is useful in overcoming the limitations of its national capacity to prosecute violations involving individuals who are outside the US or are registered under aliases. The so-called *in rem* jurisdiction allows a trademark owner to sue the infringing domain name itself. *In rem* is a legal term used to designate proceedings or actions instituted against the thing, as opposed to the more common actions that are directed against the person (*in personam*).[68] For the purposes of an *in rem* action, a domain name can be sued according to the judicial district of its registry or registrar.[69]

While it stands alone, the ACPA's claim to jurisdiction cannot be regarded as being superior in relation to the jurisdiction of the UDRP,[70] the actual practice of courts when reviewing UDRP decision express the extraterritorial philosophy of the US approach. In more general terms, this may indicate that with respect to court review as the second way to contest the jurisdiction of the transnational solution, we find similar differences between the US and other national claims to compete with the adjudicative authority of the transnational jurisdiction of the UDRP.

External Judicial Review

According to the UDRP provisions, if the decision is in favour of the complainant, ICANN rules require a cancellation of the domain name or a transfer to the complainant. During and after the decision, the respondent's only option to avoid the implementation of the decision is to file a lawsuit in a court of mutual jurisdiction. Mutual jurisdiction here refers either to the location of the domain name registrar's principal office or to the domain name holder's residence. The appeal to a court of mutual jurisdiction is not restricted to procedural aspects, but starts the entire process anew.

Given the dispersion of information on the role of national courts in reviewing UDRP decisions, a systematic gathering of data is almost impossible. Nevertheless, compiling information from different sources allows for some interesting

---

66 Serena C. Hunn, 'AntiCybersquatting Consumer Protection Act: A Powerful Remedy In Domain Name Disputes? Or a Threat to Electronic Commerce?' Available from <http://www.fmew.com/archive/cybersquat/>, accessed 1 January 2007.

67 For other differences between the ACPA and the UDRP, see Barbara Solomon, 'Two New Tools to Combat Cyberpiracy – A Comparison', *Trademark Reporter*, 679/90 (2000): 697ff. David E. Sorkin, 'Judicial Review of ICANN Domain Name Dispute Decisions', *Santa Clara Computer & High Tech. Law Journal*, 18 (2001): 50ff.

68 Thomas R. Lee, 'In Rem Jurisdiction in Cyberspace', *Washington Law Review*, 75 (2000): 97–145.

69 Domain-name registries maintain top-level domains that are used for assigning addresses in the Internet. Registrars are the companies that actually register domain names in the registries, usually charging registrants for the service.

70 Laurence R. Helfer, 'Whither the UDRP: Autonomous, Americanized, or Cosmopolitan?', *Loyola Law School Public Law and Legal Theory Research Paper* (2003–1), p. 4.

observations.[71] The most noticeable impression confirms the reluctance of most courts in the world to accept cases on TLDs involving foreign firms and, at the same time, an absolute dominance of US cases: from 73 cases collected in a specialised database on this topic, only 9 had been outside the US.[72]

Whereas most national courts obviously accept UDRP decisions as a relevant and legitimate mode of conflict resolution,[73] US courts take a quite different stance. For instance, in the case *Sallen v. Corinthians Licenciamentos LTDA*, the First Circuit of Appeals had to decide whether appeals against UDRP awards were legitimate according to the ACPA. Reviewing the legislative history regarding the drafting of the ACPA, the court came to the conclusion that the ACPA had been created to provide a cause of action for a domain name registrant in cases in which US citizens or companies feel violated by UDRP awards. Thus, by issuing the ACPA, the US Congress has not only asserted jurisdiction in an encompassing sense, that is that domain-name-vs.-trademark conflicts have to be adjudicated according to US rules and enforced according to the logic of court decision. Also, the US Congress created the ACPR specifically to override UDRP provisions when necessary according to US laws.[74]

In conjunction with the ACPA, the UDRP provisions themselves entail an important factor for the US predominance. Appeals against UDRP decisions before national courts are not only regarded as an important pillar contributing to the acceptance and legitimacy of the transnational solution.[75] The clause that allows for appeal in a court of mutual jurisdiction, that is a court at the domain name registrar's principle office or the domain name holder's residence, has given the federal district

---

71 See, e.g., <http://www.adlawbyrequest.com/legislation/antisquatting.shtml>, accessed 31 July 2003; <http://cyber.law.harvard.edu/property00/domain/CaseLaw.html>, accessed cited 31 July 2003; <http://www.cov.com/new/pressreleases/147.html>, accessed 31 July 2003; <http://www.ladas.com/BULLETINS/2002/0502Bulletin/0502Bulletin28.html>, accessed 31 July 2003; <http://www.udrplaw.net/UDRPappeals.htm>, last updated 27 March 2003, accessed 31 December 2003; <http://www.phillipsnizer.com/library/alldecisions.cfm?jsenabled=True&javaenabled=True>, accessed 31 July 2003.

72 Non–US cases involved India (1), Israel (1), Malaysia (1), Norway (1), South Korea (3), and the United Kingdom (2), see <http://www.udrplaw.net/UDRPappeals.htm>, accessed 31 December 2003.

73 André Bertrand, *Le droit des marques, des signes distinctifs et des noms de domaine* (Paris, 2002), p. 571 ; Pascaline Colombiani, 'Droit des marques et des noms de domaine. Du conflit à la co-existence', *Avocats-Publishing.com*, available from <http://www.avocats-publishing.com/article.php3?id_article=10>, accessed 31 October 2003; Hughes, 'The Internet and the Persistence of Law', p. 397.

74 Corinthians Licenciamentos LTDA v. Sallen, WIPO Case No. D2000–0461 (17 July 2000), see <http://www.arbiter.wipo.int/domains/decisions/html/2000/d2000-0461.html>, accessed 1 January 2007 Sallen v. Corinthians Licenciamentos LTDA, 2000 U.S. Dist. LEXIS 19976 (D. Mass.); See Margaret Mendenhall, 'Post Arbitration Domain Name Litigation: Settling Claims on the Cyberspace Frontier 2002', *Quelle*, 20, available from <http://www.udrplaw.net/UDRPappeals.htm>, accessed 31 July 2003.

75 <http://www.interesting-people.org/archives/interesting-people/200112/msg00112.html>, accessed 1 January 2007.

of Virginia a prominent position because the registry for the most important dotcom domain, VeriSign, is located in California.[76]

In one of the most notorious cases, the District Court for the Eastern District of Virginia held that trademark protection under the ACPA extended to foreign trademarks. In *Barcelona.com, Inc. v. Excelentisimo Ayuntamiento de Barcelona*[77] of the two parties, neither the two Spanish registrants nor the City Council of Barcelona had trademarked 'Barcelona' under US law. Applying the ACPA to affirm a UDPR panel's transfer to the City Council of Barcelona, the federal district court interpreted Spanish trademark law and found the City Council possessed a valid Spanish trademark in 'Barcelona'. According to the federal court's view, the text of the ACPA could be applied to domestic and foreign trademarks because, even though trademark protection has been historically national, the APCA had been enacted specifically to address domain name registration on the Internet, which is international in scope. Therefore, the intent of Congress must have been to protect both domestic and foreign marks, as no distinction was made between the two in the text of the statute.[78] In June 2003, however, the US Fourth Circuit of Appeals reversed this decision, stating that the district court had improperly applied Spanish trademark law to decide which of the parties was entitled to own the disputed domain name. Most importantly, the Court of Appeals quashed the verdict of the federal court by stating that the original registration of the domain name 'Barcelona' by the Spanish registrants was not unlawful under the ACPA because the City of Barcelona had no trademark rights to the word 'Barcelona' under US law. The far-reaching implication of this decision is that

...unless foreign mark owners can also demonstrate trademark rights under U.S. law, nothing will prevent registrants from proving that their use of the domain name embodying a foreign mark was lawful under the Lanham Act. This is so even if their conduct was egregious and would qualify as cybersquatting under the UDRP or the ACPA (had it been challenged by a mark owner with U.S. rights).[79]

Both the assertion of jurisdiction and the conclusion that (district and federal) court interpretations of the ACPA override UDRP awards were confirmed in a number of decisions. With their willingness to assert prescriptive and adjudicative jurisdiction in domain name-related trademark infringements, US judges trump the transnational UDRP approach of providing a balance of competing interests for parties from different national backgrounds.[80] Actually, US courts not only confirmed that national review of UDRP decisions is legitimate, but also that national rules supersede transnational regulation.

---

76 By end of December 2006, over 59 million active dotcom domains have been registered; <http://www.whois.sc/internet-statistics>, accessed 1 January 2007.

77 189 F. Supp. 2d 367 (E.D. Va. 2002).

78 Mendenhall, 'Post Arbitration Domain Name Litigation: Settling Claims on the Cyberspace Frontier 2002', p. 28.

79 Helfer, 'Whither the UDRP: Autonomous, Americanized, or Cosmopolitan?', p. 5.

80 Ibid., p. 6.

Notwithstanding this parochial predominance of US prescriptive and adjudicative jurisdiction, there are some aspects that qualify the national landing of transnational dispute resolution. First, measures against the total of almost 13.500 domain-name conflicts adjudicated by the UDRP until November 2003, the relative share of the APCA, which handled about 145 cases or little more than 1 per cent, is relatively small.[81] Second, in the majority of the cases, proceedings in national courts ended without changes to the outcome handed down by the UDRP.[82] Third, there are even cases in which national courts outside the US applied transnational provisions without expressly considering whether conventional national trademark law should be applied instead.[83] Fourth, these decisions and other indicators indicate a trend towards a dialogue between national and transnational procedures to settle conflicts at the interface between trademark provisions and the domain-name system. For instance, the Northern District of Illinois declined in *Weber-Stephen Products Co. v. Armitage Hardware and Building Supply, Inc.* to stay an UDRP panel's decision, reasoning that since the UDRP allowed for parallel proceedings in national courts, both parties had adequate recourse should they be dissatisfied with the panel's conclusion.[84] Also, in *Retail Services, Inc. v. Freebies Pub* the district court engaged in a discussion of the 'bad faith' requirement common to the ACPA and the UDRP.[85] The 'court's extensive assessment of the panel's conclusions and its focus on a key point of commonality in both the ACPA and the UDRP suggests a deliberate effort to cross-fertilize between national and non-national systems'.[86]

Conclusion

Examining the relationship between denationalizing and renationalizing regulatory activities, this paper introduced the concept of jurisdiction to cope analytically with the way in which governance occurs at the interface between national approaches to protect trademarks and the need to establish a globally unique system of Internet domain names. Jurisdiction as the conceptual point of departure specifies the notion of authority in global governance by introducing the categories of prescription, adjudication, and enforcement to assess the ambiguities of governance patterns in this specific problem area.

In empirical terms, we have described how dissatisfaction with national approaches to solve trademark vs. domain-name conflicts led to the establishment of a transnational solution in the first place. In an act of unilateral globalisation,

---

81 A Westlaw search in October 2003 yielded 145 ACPA decisions.

82 <http://www.udrplaw.net/UDRPappeals.htm>, accessed 31 October 2003.

83 Douglas Black v. Molson Canada, Court File No. 02–CV–231–828CM3, 18 July 2002 (Ont. S.C.J.)

84 Mendenhall, 'Post Arbitration Domain Name Litigation: Settling Claims on the Cyberspace Frontier 2002', p. 24.

85 Retail Services, Inc., et al. v. Freebies Publishing, et al., 2003 U.S. Dist. LEXIS 2934, 02–CV–1111 (E.D. Va. Feb. 27, 2003). National Law Journal Vol. 25; No. 26; Pg. B4, 17 March 2003.

86 Helfer, 'Whither the UDRP: Autonomous, Americanized, or Cosmopolitan?'.

ICANN was given the jurisdiction to prescribe a specific intention in registering a domain name as tort and has established its Uniform Dispute Resolution Policy as a transnational jurisdiction to govern trademark violations in the domain-name area. In turn, ICANN has delegated the jurisdiction to adjudicate cases of potential violations to a limited number of arbitration service providers, one of which is an international organisation, while the other three are private organisations. Finally, the jurisdiction to enforce court decisions occurs within the Internet's technical architecture, which allows for a relatively easy change of the status of property rights by either cancelling the domain name or by transferring it to the complainant.

Yet, the take-off of the transnational jurisdiction has its limits as national institutions claim the right not only to review the outcome of transnational awards, but also to override these when necessary. In the absence of internal appeal mechanisms, the external control mechanisms contribute significantly to the acceptance of both the UDRP provisions and its outcomes. At the same time, this external review is conducted unevenly. While most European courts restrict judicial review to cases involving national citizens and firms, the national touchdown is most explicit in the US, where the national legislator has created a specific set of rules that not only competes with the transitional procedure, but also claims to override it. Both district and federal courts in the US are very willing to maintain this claim to hand down prescriptive jurisdiction when it comes to adjudication.

For the analysis of how economic globalisation affects patterns of governance, three aspects need to be highlighted. A first important aspect relates to the analytical potential of state-centric approaches, be they neorealist or liberal institutionalist in origin, on the one hand and the global governance perspective on the other. What follows from the empirical account is the overall impression of US dominance in the setting and framing of solutions in the domain name area. This holds true not only for the early phases of the process of rule-making and the delegation of jurisdiction to ICANN, but also for the judicial review of the UDRP process and its outcomes. Hence, contrary to the observation that ICANN in general and the UDRP in particular are frequently regarded as *the* prime example of an 'island of transnational governance',[87] the empirical story tells us that transnational governance coincides with an all-too visible national caveat. Put differently, the transnational take-off of governance patterns may always experience a national landing.

Second, however, the variance of national claims and the simultaneity of complementary and competing claims for jurisdiction between transnational solutions and national institutions have two important implications. On the one hand, it implies a bridging of the gap between sub-disciplines of political science, as international relations and comparative politics become integral parts of the same inquiry. The analysis of constellations under which transnational arrangements emerge and operate dovetails with the current discussion in international relations on the vertical and horizontal migration of authority from the state either to supranational and subnational units, or to private actors. At the same time, variations in the way in which national institutions review outcomes of transnational governance arrangements account for the way in which national institutions matter and differ, and as such are

---

87 Shapiro, and Stone Sweet, *On Law, Politics, and Judicialization*, chapter 5.

at the heart of comparative politics. For the present context, one might ask for the factors that help to explain the US dominance and the relative hesitance of other national governments and courts to claim jurisdiction in trademark vs. domain name conflicts: Is it just the location of the registry; does the size of the market matter; does the difference between common law and civil law systems play a role; or is there a cultural dimension involved in a country's disposition to apply national provisions extraterritorially? Put more generally, a systematic comparative account for the role and stance of domestic institutions may generate important information for the analysis of global governance arrangements, centralizing and decentralizing powers and the importance of domestic institutions for both the national and – in case of an extraterritorial implication – the international level.

On the other hand, rather than operating with mutually exclusive claims deduced from either state-centred or society-centred theoretical accounts, it seem more fruitful to conceive of the relationship between transnational solutions and national claims to exert control as interacting and mutually reinforcing factors.[88] The important task, then, is to elaborate on the factors that characterise this dialectical relationship and to assess its outcome. While what was called a 'robust dialogue'[89] between panellists and judges in their efforts to resolve a dispute at hand is an expression for the mutual influence of the two different prescriptive and adjudicative assertions for jurisdiction, the assessment of the outcomes provides us with a final important conclusion.

Third, there is some reason to claim that the mutual influence of transnational and national efforts to define the framework of the jurisdiction for trademark-vs.-domain-name solutions has significant normative implications. These can be described in a twofold convergence. Although the domain-name system is not a corollary to the trademark system, at the transnational and at the national levels, this equitation has increasingly been accepted by trademark holders, panellists, national legislators, and courts. This holds true not only for the formulation of both the transnational rules by WIPO and the US Anti-Cybersquatting Consumer Protection Act, but also for the adjudication by UDRP panellists and national judges not only in the US, but throughout the world.

What is more, there is some evidence that the national landing tends to reinforce the bias toward well-known trademarks, while it discriminates against 'average Joe' trademark owners. In this respect, it is of interest to see how the structural features of transnational solution and national landing tend to contribute to an overall pattern. In the framework of the UDRP, the mechanism of forum-shopping for favourable service providers has been identified as an important feature contributing to a significant bias favouring the owners of well-known trademarks. This preferential treatment of well-known trademarks is reinforced by the framework of the ACPA, which covers only 'famous' and 'distinctive' trademarks. As a consequence, it seems that national efforts to solve conflicts at the interface between trademarks and domain names suffer from the same flaws that the UDRP is accused of, namely, a significant

---

88 Robert Wai, 'Transnational Liftoff and Juridical Touchdown: The Regulatory Function of Private International Law in an Era of Globalization', *Columbia Journal of Transnational Law*, 40 (2002): 209–74.

89 Helfer, 'Whither the UDRP: Autonomous, Americanized, or Cosmopolitan?', p. 10.

bias in favour of holders of well-known trademarks. Put more bluntly, justice at the interface between trademark regulation and the administration of domain names tends to favour famous and well-known trademarks, regardless of whether decisions are handed down by transnational or national authorities.

Bibliography

Arts, Bas, 'Non-State Actors in Global Governance: Three Faces of Power', *Preprints of the Max-Planck-Projekt Group on Common Goods, Bonn*, 2003/4, <http://www.mpp-rdg.mpg.de/pdf_dat/2003_4.pdf>, accessed 1 January 1007.

Berman, Harold J., *Law and Revolution. The Formation of the Western Legal Tradition* (Cambridge: Harvard University Press, 1983).

Bertrand, André, *Le droit des marques, des signes distinctifs et des noms de domaine* (Paris: CEDAT Collection Théorie et Pratique, 2002).

Cohn, Theodor, Stephen McBride, and John Wiseman (ed.), *Power in the Global Era. Grounding Globalization* (Houndmills/Basingstoke: Macmillan, 2000).

Colombani, Pascaline, 'Droit des marques et noms de domaine. Du conflit à la co-existence', *Avocats-Publishing.com*, <://www.avocats-publishing.com/article. php3?id_article=10>, accessed 31 October 2003.

Condliffe, John B., *The Commerce of Nations* (London: Allen&Unwin, 1951).

Cutler, A. Claire, *Private Power and Global Authority: Transnational Merchant Law and the Global Political Economy* (Cambridge: Cambridge University Press, 2003).

Cutler, A. Claire, Virginia Haufler, and Tony Porter, 'The Contours and Significance of Private Authority in International Affairs', in A.C. Cutler, V. Haufler and T. Porter (eds.), *Private Authority and International Affairs* (Albany: State University of New York Press, 1999), pp. 333–76.

Cutler, A. Claire, Virginia Haufler, and Tony Porter, 'Private Authority and International Affairs', in A.C. Cutler, V. Haufler and T. Porter (eds.), *Private Authority and International Affairs* (Albany: State University of New York Press, 1999).

Cutler, A. Claire, Virginia Haufler, and Tony Porter, *Private Authority and International Affairs* (Albany: State University of New York Press, 1999).

Farrell, Henry, 'Hybrid Institutions and the Law', *Zeitschrift für Rechtssoziologie*, 23/1 (2002): 18–34.

Farrell, Henry, 'Constructing the International Foundations of E-Commerce – The EU-US Safe Harbor Arrangement and Transnational Relations', *International Organization*, 57/2 (2003): 277–306.

Florini, Ann M. (ed.), *The Third Force. The Rise of Civil Society* (Tokyo/Washington, D.C.: Japan Center for International Exchange/Carnegie Endowment for International Peace, 2000).

Franda, Marcus, *Governing the Internet. The Emergence of an International Regime* (Boulder and London: Lynne Rienner, 2001).

Froomkin, A. Michael, 'A Commentary on WIPO's The Management of Internet Names and Addresses: Intellectual Property Issues', *University of Miami School of Law*, <www.law.miami.edu>.

Froomkin, A. Michael, 'ICANN's 'Uniform Dispute Resolution Policy' – Causes and (partial) Cures', *Brooklyn Law Review*, 67/3 (2002): 605–718.

Frydman, Benoit, and Isabelle Rorive, 'Regulating Internet Content through Intermediaries', *Zeitschrift für Rechtszoziologie*, 23/1 (2002): 41–59.

Galtung, Frederik, 'A Global Network to Curb Corruption: The Experience of Transparency International', in A. M. Florini (ed.) *The Third Force. The Rise of Civil Society* (Tokyo/Washington, D.C.: Japan Center for International Exchange/ Carnegie Endowment for International Peace, 2000), pp. 17–48.

Geist, Michael, 'Fair.com?: An Examination of the Allegations of Systemic Unfairness in the ICANN UDRP', <http://www.udrpinfo.com/resc/fair.pdf>, accessed 1 January 2007.

Geist, Michael, 'Fundamenatlly Fair.com? An Update on Bias Allegations and the ICANN UDRP', <www.lawbytes.ca>, accessed 24 August 2002.

Geist, Michael, 'The Shift Toward 'Targeting' for Internet Jurisdiction', in A. Thierer and C.W.J. Crews (eds.), *Who Rules the Internet? Internet Govenance and Jurisdiction* (Washington D.C.: CATO Institute, 2003), pp. 91–118.

Goldsmith, Jack L., 'Against Cyberanarchy', in A. Thierer and C.W.J. Crews (eds.), *Who Rules the Net? Internet Governance and Jurisdiction* (Washington D.C.: CATO Institute, 2003), pp. 31–70.

Goldsmith, Jack L., 'Against Cyberanarchy', *The University of Chicago Law Review*, 65/4 (1998): 1199–1250.

Goverde, Henri, Philip G. Cerny, Mark Haugaard, and Howard H. Lentner (eds.), *Power in Contemporary Politics* (London: Sage, 2000).

Grieco, Joseph M., and G. John Ikenberry, *State Power and World Markets. The International Political Economy* (New York and London: W.W. Norton & Company, 2003).

Hall, Rodney Bruce, and Thomas J. Bierstecker (eds.), *The Emergence of Private Authority in Global Governance* (Cambridge: Cambridge University Press, 2002).

Held, David, Anthony McGrew, David Goldblatt, and Jonathan Perraton, *Global Transformations. Politics, Economics, and Culture* (Stanford: Stanford University Press, 1999).

Helfer, Laurence R., and Graeme B. Dinwoodie, 'Designing Non-National Systems: The Case of the Uniform Donaim Name Dispute Resolution Policy', *William and Mary Law Review*, 48 (2001): 141–273.

Helfer, Laurence R., 'Whither the UDRP: Autonomous, Americanized, or Cosmopolitan?', *Loyola Law School Public Law and Legal Theory Research Paper*, (2003-1), <http://ssrn.com/abstract=437182>, accessed 31 October 2003.

Hoffmann, Stanley, 'Notes on the Elusiveness of Modern Power', *International Journal*, 30 (1975): 183–206.

Holitscher, Marc, *Internet Governance: Die Reform des Domain Namen Systems und die Entstehung der Internet Corporation for Assigned Names and Numbers.*

Eine Fallstudie zur Rolle privater Akteure jenseits des Nationalstaates (Zürich: U. Zürich, Institut für Politikwissenschaft, 2002).

Hooghe, Lisbeth, and Garry Marks, 'Unravelling the Central State, but How? Types of Multi-level Governance', *American Political Science Review*, 97/2 (2003): 233–43.

Hughes, John, 'The Internet and the Persistence of Law', *Boston College Law Review*, 43/2 (2003): 359–96.

Hunn, Serena C. 'AntiCybersquatting Consumer Protection Act: A Powerful Remedy In Domain Name Disputes? Or a Threat to Electronic Commerce?', <http://www.fmew.com/archive/cybersquat/>, accessed 1 January 2007.

Johnson, David R., and David Post, 'Law and Borders – The Rise of Law in Cyberspace', *Stanford Law Review*, 48 (1996): 1367–1402.

Kahler, Miles, and David A. Lake, 'Globalization and Governance', in M. Kahler and D. A. Lake (eds.), *Governance in A Global Economy. Political Authority in Transition* (Princeton and Oxford: Princeton University Press, 2003), pp. 412–38.

Karl, Rolan, 'Die Verletzung von Serien- und Wort-Bild-Marken durch Domain-Namen', *Östereichische Juristen-Zeitung ÖJZ*, 58/4 (2003): 128–38.

Keohane, Robert O., and Joseph S. Nye, ‚Introduction' in J. S. Nye and J. D. Donahue (eds.), *Governance in a Globalizing World* (Washington, D.C.: Brookings Institution Press, 2000).

Keohane, Robert O., and Joseph S. Nye, 'Redefining Accountability for Global Governance', in M. Kahler and D. A. Lake (eds.), *Governance in A Global Economy. Political Authority in Transition* (Princeton and Oxford: Princeton University Press, 2003), pp. 412–38.

Knill, Christoph, and Dirk Lehmkuhl, 'Private Actors and the State: Internationalization and Changing Patterns of Governance', *Governance: An International Journal of Policy, Adminstration and Institutions*, 15/1 (2002): 41–63.

Kobayashi, Bruce H., and Larry E. Ribstein, 'Multi-Jurisdictional Regulation of the Internet', in A. Thierer and C.W.J. Crews (eds.), *Who Rules the Net? Internet Governance and Jurisdiction* (Washington D.C.: CATO Institute, 2003): 159–215.

Kur, Annette, *UDRP* (9 January 2002). Max-Planck-Institute for Foreign and International Patent, Copyright and Competition Law, Munich in cooperation with the Institute for Market Law and Intellectual Property at the University of Stockholm and the Institute for Information Law at the Technical University of Karlsruhe, <http://www.intellecprop.mpg.de/Online-Publikationen/UDRP-e.htm>, accessed 12 January 2002.

Lee, Thomas R., 'In Rem Jurisdiction in Cyberspace', *Washington Law Review*, 75 (2000): 97–145.

Lukes, S., 'Perspectives on Authority', in J. Raz (ed.) *Authority* (Oxford: Basil Blackwell, 1990), pp. 203–17.

Mann, Michael, 'A History of Power from the Beginning to AD 1760', in Michael Mann (ed.), *The Sources of Social Power* (2 vols. Cambridge: Cambridge University Press, 1986), vol. 1.

Mathews, Jessica T., 'Power Shift', *Foreign Affairs*, 76/1 (1997): 50–66.

Mattli, Walter, 'Private Justice in a global economy. From litigation to arbitration', *International Organization*, 55/4 (2001): 919–48.

Mendenhall, Margaret, 'Post Arbitration Domain Name Litigation: Settling Claims on the Cyberspace Frontier 2002', <http://www.udrplaw.net/UDRPappeals.htm>, accessed 31 July 2003.

Mueller, Milton, 'Rough Justice. An Analysis of ICANN's Uniform Dispute Resolution Policy', <http://dcc.syr.edu/miscarticles/roughjustice.pdf>, accessed 1 January 2007.

Mueller, Milton, 'Dancing the Quango: ICANN and the Privatization of International Governance', <http://istweb.syr.edu/~mueller/onlinepubs.htm>, accessed 1 January 2007.

Mueller, Milton, 'Success by Default: A New Profile of Domain Name Trademark Disputes unde ICANN`s UDRP', <http://istweb.syr.edu/~mueller/onlinepubs. htm>, accessed 1 January 2007.

Nye, Joseph S., *The Paradox of American Power. Why the World's Only Superpower Can't Get It Alone* (Oxford: Oxford University Press, 2002).

Pieth, Mrak, and Gemma Aiolfi, 'The Private Sector becomes active: The Wolfsberg Process in A Practitioner's Guide to International Money Laundering Law and Regulation', *Journal of Financial Crime*, 10/4 (2003): 359–69.

Post, David G. 2003, 'Against 'Against Cyberanarchy'', in A. Thierer and C.W.J. Crews (eds), *Who Rules the Net? Internet Governance and Jurisdiction* (Washington D.C.: CATO Institute, 2003), pp. 71–90.

Raz, Joseph, 'Introduction: Conceptualizing Multiple', in J. Raz (ed.), *Authority* (Oxford: Basil Blackwell, 1990), pp. 1–19.

Reich, Robert B., *The Work of Nations: Preparing ourselves for the 21-Century Capitalism* (New York: Simon and Schuster, 1991).

Risse, Thomas, Stephen C. Ropp, and Kathryn Sikkink (eds.), *The Power of Human Rights. International Norms and Domestic Change* (Cambridge: Cambridge University Press, 1999).

Rosenau, James N., 'Distant Proximities: The Dynamics and Dialectics of Globalization', in B. Hettne (ed.), *International Political Economy: Understanding Global Disorder* (London: Zed Books, 1995), pp. 46–65.

Rosenau, James N., Along the Domestic-Foreign Frontier: Exploring Governance in a Turbulent World (Cambridge: Cambridge University Press, 1997).

Rosenau, James N., *Distant Proximities: Dynamics beyond Globalization* (Princeton: Princeton University Press, 2003).

Santos, Boaventura de Sousa, Toward an New Common Sense. Law, Science and Politics in Paradigmatic Transition (New York/London: Routledge, 1995).

Sassen, Saskia, 'The State and Globalization', in R.B. Hall and T.J. Bierstecker (eds), *The Emergence of Private Authority in Global Governance* (Cambridge: Cambridge University Press, 2002), pp. 91–112.

Schiff Berman, Paul, 'The Globalization of Jurisdiction', *University of Pennsylvania Law Review*, 151/2 (2002): 311–529.

Shany, Yuval, *The Competing Jurisdictions of International Courts and Tribunals* (Oxford: Oxford University Press, 2003).

Shapiro, Martin, and Alec Stone Sweet, *On Law, Politics, and Judicialization* (Oxford: Oxford University Press, 2002).

Sinclair, Timothy J., 'Passing Judgement: Credit Rating Processes as Regulatory Mechanims of Governance in the Emerging World Order', *Review of International Political Economy*, 1/1 (1994): 133–59.

Sinclair, Timothy J., 'Bond-Rating Agencies and Coordination in the Global Political Economy', in A.C. Cutler, V. Haufler and T. Porter (eds.), *Private Authority in International Affairs* (Albany: State University of New York, 1999), pp. 153–68.

Solomon, Barbara, 'Two New Tools to Combat Cyberpiracy – A Comparison', *Trademark Reporter*, 679/90 (2000): 679–722.

Sorkin, David E., 'Judicial Review of ICANN Domain Name Dispute Decisions', *Santa Clara Computer & High Tech. Law Journal*, 18 (2001): 50ff.

Stewart, Ian L. 'The Best Laid Plans: How Unrestrained Arbitration Decisions Have Corrupted the Uniform Domain Name Dispute Resolution Policy', *Federal Communication Law Journal*, 53 (2001): 509–32.

Strange, Susan, *States and Markets: An Introduction to International Political Economy* (London: Pinter, 1988).

Strange, Susan, *The Retreat of the State. The Diffusion of Power in the World Economy* (Cambridge: Cambridge University Press, 1996).

Thornburg, Elisabeth G., 'Fast, Cheap & Out of Control: Lessons from the ICANN Dispute Resolution Process', *Journal of Small & Emerging Business Law*, 7 (2001).

Thornburg, Elisabeth G., 'Going Private: Technology, Due Process, and Internet Dispute Resolution', *U.C. Davis Law Review*, 34/1 (2000): 151–220.

Trachtman, Joel P., 'Externalities and extraterritoriality: The law and economics of prescriptive jurisdiction', in J.S. Bhandari and A.O. Sykes (eds.), *Economic dimensions in international law. Comparative and empirical perspectives* (Cambridge: Cambridge University Press, 1997), pp. 642–83.

Robert Wai, 'Transnational Liftoff and Juridical Touchdown: The Regulatory Function of Private International Law in an Era of Globalization', *Columbia Journal of Transnational Law*, 40 (2002): 209–74.

Weinberg, Jonathan, 'ICANN and the problem of legitimacy', *Duke Law Journal*, 50 (2000): 187–206.

Weiss, Linda, *The Myth of the Powerless State. Governing the Economy in a Global Era* (Cambridge: Polity Press, 1998).

Weiss, Linda, *States in the Global Economy. Bringing Domestic Institutions Back In* (Cambridge: Cambridge University Press, 2003).

Werle, Raymund, and Volker Leib, 'The Internet Society and its Struggle for Recognition and Influence', in C. Ronit and V. Schneider (eds.), *Private Organizations in Global Politics* (London/New York: Routledge, 2000), pp. 102–22.

Zittran, Jonathan, 'Be Careful What You Ask For: Reconciling A Global Internet and Local Law', in A. Thierer and C.W.J. Crews (eds.), *Who Rules the Internet? Internet Govenance and Jurisdiction* (Washington D.C.: CATO Institute, 2003), pp. 13–30.

Zürn, Michael, 'From Interdepence to Globalization', in Carlsnaes, T. Risse and B. Simmons (eds.), *Handbook of International Relations* (London/Thousand Oaks/New Dehli: SAGE Publications, 2002), pp. 235–53.

Chapter 5

The Return of the State in Cyberspace: The Hybrid Regulation of Global Data Protection

Ralf Bendrath

Introduction: The State in a Globalized Online World[1]

The emergence of the internet is regarded as a driver and a prominent example of globalization, and it is said to be the best example of why the role of the state can be expected to shrink. Unlike traditional communication infrastructures, the transnational architecture of the data network is not bound to territorial borders, nor is it controlled by national and international authorities. The internet is governed by a combination of private, public-private, and public authorities. What is more, internet users enjoy considerably more freedom than they did in the old telephone network. This, as many have suggested, also leads to new forms of transnational self-governance that are both effective and legitimate. The internet therefore can be used as a most likely case for studying the transformation of the state under conditions of globalization.

The role of states in a globalizing world is an issue that has drawn growing attention in the social sciences. Shrinking borders,[2] growing cross-border interaction,[3]

1   Research for this chapter was conducted in the ongoing project 'Regulation and Legitimacy on the Internet' as part of the Collaborative Research Center 'Transformations of the State', Bremen University, <http://www.state.uni-bremen.de>. Many ideas were therefore developed together with my colleagues Jeanette Hofmann, Volker Leib, Peter Mayer, Johannes Moes, Gregor Walter, and Michael Zürn. This chapter is based on an earlier paper that was written by me and Jeanette Hofmann and included two case studies (on data protection and on the Domain Name System). I would like to thank Stefanie Sifft, J.P. Singh and an anonymous reviewer for helpful comments. Clemens Haug, Nino David Jordan, Monika Tocha and Dulani Perera provided valuable research assistance. Funding for this project comes from the German Research Foundation.
    2   Mathias Albert and Lothar Brock, 'Entgrenzung der Staatenwelt. Zur Analyse weltgesellschaftlicher Entwicklungstendenzen', *Zeitschrift für Internationale Beziehungen*, 2/2 (1995): 259–85.
    3   For a very early concept of national and regional integration based on the growth of cross-border communication, see Karl W. Deutsch, *Nationalism and Social Communication. An Inquiry into the Foundations of Nationality* (Cambridge, 1953). For empirical data

and the rise of private authority in international affairs[4] challenge the nation state. New forms of cooperation between the public and the private sector as well as new modes of self-regulation seem to indicate an *organisational* transformation of traditional statehood. At the same time, a shift of regulatory power to international or transnational regimes questions the *spatial* dimension of modern statehood.

I want to contribute to this debate with empirical research on the changing role of the state in cyberspace. In the case study on data protection presented here, processes of privatization and transnationalisation have indeed taken place. However, contrary to what much of the theoretical literature suggests, the withdrawal of the nation state has not only slowed down, but might be reversed. There are signs that state intervention and regulation are coming back after a period of decline. Ironically, this is because of the weakness of transnational governance arrangements. The empirical findings suggest that transnational private data protection regimes struggle with compliance and legitimacy problems. Private regulation has proven to be less effective and successful than expected. Private policy arrangements also suffer from a lack of legitimacy – normatively and empirically. Private regulatory institutions fail to provide adequate forms of accountability, representation, and thus congruence between the rulers and the ruled. As a consequence, the state might now be returning to cyberspace in a new role as a legitimate and effective regulator.

It seems unlikely, though, that public authorities can go through periods of withdrawal without any change. We can expect the states to assume more political responsibility on the basis of still-evolving multi-stakeholder cooperation. In other words, states will play a more active role, but rather as 'primi inter pares' or moderators than as sovereigns.

In the next part, I will briefly flesh out the theoretical assumptions based on the literature on privatization and internationalization, and will discuss how they are applied to the internet. In the main part, the findings of a case study on data protection will be presented. Four phases in the development of data protection regimes can be identified: 1) the phase of the classical interventionist nation-state in the 1970s; 2) the phase of internationalization in the 1980s and early 1990s; 3) the phase of privatization and self-regulation in the late 1990s; 4) the phase of the return of the state that has started around 2000. The most striking outcome is the recent and unexpected return of the state to the regulation of cyberspace. I will discuss this in the final section.

---

see Marianne Beisheim et al., *Im Zeitalter der Globalisierung? Thesen und Daten zur gesellschaftlichen und politischen Denationalisierung* (Baden-Baden, 1999).

4   Claire A. Cutler et al., *Private Authority and International Affairs* (Albany/New York, 1999); Tanja Brühl et al. (eds.), *Die Privatisierung der Weltpolitik. Entstaatlichung und Kommerzialisierung im Globalisierungsprozess* (Bonn, 2001).

Assumptions: Globalization, the State, and the Internet

Spatial and Organizational Moves Away from the State

The transformation of the state in the last decades can be understood as a two-dimensional movement: it has shifted organizationally and spatially. The organizational axis is located between privatization and nationalization; the spatial axis between regionalization and internationalization. Globalization is often described as a movement towards privatization and internationalization, eventually leading to more global transnational political spaces and institutions.[5]

Much of the literature on globalization and on developments in law and regulation suggests a shrinking role of the state and a more prominent role of private actors in policy – the *organizational dimension*. This is based on two strands of research about the rise of the transnational global market and about the growing complexity of modern societies. The first assumption is that states cannot and should not regulate everything, especially not in economic affairs. Growing international trade in goods and services and an accompanying growth in foreign direct investment have led to an – at least perceived – increase in power of transnational corporations. These, in turn, are increasingly constructing their own regulatory institutions – as 'private authority in international affairs'[6] – that range from global standards bodies to transnational law firms and private trade law and judiciary institutions.[7] Apart from that, the functional differentiation of modern societies is leading to a growing complexity and dynamic of societal subsystems, which also affects the role of the state. It can neither hope to keep up with all the latest developments in this area, nor can it acquire the expertise and information to effectively control them.[8] The state therefore only has a chance to be successful in such an environment if it shares responsibilities, moderates between private interests, and delegates many forms of direct intervention in society, or of the production of public goods, to private actors. By now, privatization has reached even the core functions of the state on a scale not seen before, leading some scholars to speak of a 'public management revolution'[9] or of 'private interest government'.[10] This development has been labelled as a transformation from the 'sovereign state' to the 'negotiating state'.[11]

---

5   Stephan Leibfried and Michael Zürn (eds.), *Transformations of the State?* (Cambridge, 2005).

6   Cutler et al., *Private Authority and International Affairs.*

7   Gunther Teubner, 'Globale Bukowina. Zur Emergenz eines transnationalen Rechtspluralismus', *Rechtshistorisches Journal*, 15/6 (1996): 255–90.

8   Helmut Willke, *Ironie des Staates. Grundlinien einer Staatstheorie polyzentrischer Gesellschaft* (Frankfurt/M., 1992).

9   Janet Newman, *Modernizing Governance. New Labour, Policy, and Society* (London, 2001); Ezra Suleiman, *Dismantling Democratic States* (Princeton, 2003).

10   Renate Mayntz and Fritz W. Scharpf (eds.), *Gesellschaftliche Selbstregulierung und politische Steuerung* (Frankfurt a. M., 1995), p. 20.

11   Wolfgang Schulz and Thorsten Held, *Regulierte Selbstregulierung als Form Modernen Regierens.* Report for the German Federal Secretary for Culture and Media (Hamburg, 2002), p.A-2.

Internationalization – the *spatial dimension* of globalization that is described by the second analytical axis – generally means a shift of regulatory powers from the nation-state towards international arenas and forums. In society, we are witnessing a thickening of societal transactions across national borders. Not only markets, but also communication and cultural spaces have become more globalized, as have the cross-border impacts of national economic policies and technological developments. More international cooperation is therefore also necessary to address truly international problems – which are becoming more endemic and nowadays range from climate protection to global terrorism and currency crises. The nation-state, in the wake of these developments, is somehow forced to cooperate internationally if it wants to have an impact at all and serve as a problem-solving institution for its citizens any longer. The European Union is the most prominent example of this, but the regulatory power of organizations like the WTO, the World Bank and others is also discussed broadly. While these international institutions are composed of nation-states, it is much harder for individual governments or parliaments to defect from internationally agreed rules once they are decided.[12]

Table 5.1   Governance models in the organizational and spatial dimension

organizational dimension / spatial dimension	state	private
national	national state regulation	national private governance
international	multilateral regime	transnational self-governance

Globalization, the Internet–and the State?

Reflecting these general observations in globalization research, the internet should be a most likely case allowing us to observe changes, firstly in the spatial reach of policies, and secondly in the organizational type of public intervention. As a global space for all kinds of human interaction, it should exhibit the typical characteristics of globalized governance beyond the nation-state (spatial dimension). At the same time, it is mainly run by private and transnational companies, and its technical standards are developed by transnational bodies (organizational dimension).

The decentralized architecture of the internet was widely regarded in the late 1990s as a paradigmatic break with the prevailing organizational principles of modern infrastructures. Unlike telephone networks, which were designed by hierarchical forms of coordination in and between nation states, the internet seemed

---

12 A side-effect is the tactical use of this mechanism for governments facing opposition at home. Some scholars have started to call this 'policy-laundering', see e.g. Gus Hosein, *International Relations Theories and the Regulation of International Dataflows: Policy Laundering and Other International Policy Dynamics* (Montreal, 2004).

to be immune to any form of central steering. It is true that the core resources of the internet, like the root server for the domain-name system or the allocation of IP address ranges, are organized centrally. But normal usage is not affected by this, as routing and packet switching take place in a decentralized way. The design of TCP/IP, the technical standards that ensure the flow of information and data on the internet, was taken as evidence for the assumption that governments would not be able to control the net:

> The Internet is built on a simple suite of protocols – the basic TCP/IP suite (...) Like a daydreaming postal worker, the network simply moves the data and leaves interpretation of the data to the applications at either end. This minimalism in design is intentional. It reflects both a political decision about disabling control and a technological decision about the optimal network design.[13]

Because the internet crosses and to some extent ignores national borders,[14] it undermines territorial forms of control. However, national sovereignty and the authority of law are based on territories and intact borders between them.[15] In the view of many observers, this could only mean that cyberspace had to develop its own form of post-nation state control:

> Global computer-based communications cut across territorial borders, creating a new realm of human activity and undermining the feasibility – and legitimacy – of applying laws based on geographic boundaries. While these electronic communications play havoc with geographic boundaries, a new boundary, made up of the screens and passwords that separate the virtual world from the 'real world' of atoms, emerges. This new boundary defines a distinct Cyberspace that needs and can create new law and legal institutions of its own.[16]

Consequently, the still emerging internet community discussed various scenarios of 'nongovernmental governance' for the net[17] that ranged from Barlow's famous 'Declaration of the Independence of Cyberspace'[18] to articles on the 'virtual

---

13 Lawrence Lessig, *Code and other Laws of Cyberspace* (New York, 1999), p. 32. Lessig sees this as a property of a *specific* technical design of the internet, which might be changed to make control much easier. His book is essentially an attempt to warn against these changes.

14 The real borders of the internet exist between the different transnational network providers, not between countries.

15 William J. Drake, 'Territoriality and Intangibility', in Kaarle Nordenstreng and Herbert I. Schiller (eds.), *Beyond National Souvereignty: International Communications in the 1990s* (Norwood, 1993), pp. 259–313.

16 David R. Johnson and David G. Post, 'The Rise of Law on the Global Network', in Brian Kahin and Charles Nesson (eds.), *Borders in Cyberspace. Information Policy and the Global Information Infrastructure* (Cambridge, 1997), p. 3.

17 Walter S. Baer, 'Will the Global Information Infrastructure Need Transnational (or Any) Governance?', in Brian Kahin and Ernest J. Wilson III (eds.), *National Information Infrastructure Initiatives: Visions and Policy Design* (Cambridge, 1997), pp. 532–52.

18 Barlow, John Perry, *A Declaration of the Independence of Cyberspace* (Davos, Switzerland, 8 February 1996), <http://homes.eff.org/~barlow/Declaration-Final.html>.

state'[19] that only plays a networking role and is not primarily based on its territory anymore.

The self-regulatory mainstream discourse on internet regulation in the 1990s was closely connected to an understanding of democracy based on direct participation and networked forms of community self-governance. Legitimacy in this view is more created by deliberation and participation than by models of traditional parliamentary (i.e., representative) democracy. These ideas were further elaborated by social scientists a bit later. They saw in the internet the first opportunity for an ideal discourse situation in Habermas' sense that would also work in contexts of mass communication.[20] Others considered the net an optimizing instrument for rule by voting, which would at the same time transcend representative democracy. Some scholars went as far as to suggest that with online voting, for the first time the direct rule of the people had become possible.[21] This debate did not end with the burst of the dot-com bubble. Some years into the new millennium, we still find academic visions and findings of the 'peer-production of Internet governance',[22] the emergence of 'global civil constitutions' in cyberspace,[23] or of cyberspace as a Habermasian 'functioning example of discourse theory in action'.[24] The transnational character of the internet in this debate was and is seen as challenging the idea of democracy in the two dimensions of our research project: Spatially, it de-coupled governance from the container of the nation-state, and organizationally, it made possible more direct forms of democracy that could 'short-circuit' the long and diffuse chains of representation and compensate for the lesser influence of national parliaments. It therefore could serve as a new model for the production of legitimacy in global governance.

Like all academic discussions or political visions, this one too has its critics. Already early on in this debate, they raised their voices against the 'cyber-separatists'.[25] They viewed 'reports of the imminent death of the state as greatly exaggerated',[26]

---

19 Richard Rosecrance, 'The Rise of the Virtual State', *Foreign Affairs*, 4 (1996): 45–61.

20 Barry N. Hague and Brian D. Loader, *Digital Democracy. Discourse and Decision Making in the Information Age* (London/New York, 1999).

21 Lawrence K. Grossman, 'Der Traum des Nebukadnezar. Demokratie in der Ära des Internet', in Claus Leggewie and Christa Maar (eds.), *Internet und Politik. Von der Zuschauer- zur Beteiligungsdemokratie* (Köln, 1998), p. 85.

22 David R. Johnson, Susan P. Crawford, and John G. Palfrey, Jr., *The Accountable Net: Peer Production of Internet Governance* (Cambridge, 2004).

23 Gunther Teubner, 'Globale Zivilverfassungen: Alternativen zur staatszentrierten Verfassungstheorie', *Zeitschrift für ausländisches öffentliches Recht und Völkerrecht*, 63/1 (2003): 1–28.

24 A. Michael Froomkin, 'Habermas@Discourse.Net: Toward a Critical Theory of Cyberspace', *Harvard Law Review*, 116/3 (2003): 872.

25 For the following, see Viktor Mayer-Schönberger, 'The Shape of Governance: Analyzing the World of Internet Regulation', *Virginia Journal of International Law*, 43 (2003): 605–73.

26 David G. Post, 'The "Unsettled Paradox": The Internet, the State, and the Consent of the Governed', *Indiana Journal of Global Legal Studies*, 5 (1998): 521.

and deconstructed the libertarian cyber-optimism as a new 'Californian ideology'.[27] There were two groups of scholars that still believed in a role of the state.[28] According to the 'traditionalists', their opponents were overlooking that people and corporations acting online are still present in the physical space, and that the internet also depends and runs on a physical infrastructure comprised of cables, servers, and routers. As these are located in national territories, they can become subject to the state monopoly of force. Implementation of regulations and the enforcement of law on the internet might be more difficult, but not impossible. The 'internationalists' were more concerned about the non-Cartesian characteristics of cyberspace, where physical distance is replaced by virtual distance, measured by the number of links separating two websites, and where 'safe havens' – the proverbial server on the Antilles – can be used for escaping regulation while still providing worldwide services. Because of the global extension of cyberspace, the internationalists saw multilateral cooperation between states as necessary for functioning regulation. The proper medium for global governance of cyberspace therefore would be international law – still state-based and democratically legitimized, but with global reach.[29]

The utopian vision of 'cyberian' self-governance was also criticized on normative grounds by both traditionalists and internationalists. According to them, the proponents of non-state internet governance, who often see themselves as the true liberals or libertarians, give insufficient weight to the support extended by representative democracy for liberal ideals and greatly exaggerate the propensity of online communication for the support their visions of self-governance. Their claim that liberal 'government' could emerge from individual non-hierarchical decision-making in cyberspace was also subject to many of the standard criticisms from the offline world, e.g. the need for countering discrimination, protecting privacy, and promoting a fair distribution of resources.[30]

Much of this debate has still been theoretical. It has certainly helped us to arrive at a better understanding with regard to both the regulatory and the legitimacy aspects of internet governance. It has also clarified some political problems related to the emergence of the internet as a new virtual reality. What is needed, though, is a virtual reality check. This chapter sets out to contribute to this debate with empirical research on the role of the state in cyberspace.[31] What kinds of privatized and internationalized governance can really be found on the internet ten years after its break-through as a mass medium, and which forms of legitimacy and legitimation have developed there? Reflecting the general observations in globalization research, the working hypothesis assumes that the internet's drive toward de-nationalization

---

27 Richard Barbrook and Andy Cameron, *The Californian ideology* (1995).

28 Mayer-Schönberger, 'The Shape of Governance: Analyzing the World of Internet Regulation'.

29 Terrence Berg, 'www.wildwest.gov: The Impact of the Internet on State Power to Enforce the Law', *Brigham Young University Law Review*, 25/4 (2000): 1305–62.

30 Neil Weinstock Netanel, 'Cyberspace Self-Governance: A Sceptical View from Liberal Democratic Theory', *California Law Review*, 88 (2000): 395–498.

31 The existing empirical studies on internet governance have almost exclusively focused on ICANN as a prominent example, without clarifying the theoretical leverage of the findings made there.

Table 5.2   Governance models and their specific aspects

specific aspects / governance model	role of the state	regulation model	basis of legitimacy
national state regulation (traditionalist)	regulator	public intervention	democratic representation
national private governance (cyber-separatist)	limited oversight through general law	national self-regulation	effectiveness, legality
multilateral regime (internationalist)	interdependent, constrained regulator	multilateralism, national compliance	international consensus, congruence
transnational self-governance (cyber-separatist)	none	transborder private self-regulation	effectiveness, participation

challenges the traditional form of national statehood. The internet is a 'most likely case' for observing changes in the type of public intervention, in the spatial reach of policies, and in the generation of legitimacy. If effective and legitimate governance beyond the nation-state is not found on the internet, where else could it develop?

We can derive some possible ideal-type outcomes that we can expect after doing the empirical work. The zero-hypothesis would be no change at all, which would mean that the nation-state has never disappeared in the reality of the globalized online world. The opposite would be the hypothesis that 'the internet changed everything', implying that we had actually found modes of internationalized and privatized governance on the internet that are at the same time effective and legitimate, but derive their legitimacy from democratic models beyond the nation-state-based representative democracy. And of course we could find mixtures of the two, such as instances of effective transnational internet governance that is lacking legitimacy, or legitimate transnational internet governance that is not effective. In the organizational dimension, we may also find variations where internet governance is either more state-based or more privatized. Table 5.2 shows the specific aspects of the governance models developed above and summarized in Table 5.2. Of interest here are the role of the state, the regulation model, and the basis of legitimacy. According to globalization and internet governance theory, we should expect a movement from the upper to the lower row over the last decades.

Findings: The Change of Data Protection Regulation

The Nation-State and the Birth of Data Protection Regulation in the 1970s

'Privacy' has been internationally regarded as a fundamental civil liberty since the 1940s. The Universal Declaration of Human Rights (1948) already had a paragraph on privacy. The 1950 Council of Europe's Human Rights Convention included a similar clause, and even established a court for enforcement.[32] The US has already had a judicial tradition of privacy protection since the 1890 seminal article by Samuel Warren and later Supreme Court judge Louis Brandeis, who coined the phrase of the 'right to be let alone'.[33]

These early privacy rules were originally intended as a protection against unreasonable police searches of private property or against an overly intrusive press. As a result of World War II and the experiences with the Nazi regime, people became more afraid of too much personal information in the hand of powerful government bureaucracies.[34] This historical memory had a much bigger impact on European than on US privacy

---

32 Citizens could sue their governments if the latter did not translate the convention's protections to the national level.

33 Louis Brandeis and Samuel Warren, 'The Right to Privacy', *Harvard Law Review*, 4 (1890): 193–220.

34 The Netherlands had maintained comprehensive population registers since the 1930s, which were seized by the German government in the first three days of the occupation. The Dutch Jews as a result had the highest death rates in all occupied countries in Western Europe – including Germany. See William Seltzer and Margo Anderson, 'The Dark Side of Numbers:

debates and mainly affected the framing of the first data protection laws in Europe, as US political culture has always had a more sceptical view of the government.[35]

The use of computers for accounting and personnel management since the 1960s transformed the policy problem of limiting the compilation, access, and use of personal files from a purely bureaucratic task into a political-technological endeavour. Now, it became a matter of 'informational privacy' (the US term) and 'data protection' (in Europe).[36]

> The first data-protection laws were enacted in response to the emergence of electronic data processing within government and large corporations.[37]

The discussion on the 'Big Brother state' was increasing at the same time.[38] The rise of computer use and the special political situation in the late 1960s then led to enough public pressure to open policy windows. The first parliaments started to enact laws to protect personal information against unlimited use. The world's first data protection law was enacted in the German state of Hesse in 1970. Shortly afterwards, Sweden (1973) and the US (1974) followed, as West Germany did on the federal level soon thereafter (1977); Denmark, Austria, France, Norway and Luxembourg (all 1978) also had privacy protection laws. Until the beginning of the 1980s, seven countries – all in Western Europe – had enacted data protection laws, and in the 1980s ten more followed, among them Israel, Japan, Canada, and Australia.[39] In the 1990s, 22 more states from all continents joined the crowd, while a few more did so in the new millennium.[40] The reasons for this general spread of privacy legislation are not the topic of this paper.[41] We can keep in mind that there were some 'waves' or 'generations' of data protection legislation.[42]

The Role of Population Data Systems in Human Rights Abuses', *Social Research*, 68/2 (2001): 481–513.

35 Colin J. Bennett, *Regulating Privacy. Data Protection and Public Policy in Europe and the United States* (Ithaca, 1992).

36 In the US, the term 'fair information practices' is also widely used.

37 Viktor Mayer-Schönberger, 'Generational Development of Data Protection in Europe', in Philip E. Agre and Marc Rotenberg (eds.), *Technology and Privacy: The New Landscape* (Cambridge, 1998), p. 221.

38 Lyon has elaborated the thesis that 'privacy' only became a social value when the technologically enabled surveillance society was already a fact. David Lyon, *Surveillance Society. Monitoring Everyday Life* (Buckingham & Philadelphia, 2001).

39 For a systematic four-country comparison of the USA, Germany, Sweden and the UK from 1960-1980, see Bennett, *Regulating Privacy*.

40 In 2004 the annual survey done by EPIC and Privacy International lists 62 States, among them only two from Africa, see: EPIC, *Privacy & Human Rights 2004. An International Survey of Privacy Laws and Developments* (Washington D.C., 2004).

41 Bennett and Raab mention a change in public opinion, policy-learning, diffusion through epistemic communities and the influence of external actors (EU, Council of Europe, OECD), see Colin J. Bennett and Charles D. Raab, *The Governance of Global Issues: Protecting Privacy in Personal Information*, paper presented at the ECPR Joint Sessions of Workshops, Edinburgh (28 March–2 April 2003), p.3.

42 Mayer-Schönberger, 'Generational Development of Data Protection in Europe'.

National Rules, Different Regulatory Models In the spatial dimension, the first data protection laws in the 1970s were purely national endeavors. Though they were influenced by cross-border exchange among the expert community, significant national differences in the institutional design and the scope of protection can be found, and there was no international regime. A rough consensus was emerging internationally, though, with the Council of Europe's ministerial resolutions 22 (1973) and 29 (1974) on the automatic processing of data as the first internationally agreed basic principles. But at that time, no body of international law or multilateral regime of data protection was in sight yet.

Organizationally, the regulatory model was mainly state-interventionist. This was linked closely to the specific technical structure of the problem. Computers at that time were mainframe computers in the hands of huge bureaucracies or corporations. The laws of the first generation were therefore aimed at the technical systems that stored and processed data. They set up registration or even licensing mechanisms for databases, they regulated access controls, and they were full of terms like 'data', 'data file', or 'data record'. The technical systems then were envisioned as centralized large computer facilities that would be easy to control and supervise.

> In other words: There were huge cabinets full of digitized data where before there had been huge cabinets full of files, but still, they were huge cabinets.[43]

The regulation model that followed was direct oversight, control, and intervention. All data protection laws had two things in common: They mandated the listing of all or most databases in a public register, and they all (with the US being the only exception) created independent regulatory agencies with far-reaching rights. Because of the obligation to register, these supervisory bodies or data protection commissioners had a good overview of the few, but large existing databases, and regular inspections ensured high compliance. Beyond that, there were different degrees of freedom for the agencies.[44] The Swedish model had the greatest degree of delegation to the oversight agency, which could not only intervene in the design of the databases, but also was the only one that could fine wrongdoers, while in other countries, this was left to the courts. It was similarly adopted in Denmark, Norway, and France. The German model, on the other hand, tried to institutionalize some oversight function in the private sector. Companies with more than four employees processing personal data were mandated to create an internal independent data protection commissioner, whose job it was to ensure compliance with the rather broad principles of the data protection law. A similar model was adopted in the UK and later in Canada. The

---

43 Simon Fink, *Datenschutz zwischen Staat und Markt. Die 'Safe Harbor'-Lösung als Ergebnis einer strategischen Interaktion zwischen der EU, den USA und der IT-Industrie*, Master Thesis (Department of Political and Administrative Science, University of Konstanz, 2002), <http://www.ub.uni-konstanz.de/v13/volltexte/2003/1012//pdf/magarbsfink.pdf>, p. 85, translation R.B.

44 For the different models, see Godfrey Stadlen, 'Survey of National Data Protection Legislation', *Computer Networks*, 3 (1979): 174–86. Bennett distinguishes four models, but the 'British' and the 'German' model can roughly be but in the same category, see Bennett, *Regulating Privacy*.

independent public data protection commissioners on the federal and state (Länder) level functioned more as ombudsmen and less as interventionist regulators, while still retaining an oversight function. The US model, adopted only in the US, was and still is limited in scope, as the Federal Privacy Act of 1974 only applies to the state processing of personal data. It also did not create an independent body, but instead relied on the courts for enforcement. This was done through tort claims for violation of one's [own] personal data.[45] Until today, data processing by US private enterprises is not regulated through an omnibus act, but only in a few sectors like health or financing. This is mainly due to the specific history of the Privacy Act[46] and to the general aversion in the US against government intervention in the market and in the 'free flow of information'.

High Legitimacy of First-generation Data Protection Laws   The legitimacy of national data protection legislation in the 1970s and early 1980s was as high as any other public law – maybe even higher. The parliamentarians who decided about the level and institutional design of data protection were elected by the national constituency whose personal data they wanted to protect. Transnational data flows were not really an issue then. The data, once it had entered a system, was to stay there. Transparency was also high: The parliaments had lengthy debates on the shape of the law; they held public hearings and wrestled with government departments and outside experts.[47] The public was very interested in this topic then, and even the fictional horror stories in novels and movies like '2001 – A Space Odyssey' were an important part of forming a public opinion on these matters. It was clear to everybody involved that the citizens were afraid of the power of computers.

Compliance, or output legitimacy, was also good. The technical systems then were centralized large computer facilities that were easy to control and supervise. There were only a small number of databases in each country, and they were run by large corporations or by the government authorities. These also had the expertise and the resources to employ specialized internal data protection commissioners or to take care of the complicated processes for registering a database and complying with the data protection laws.

International Coordination in the 1980s and Early 1990s

International Harmonization   The accelerated globalization of the economy in the 1980s created pressure against national sovereignty in data protection policy. On the one hand, more and more data was being transferred within transnational

---

45 The *Office of Management and Budget* got the task of producing guidelines fort he Federal bureaucracy, but has no enforcement power.

46 The policy window that made its passage possible was opened by the Watergate scandal. The Privacy Act became law only five months after Nixon had stepped down, but with the republican majority still controlling the House of Representatives. See Colin Bennett, *Regulating Privacy*.

47 German federal data protection legislation took years of debate and reports and produced several drafts from 1971 on, before the law finally was passed in 1978. The US Privacy Act was built on more than 200 bills and 47 congress hearings.

corporations; on the other hand, one of the official goals of international economic policy was (and is) free trade. Personal data, as soon as it was more widely available than before, also became a commodity.[48] An expert group set up by the Council of Europe had stated the need for international regulatory harmonization as early as 1970:

> It was felt that common European norms were highly desirable because [...] the computer medium was itself international in character.[49]

Many of the data protection laws of the 1970s prohibited transferring personal data to other countries under certain conditions. Usually, such conditions included a lack of adequate or comparable levels of legal and institutional data protection in the target country. This could become a problem for multinational corporations. The different laws often had different procedural instruments for regulating data protection, even though they would rest on the same set of basic principles. This could lead to difficult legal conflicts.[50]

The objective soon became clear in forums like the Council of Europe and the EC Parliament: International harmonization of data protection was needed. The goal was not the protection of the citizens' data (there were already many national laws for this), but to make data protection compatible with the increasingly internationalized or even globalized market. The driving force here was not a civil liberties perspective, but a functional view on privacy regulation. The European Parliament made this very clear. A 1979 resolution called for the

> creation of a genuine common market in data-processing in which the free movement of goods and freedom to provide services are assured and competition is not distorted.[51]

The 1981 'Sieglerschmidt report' to the European Parliament explicitly asked for international market competition over personal data:

> Transborder competition in data banks and free data flow within the Community are possible only if data protection is harmonized.[52]

---

48 ThiloWeichert, 'ZurÖkonomisierungdesRechtsaufinformationelleSelbstbestimmung', in Helmut Bäumler (ed.), *E-Privacy. Datenschutz im Internet* (Braunschweig and Wiesbaden, 2000), pp. 158–84.

49 Bennett, *Regulating Privacy*, p. 134.

50 EU-JRC, *Security and Privacy for the Citizen in the Post-September 11 Digital Age: A Prospective Overview. Report to the European Parliament Committee on Citizens Freedoms and Rights, Justice and Home Affairs (LIBE)* (Brussels, 2003), p. 90.

51 European Parliament, Resolution on the protection of the rights of the individual in the face of technical developments in data processing, *Official Journal of the European Communities*, No. C 140/35, (5 June 1979).

52 European Parliament, *Second Report drawn up on behalf of the Legal Affairs Committee on the protection of the rights of the individual in the face of technical developments in data processing*. Rapporteur: Mr. H. Sieglerschmidt, Document 1-548/81, PE 70.166/final (12 October 1981), p. 31.

Several international documents that tried to harmonize international data protection were developed in the following years. The most binding international agreement for 15 years was the Council of Europe's 1980 'Convention for the Protection of Individuals with Regard to Automatic Processing of Personal Data'. This 'influential treaty',[53] which constitutes binding international law for its signatories, included regulations on transborder data flows and allowed restrictions on these if the data was to be transferred to a country with lower protection levels. Citizens could even sue their governments in the European Court of Human Rights if their country was a treaty member, but had not transposed its provisions into national law. The Council of Europe subsequently adopted a number of recommendations for implementing the convention in specific areas ranging from medical databases (1981) to privacy protection on the internet (1999).[54] Here, we can clearly see that the globalization of data networks and information flows was a strong driver towards international law and multilateral agreements.

The OECD developed its 1980 'Guidelines on the Protection of Privacy and Transborder Flows of Personal Data' in close coordination with the council of Europe, in order to avoid further complications. The guidelines were preceded by fierce conflicts between the US and some European governments. The Europeans regarded the very low or (for the private sector) non-existing level of data protection in the US as unacceptable and as an attempt to globalize the dominance of the US computer industry with the buzz phrase 'free flow of information'. The US, in turn, accused the Europeans of protectionism by means of data protection.[55] The OECD guidelines were a compromise and already weakened the international commitment to states' intervention into the private sector's handling of data. They are not binding for the OECD member states in the same way as the Council of Europe's convention is. On the other hand, the OECD has repeatedly and actively tried to make the private sector adopt them as industry guidelines and commit to their principles as well. International business associations like the International Chamber of Commerce have been constantly involved in the work of the OECD Committee for Information, Computer and Communications Policy.

The OECD followed up in 1985 with another declaration on 'transborder data flows' that dealt with trade barriers, information-handling within transnational corporations, and related aspects of data protection, and envisioned better cooperation and harmonization.[56] The organization has also developed a comprehensive 'best practices' handbook, and later even developed an online privacy-statement generator,[57] both of which were produced in order to help corporate data handlers be more conscious and transparent about what data they collect and how they use it. The OECD for a decade remained the only international organization with a reach beyond Europe that dealt with privacy and data protection. Only in 1990 did the UN

53 Bennett and Raab, *The Governance of Global Issues*, p.3.
54 EU-JRC, p. 120.
55 Bennett, *Regulating Privacy*, pp. 136f.
56 OECD, *Declaration on Transborder Data Flows*, Adopted by the Governments of OECD Member countries (11 April 1985).
57 <http://www.oecd.org/sti/privacygenerator>.

General Assembly adopt the voluntary 'Guidelines concerning computerized data files', which had no follow-up mechanism and therefore no real impact.[58] As we will see later, the OECD guidelines marked a transition away from the state-based laws of 1970s and the multilateral harmonization of the 1980s towards a more voluntary approach that relies on good corporate governance.

European Integration and Third-Party Rules   The European Parliament, as was mentioned above, had adopted several resolutions on data protection since 1975 and repeatedly urged the EC Commission to draft an EC directive for harmonizing national legislation. The commission was rather hesitant to become active in this field. It therefore only recommended that the member states join the Council of Europe's convention. It was only in 1990, with the common European market approaching fast, that the Commission reacted and issued a draft data protection directive. This step was a surprise to many, as the EC was still seen as an economic community that did not deal with human rights issues. But the Commission used the same argument as the EC parliamentarians had: It referred to Article 100a of the EC treaty and presented its move as necessary for the functioning of the common European market.[59] It took five more years of negotiations in Brussels and the Bangemann report on 'Europe and the global information society',[60] which made the common European information space a top priority, before the directive 95/46/EC[61] was enacted.

The EU data protection directive is unanimously described as 'the most influential international policy instrument to date'.[62] It contains regulations on the private and public sector use of personal data, applies to manual and automated data processing, prescribes permitted and prohibited uses of personal data as well as the rules on implementation and data protection commissioners, creates an advisory body on the European level (the 'Article 29 Working Party', consisting of the national commissioners), and gives considerable discretion to the commission for determining adequate levels of data protection, certifying industry codes of conduct, and issuing model contracts for data subcontractors. It was supplemented in 1997 by a special directive for privacy in the electronic communications sector.[63] Since the 1999 treaty of Amsterdam, the directive has also applied to data processing within the EU bureaucracy, which got its own data protection supervisor.

---

58 They might have had an impact by carrying the discussion on data protection into non-OECD countries, but this is beyond the scope of this paper.

59 Nick Platten, 'Background and History of the Directive', in David Bainbridge (ed.), *The EC Data Protection Directive* (London, 1996), pp. 13–32.

60 EU, *Europe and the global information society. Recommendations to the European Council. Report of the High-Level Group on the Information Society* (1994).

61 EU, *Directive 95/46/EC of the European Parliament and of the Council, on the protection of individuals with regard to the processing of personal data and on the free movement of such data* (24 October 1995); see Platten, pp. 23–32.

62 Raab and Bennett, *The Governance of Global Issues*, p. 5.

63 EU, *Directive 97/66/EC of the European Parliament and of the Council, concerning the processing of personal data and the protection of privacy in the telecommunications sector* (15 December 1997).

Directive 95/46 also contained, for the first time on the international level, binding regulation for data transfers to third-party countries. This feature made it have an impact far beyond the EU, and this is why we can speak of 'globalization', and not just 'European integration', in this context. EU member states are only allowed to approve data exports of personal data if there is an 'adequate level of protection' in the recipient country. If there is no comparable legislation in place, the companies wanting to export the data can do so only if this is based on a contract with the company that receives the data, which also has to ensure adequate protection for further re-export. This clause has created significant adaptational pressure on third countries.[64] The EU later also developed standard contract clauses for data exports.[65] Unexpected help for this came from international trade regulation. The 1994 General Agreement on Trade in Services (GATS) mentions privacy, but as an exception from otherwise liberalized trade in services, including data services.[66] This case of non-integration of world trade created a stronger role for national or supranational privacy regulations. By doing this, the WTO constrained other states' ability to retaliate with other trade restrictions.[67]

> In effect, the EU's adequacy provisions are the *de facto* rules of the road for the increasingly global character of personal data processing activities, and have been a main focus of international attention, debate and controversy.[68]

The EU directive also had an impact on the older international legal agreement on data protection, the Council of Europe convention from 1980. There were early concerns that the directive could collide with the convention and create legal problems for members of both the EU and the Council of Europe. This was avoided by adapting the convention to the EU directive. The Council of Europe allowed the EU to join its convention as a member in 1999, and an additional protocol in 2001 added two core features of the EU directive to the convention: The institution of independent data protection commissioners, and the mandatory restrictions on data transfers into third countries that lack an adequate level of protection.[69]

---

64 Andrew Charlesworth, 'Clash of the Data Titans? US and EU Data Privacy Rules', *European Public Law*, 6/2 (2000): 253–74.

65 EU Commission, *2002/16/EC, Commission Decision on standard contractual clauses for the transfer of personal data to processors established in third countries* (2002).

66 'nothing in this Agreement shall be construed to prevent the adoption or enforcement by any Member of measures (…) necessary to secure compliance with laws or regulations (…) including those relating to (…) the protection of the privacy of individuals in relation to the processing and dissemination of personal data and the protection of confidentiality of individual records and accounts.' WTO, *General Agreement on Trade in Services (GATS), article XIV* (Geneva, 1994).

67 Shaffer, p. 86.

68 Bennett and Raab, *The Governance of Global Issues*, p.6.

69 Council of Europe, *Additional Protocol to the Convention for the Protection of Individuals with regard to Automatic Processing of Personal Data regarding supervisory authorities and transborder data flows (ETS No. 181), Explanatory Report* (2001).

Lower Legitimacy of Internationalized Data Protection Regulation What is the democratic quality of the internationalized or supra-nationalized privacy regulation that emerged between 1980 and 1995? One finding is a shift away from directly elected decision-makers to the international level. This prolongs the representation chains, and it moves the discussion towards international diplomacy. At the time when these regulatory mechanisms were developed, international negotiations in general meant less transparency. Not even the national parliaments were involved directly in the process, much less consumer groups or the general public. The ministers negotiated behind closed doors, and the citizens and parliamentarians only found out about the outcome later. The European Parliament, in particular, had no real impact on the 1995 directive. It was mainly shaped by the struggle among influential governments in the European Council.[70] European and US interest groups were voicing their concerns, but because of the deadlock in the Council of Ministers had no significant impact.[71]

The third-party rules of the EU directive are a delicate case of democratic congruence. The data export conditions of the directive have had a direct impact on data processing actors outside of the EU. The EU because of its sheer size and economic weight is setting standards that can no longer be ignored outside its borders. The 1995 directive has already set the terms for data protection laws from Australia to Argentina. The citizens in these third-party countries never had a chance to participate (however indirectly) in the genesis of the regulation.

Looking at output legitimacy, the effectiveness of the EU directive is not too high.[72] An intial commission evaluation of the reality of data protection – eight years after the adoption of the directive – found 'reasons for serious concern'[73] and 'very patchy compliance', as 'the risks of getting caught seem low'.[74] Slowly, Europe's data protection commissioners have started to coordinate their work to improve EU-wide compliance. They have agreed to focus on specific business sectors at the same time, and they even try to coordinate and synchronize their inspections in the respective companies.

The Rise of Self-Regulation in the mid-1990s

The Internet and the Hegemony of the US Approach As early as the mid-1980s, when the personal computer hit the market, the use and processing of all kinds of data – including personal data – had finally increased to a volume that was beyond

---

70 The German government was the veto-player here until it took over the EU presidency in July 1994, see Platten.

71 Platten, pp. 22–32; Priscilla M. Regan, 'American Business and the European Data Protection Directive: Lobbying Strategies and Tactics', in Colin J. Bennett and Rebecca Grant (eds.), *Visions of Privacy. Policy Choices for the Digital Age* (Toronto, 1999), pp. 199–216.

72 As this is the most binding agreement, is will suffice here to only look at the compliance to this directive and assume that the weaker OECD and Council of Europe principles are included.

73 EU Commission, *Report from the Commission. First report on the implementation of the Data Protection Directive (95/46/EC), COM* (Brussels, 2003), p. 13.

74 Ibid, p. 12.

the reach of effective government oversight with traditional registrations and inspections. After the advent of the internet as a mass medium in the 1990s, this problem became even worse, because the trade and flow of personal data across borders was only a matter of seconds now. The adoption of the EU directive had been accelerated by the high-level report on the 'European Information Society', but its adoption came just a bit too early to reflect the internet breakthrough in the mid-1990s. Quickly afterwards, it became clear that new regulatory problems would arise. With the internet, the number and diversity of data-collecting agents increased dramatically; data on user behaviour online could be automatically collected through web servers even without the users filling in forms, and the transnational nature of cyberspace made it difficult to apply and enforce national laws.

The EU tried to adapt the European legal approach to data protection, but with its slow policy processes had considerable problems following the internet's dynamic. Its directive on privacy in telecommunications[75] was adopted in December 1997, but only related to digital telephony (ISDN). The word 'internet' did not appear a single time in the whole text. It took the EU five more years to replace it with the new directive on privacy in electronic communications in 2002.[76] From the beginning, the US government had followed a clear 'hands-off'[77] policy towards the internet in general and data protection in particular. Both sides, on the other hand, had a common interest in supporting the growth of the new global electronic marketplace. They were soon joined by the private sector in accepting that consumers' trust in e-commerce would only grow if there were significant safeguards for personal data.[78] The EU and its member states still wanted to ensure compliance with their data protection legislation, but were also driven by the economic optimism of the dot-com bubble, and viewed the dominance of US companies in the technological developments with envy.

Because of the high technological dynamic and the multiplicity of users and developers of the internet, the ability of states to control this field seemed very limited anyway. The big corporations were still easy to control, but they also had the resources to fight what they regarded as overly intrusive government controls and prohibitions.[79] Swire and Litan use the instructive metaphor of elephants and mice: Elephants – big corporations – are large and easy to spot, but they also have the ability to inflict considerable damage on their environment. The more complicated

---

75 EU, *Directive 97/66/EC*.

76 EU, *Directive 2002/58/EC of the European Parliament and of the Council, concerning the processing of personal data and the protection of privacy in the electronic communications sector* (12 July 2002).

77 White House, *A Framework for Global Electronic Commerce* (1 July 1997).

78 This is a recurring theme, see the 1997 'European Initiative in Electronic Commerce' (EU Commission 1997), the US-'Framework For Global Electronic Commerce' (White House 1997), the OECD conferences on 'Dismantling the Barriers to Global Electronic Commerce' 1997 (OECD 1998b) and 'Realising the Potential of Global Electronic Commerce' 1998 (OECD 1998c), the 'Declaration of Principles' of the UN Summit on the Information Society 2003 (WSIS 2003).

79 For the lobbying efforts of the US computer industry in Europe, see Regan.

problem, though, are mice – the small companies that easily re-locate and are hard to control:

> The situation is far different for mice, which are small, nimble, and breed annoyingly quickly.[80]

Data protection therefore could only work if government oversight was combined with functioning self-regulation in the private sector. Therefore, the expert discussions as well as the political discourse on data protection in the mid-1990s focused on self-regulation and technical approaches. Interestingly enough, the EU directive with its third-party rules helped to create some dynamic in the US in this field. The Clinton administration was afraid the EU Commission could shut US companies out of the large European market for e-commerce, because the lack of comprehensive data protection legislation in the US could mean an 'inadequacy' rating. Before the directive had to be implemented on the national levels in 1998, the US government therefore tried to convince the EU that self-regulation worked.[81] At the same time, it also started pushing the private sector into seriously self-regulating data protection. Some parts of the administration, especially in the Federal Trade Commission, even threatened to adopt legal measures if self-regulation would not work quickly. Therefore, the self-regulatory instruments have been called 'the Directive's bastard offshoots'.[82]

Mainly in the US, a number of codes of conduct were developed early on by different industry and trade associations, ranging from the Direct Marketing Association to the Associated Credit Bureaus. These sectoral codes[83] have become quite popular in the last few years. Many of the self-regulating institutions award 'privacy seals' to websites that publicly declare their adherence to the specific data protection standard. The most popular ones are *TRUSTe* and *Better Business Bureau (BBB) Online*. These mostly US-based certificate schemes are often less supportive of privacy than comparable EU legislation. For instance, for commercial marketing mails, opt-out instead of opt-in mechanisms are the norm. While seal providers have no way of taking action against companies that do not participate in these voluntary agreements, their reach has constantly grown,[84] and compliance checks nowadays

---

80 Peter P. Swire and Robert E. Litan, *None of Your Business: World Data Flows, Electronic Commerce, and the European Privacy Directive* (Washington DC, 1998), p. 201.

81 E.g. with a comprehensive compendium: U.S. Department of Commerce, *Privacy and Self-Regulation in the Information Age* (Washington/DC, 1997), <http://www.ntia.doc.gov/reports/privacy/privacy_rpt.htm>.

82 Gregory Shaffer, 'The Power of Collective Action: The Impact of EU Data Privacy Regulation on US Business Practice', *European Law Journal*, 5/4 (1999): 433.

83 Colin J. Bennett, 'Privacy Self-Regulation in a Global Economy: A Race to the Top, the Bottom or Somewhere Else?', in Kernaghan Webb (ed.), *Voluntary Codes: Private Governance, the Public Interest and Innovation* (Ottawa: Carleton Research Unit for Innovation, Science and Environment), pp. 227–48, <http://www.carleton.ca/spa/VolCode/Ch8.pdf>.

84 In fiscal year 2005, 1,975 websites participated in TRUSTe's seal programme, among them 28 Fortune 500 companies and 115 Safe Harbor seal holders (see below), TRUSTe, *TRUSTe Fact Sheet* (2006), <http://www.truste.org/about/fact_sheet.php>.

are better and partly automated. While not mandated by law, more and more US companies have created the position of a 'Chief Privacy Officer', who has broadly the same functions as the internal data protection commissioners in Europe.

Most of these instruments fit into the model of national self-regulation, as their prime users are US companies. But they were also developed on an international scale, the most prominent being the work of the *International Commerce Exchange* on a 'Global Code of Conduct'[85] and the *Global Business Dialogue on electronic Commerce's* guidelines for 'consumer confidence'.[86] Other approaches included the use of private transnational law for model contracts on personal data flows in international commerce, and developments towards a data protection standard. The first real privacy standard was the Canadian 'Model Code for the Protection of Personal Information' of 1992, which was officially recognized as a 'National Standard of Canada' in 1996. The Japanese Standards Association in 1999 published the standard JIS Q 15001, which was modelled on the environmental management standard ISO 14001. On the international level, the International Standards Organization (ISO) in 1996 initiated a process for the development of an international standard after pressure from its Consumer Policy Committee, but because of heavy lobbying from US corporations and criticism from European data protection commissioners, has not been able to agree on a standard yet. The European standards body Comité Européen de Normalisation (CEN) has also been studying the feasibility of an international privacy standard.[87]

The different self-regulatory instruments also can re-enforce each other, with one instrument referencing another, even across the different national, European, and international levels. A data-handling contract between a European and a Canadian company, for example, can reference the CSA model code and thereby comply with the EU directive's regulation for the transborder flow of personal data. Nationally, standards can be used by government agencies that hire private contractors. And providers of national privacy seals can build on the guidelines developed by transnational industry associations and projects like the *Global Business Dialogue on electronic Commerce*.

This technologically driven move towards self-regulation converged with another development that had already started in the 1980s: The new legal and political concept of 'informational self-determination' that the German constitutional court had developed in a landmark census ruling in 1983.[88] Contrary to the first data protection laws that tried to regulate the technology, the new ones enacted in the 1980s gave the citizens a say in the process. 'Informational self-determination' also reached further than just the collection of the data and included the control of the individual over all later stages of the processing and use of the data. But 'self-determination' also meant

---

85 Colin J. Bennett and Charles D. Raab, *The Governance of Privacy. Policy Instruments in Global Perspective* (Aldershot, 2003), p. 134.

86 Global Business Dialogue on electronic commerce, *Consumer Confidence: Trustmarks* (14 September 2001), <http://www.gbd.org/pdf/recommendations/trustmark00.pdf>.

87 Bennett, 'Privacy Self-Regulation in a Global Economy'.

88 Bundesverfassungsgericht, *BVerfGE 65, 1 – Volkszählung. Urteil des Ersten Senats* (15 December 1983).

that the consent of the individual could override default legal prohibitions against the use of personal data.[89]

This development got a new boost with the internet. Initially, cyberspace was seen as a great place for user empowerment. In the early days of the internet, most of the netizens did not want the government to play a role in this new frontier territory. Even many privacy activists believed that they could not rely on the government for protection (instead, they still feared the Big Brother), but instead placed their trust in technology and mathematics. The invention of public-key cryptography[90] and the publication of end-user tools like Pretty Good Privacy (PGP) furthered this mind-set. A whole plethora of so-called 'privacy enhancing technologies' (PETs) have been developed since then, which include anonymising services, tools for automatically administering and deleting cookies, anonymous re-mailers, and many more.[91]

The governments, on the other hand, took up this libertarian self-help approach. The Council of Europe 1999 recommendations for privacy on the internet read like a capitulation of state regulation:

> For Users: Remember that the Internet is not secure. However, different means exist and are being developed enabling you to improve the protection of your data. Therefore, use all available means to protect your data and communications.[92]

Low Legitimacy of Self-Help and Self-Regulation   Self-regulatory mechanisms are generally not representative. Elected representatives of the people are only indirectly involved through the different expert networks and professional communities, if at all. Some of these self-regulatory mechanisms have been developed with the participation of consumer and civil liberties groups.[93] The internet also helped more NGOs and watchdog groups concerned about privacy to play an increasing role in international privacy policy. Their representatives are now routinely invited for presentations at the World Conference of Data Protection Commissioners or the OECD privacy meetings, and the more professional ones with international reach, like Privacy International, have been working closer with industry in the last few years. This participation of civil society is probably a general new feature of global and private governance, but it cannot replace the democratic quality of legislation by the elected representatives of the people. Neither does private-sector regulation fulfill

---

89 Mayer-Schönberger, 'Generational Development of Data Protection in Europe'.

90 David Chaum, 'Achieving Electronic Privacy', *Scientific American,* 267 (1992): 76–81.

91 For an overview, see <http://www.epic.org/privacy/tools.html>.

92 Council of Europe, *Recommendation No R(99)5 of the Committee of Ministers to Member States for the Protection of Privacy on the Internet. Guidelines for the Protection of Individuals with Regard to the Collection and Processing of Personal Data on Information Highways*, adopted by the Committee of Ministers at the 660th meeting of the Ministers' Deputies (23 February 1999).

93 TRUSTe was even founded by Commerce Net and the Boston Consulting Group together with the Electronic Frontier Foundation, a Silicon Valley-based civil liberties group (Abraham L. Newman and David Bach, 'Self-Regulatory Trajectories in the Shadow of Public Power: Resolving Digital Dilemmas in Europe and the United States', *Governance: An International Journal of Policy, Administration, and Institutions,* 17/3 (2004): 387–413.

the democratic criterion of congruence of the ruled and the rulers. As the guidelines are set up by business associations with arbitrary membership and a specific economic interest structure, the consumers or users are not necessarily a formal part of the regulation-setting process. The degree of transparency of the privatized regulation-setting processes is not very high, either. Unlike parliament decisions, the industry guidelines do not have to be developed under public observation or keep records of the discussions. On the other hand, they are not binding, so they need less input legitimacy. But at the same time, this creates the problem of defection, lowering their output legitimacy. The effectiveness of privatized data protection in cyberspace is low. Surveys routinely find a lack of privacy policy statements, and an overly broad tendency to collect all kinds of personal data that are not necessary for the online transaction in question. The 1999 Georgetown Internet Privacy Policy Survey concluded that collecting of personal data was the norm on commercial websites. At least one piece of personal information (name, e-mail, address) was collected by almost all (92.8 per cent) of the sites. Only 6.6 per cent of the sites collected no information, and one third (34.1 per cent) had no privacy policy at all.[94] The OECD openly questioned the effectiveness of any of the official or self-governance instruments on the web:

[T]here is a marked discrepancy between the world of the various institutions and organizations that develop ideas and instruments for data protection on the one hand, and the world of Web sites on the other.[95]

The existing mechanisms for an effective enforcement of these industry codes of conduct have repeatedly been called into question. The certifying companies depend on funding by their members, so tough measures against the ones who break the rules are unlikely. TRUSTe, for example, came under public pressure after it did not properly follow up on accusations against its member Microsoft.[96] Around 2000, some well-published cases of misuse of personal information by companies like online marketing giant DoubleClick, the steady rise of spam and junk mail, security holes in customer databases, and a growing fear of credit card data being stolen on the net[97] led to public pressure for more effective privacy protection on line. The users, according to a number of other surveys, are still not satisfied with the state of online data protection.[98] A March 2004 EuroBarometer survey found that out of the

94 Mary J. Culnan, *Georgetown Internet Privacy Policy Survey: Report to the Federal Trade Commission* (1999).

95 OECD, Directorate for Science, Technology, and Industry, Committee for Information, Computer and Communications Policy, Group of Experts on Information Security and Privacy, *Practices to Implement the OECD Privacy Guidelines on Global Networks* (1998), p. 23.

96 Paul Boutin, 'Just How trusty is Truste?', *Wired News* (9 April 2002); Lee Richardson, 'History of Self-Regulation Cast Doubt on its Effectiveness', *Privacy Times* (12 July 2000).

97 For an overview, see Junkbusters, *News and Opinion on Marketing and Privacy* (2006, constantly updated), <http://www.junkbusters.com/new.html>.

98 For an overview, see Colin J. Bennett, 'Privacy in the Political System: Perspectives from Political Science and Economics', in Alan Westin (ed.), *Privacy and Freedom Updated:*

84 per cent of EU citizens who do not shop online, 25 per cent avoid this form of purchase because they do not trust the medium.[99]

Hybrid Regulation and the Return of the State since 2000

Effectiveness and Legitimacy Problems By the late 1990s, data protection regulation had a legitimacy problem. Input legitimacy, that is the democratic quality of privacy protection, was eroding, as more regulation had been shifted to the European, international, or private levels, and the participation of civil society or citizens was still limited to a few insiders and professional NGO workers. The hope of the 1980s and early 1990s had been that this democratic deficit could be outweighed by a higher effectiveness of these rules. Output legitimacy, though, was also quite low, especially in the field of online privacy. Comparably few corporations adhered to privacy protection standards, whether they were mandated by law or recommended by private organizations. Neither did the reality of privacy protection on the internet live up to the letters of international or private agreements, nor did it meet the users' demands, expectations, or fears.

This lack of legitimacy was noted by many. The lack of consumer trust in privacy and other rights on the web were and are still perceived as major problems that stand in the way of a large-scale breakthrough of e-commerce. This was stated repeatedly in a number of national and international forums from 1997 on, from the White House to the EU, the OECD, and the World Summit on the Information Society.[100] It led to a push by politicians as well as NGOs for a more prominent role of the state in privacy regulation. In the private sector, the growing complexity of overlapping national and state-level legislation, international guidelines, industry codes and self-regulatory mechanisms, contract law, and technical approaches created headaches

---

Social Science Perspectives on Privacy (forthcoming), <http://web.uvic.ca/~polisci/bennett/pdf/westinbook.pdf>.

99 EuroBarometer, *E-Commerce Survey* (2004).

100 See e.g. the the EU Commission's 1997 'European Initiative in Electronic Commerce' (EU Commission, *COM(97) 157: A European Initiative in Electronic Commerce. Communication to the European Parliament, the Council, the Economic and Social Committee and the Committee of the Regions* (1997)), the White House's 1997 'Framework For Global Electronic Commerce' (White House, *A Framework For Global Electronic Commerce* (1997)), the OECD 1997 Turku conference on 'Dismantling the Barriers to Global Electronic Commerce' (OECD: Directorate for Science, Technology, and Industry, Committee for Information, Computer and Communications Policy, *'Dismantling the Barriers to Global Electronic Commerce' OECD Doc. No. DSTI/ICCP(98)13/FINAL* (1998)), the OECD 1998 Ottawa ministerial conference on 'Realising the Potential of Global Electronic Commerce' (OECD: Directorate for Science, Technology, and Industry, Committee for Information, Computer and Communications Policy, Working Party on Information Security and Privacy, *Ministerial Declaration on the Protection of Privacy on Global Networks, OECD Doc. No. DSTI/ICCP/REG(98)10/FINAL OECD Doc. No. DSTI/ICCP/REG(98)10/FINAL*, (Ottawa, 1998)), the 2003 World Summit on the Information Society's 'Declaration of Principles' (World Summit on the Information Society, *Declaration of Principles. Building the Information Society: a global challenge in the new Millennium* (Geneva, 12 December 2003)).

for the corporate lawyers and chief privacy officers. They increasingly saw the need for a harmonization of these different instruments, functionally and spatially. This created a growing pull-factor in the private sector for a stronger role of the state, which could use its influence to set some common privacy baselines.

Regulated Self-Regulation: The 'Safe Harbor' Compromise   As the US does not have comprehensive data protection legislation for the private sector, there was a dilemma after the EU directive had been enacted: Either the EU Commission could have treated the US data protection regulation as 'not adequate' and risked another transatlantic trade war, or it could have declared the limited self-regulatory instruments to be 'adequate' and seriously damage the credibility of the whole directive. Of course, it did neither, but entered into discussions with the US government, eventually leading to a compromise.[101] In July 2000, the EU Commission and the US Department of Commerce signed the 'Safe Harbor' agreement.

The 'Safe Harbor' agreement can be regarded as a 'hybrid' or 'interface solution'[102] because it is a combination of two different regulatory approaches: The European law-based and comprehensive privacy regulation and the US private sector-based and sectoral privacy regulation. Under Safe Harbor, the object of the important adequacy rating by the EU Commission is not a country anymore, but a single company. Therefore, the US could keep its data processing industry partly unregulated, and the EU could allow data transfers to US companies on the condition that they submit to the Safe Harbor principles. The mechanism is quite simple:

> The decision by U.S. organizations to enter the safe harbor is entirely voluntary. Organizations that decide to participate in the safe harbor must comply with the safe harbor's requirements and publicly declare that they do so.[103]

As of May 2006, 950 companies had entered the Safe Harbor.[104] Due to the nature of the compromise, this agreement is weaker than the respective EU regulation. There is no possibility for EU citizens to legally insist on getting information about what is happening to their data in the US, or for European data protection commissioners to inspect the processing companies on the other side of the Atlantic. The European Parliament therefore strongly resisted the agreement, but because the assessment of 'adequacy' according to the 1995 directive is delegated to the Commission, it could not do much against it. But the agreement still comes with public oversight and

---

101 For details on the process, see Fink, *Datenschutz zwischen Staat und Markt;* Henry Farrell, 'Constructing the International Foundations of E-Commerce: The EU-U.S. Safe Harbor Arrangement', *International Organization*, 57/2 (2003): 277–306; Dorothee Heisenberg, *Negotiating Privacy. The European Union, the United States and Personal Data Protection* (Boulder, 2005).

102 Henry Farrell, 'Hybrid Institutions and the Law: Outlaw Arrangements or Interface Solutions?', *Zeitschrift für Rechtssoziologie*, 23/1 (2002): 25–40.

103 U.S. Department of Commerce, *Safe Harbor Overview* (2005), <http://www.export.gov/safeharbor/sh_overview.html>.

104 U.S. Department of Commerce, *Safe Harbor List* (2006), <http://web.ita.doc.gov/safeharbor/shlist.nsf/webPages/safe+harbor+list>.

enforcement, because it used a general clause in US trade regulation. Companies that have joined Safe Harbor and are caught red-handed contravening it can be fined by the Federal Trade Commission for 'unfair and deceptive trade practices'. There is also an arbitration procedure in cases of complaints, where the arbitrator can be chosen from either private providers like TRUSTe or public authorities like the EU data protection commissioners.

The regulatory regime of Safe Harbor therefore consists of several layers: The EU sets the substantive data protection standards, the companies voluntarily commit to them, private or public bodies provide arbitration services, public enforcement is undertaken by a US agency, and the EU Commission still has the last word and can terminate the whole agreement if compliance or public oversight in the US do not work properly. Safe Harbor can therefore be seen as a hybrid arrangement that integrates transnational self-regulation on the one hand, and nation-state based and intergovernmental public regulation on the other hand, into a complex, layered regime.

The State's Seal on Private Regulation Efforts   The EU Commission's 'adequacy' rating in a way corresponds to the work of rating agencies in the financial sector. Elsewhere in the data protection universe, states have also started to certify private instruments like technical standards, organizational procedures, or legal arrangements. The Canadian 'Model Code for the Protection of Personal Information', for example, is a model in a twofold sense: A model for good privacy practices, and a model for an incrementally growing role of the state. The code had been developed since 1992 by trade associations and consumer organizations together with the Canadian government and the Canadian Standards Association (CSA). It was officially recognized ('rated') as a 'National Standard of Canada' in 1996. Organizations that voluntarily adopt the standard are then bound to mandatory quality controls by the CSA, comparable to the web privacy seals in the US. The model code even served as the basis for comprehensive privacy legislation for the private sector – the 2001 Personal Information Protection and Electronic Documents Act (PIPEDA).[105]

The 1995 EU directive also contains options for state certification of private self-regulation instruments. These options had been conceived as exceptions that should be rarely used, but since the Safe Harbor breakthrough, even the European data protection commissioners have actively supported and promoted them. The basic idea is to let business associations develop codes of conduct for privacy, but to embed them in a legal framework and have them certified by public authorities. The data protection commissioners have a strong role here. The EU directive envisions consultations between them and the business associations on the national level for country-wide codes of conduct, and an examination by the group of national commissioners (the 'Article 29 Working Party') for EU-wide regulation. The European Union has recently started using this model of regulated self-regulation in order to certify global adherence within multinational corporations to its data protection standards. The procedure for this has already been harmonized among

---

105   Bennett and Raab, *The Governance of Global Issues*, p. 15.

the EU data protection commissioners.[106] In May 2005, DaimlerChrysler became the first corporation to be awarded a certificate that is valid in the whole EU from the French supervisory agency CNIL for its global *Privacy Code of Conduct*. Others, like General Electric, have since followed. The EU Commission, in its first report on the implementation of the 1995 Data Protection Directive in 2003, noted that 'certification schemes play a crucial role'.[107]

Several adaptations of this certified self-regulation have been developed on the national level. Under the reformed German Federal Data Protection Law of 2001, companies can submit their individual products or privacy policies to an official audit mechanism and thereby get a certificate and a seal of approval.[108] Interest among German corporations for this official auditing is high, which is evidence of a greater trust in the state even in the private sector.[109] In the US, the 1998 *Children's Online Privacy Protection Act* also introduced the possibility of an official certification of private privacy programmes by the FTC. Companies that have this certificate significantly reduce their risk of liability lawsuits if problems should arise. Because it fits into the US model of privacy protection through the courts, this certification could become a model for other sectors as well.[110]

The State's Regulation of Technological Design   The internet is an infrastructure, but it also is a social space that enables and shapes online interactions between individuals and groups. Because all of these interactions take place in a technically mediated environment, the range of freedoms and individual options for behavior is also determined by the way the network architecture is built.[111] The amount of personal data that is collected therefore depends on the design of the web servers, databases, browsers, and networks. If data protection is built into them, one can expect an extremely high level of compliance, as the 'law of code' works with ex-ante enforcement. That differs significantly from the normal law or self-regulation based mechanisms, where enforcement can only be pursued after the fact. Therefore, data protection principles have to be applied in the early stages of computer systems design and development. The first country to make so-called 'privacy impact

---

106 Article 29 Working Party, *Working Document: Setting Forth a Co-Operation Procedure for Issuing Common Opinions on Adequate Safeguards Resulting From 'Binding Corporate Rules'*, Document WP 107 (Brussels: EU Commission, 2005).

107 EU Commission, *Report from the Commission. First report on the implementation of the Data Protection Directive (95/46/EC), COM (2003) 265 final*, (15 May 2003), p. 16.

108 Berlin Data Protection Commissioner, *Neuregelungen im Bundesdatenschutzgesetz* (Berlin, 2001); Alexander Rossnagel, *Datenschutzaudit. Konzeption, Durchführung, gesetzliche Regelung* (Braunschweig/Wiesbaden, 2000).

109 Richard Sietmann, 'Bundestag will Datenschutzreform anmahnen', *heise news* (1 December 2004).

110 Lorrie Faith Cranor and Joel R. Reidenberg, *Can user agents accurately represent privacy notices?*, paper for the Telecommunications Policy Regulation Conference 2002, <http://tprc.org/papers/2002/65/tprc2002-useragents.PDF>, p. 19.

111 Lessig, *Code and other Laws of Cyberspace*; Joel R. Reidenberg, 'Lex Informatica: the Formulation of Information Policy Rules Through Technology', *Texas Law Review*, 76 (1998): 553–84.

assessments' (PIAs) mandatory for federal agencies and departments in exactly these early stages was Canada.[112] The US, with its e-Government Act of 2002, has also begun to mandate privacy impact assessments for government databases in order to ensure compliance through the technology. All government agencies have to use the P3P standard ('Platform for Privacy Preferences Project') developed by the World Wide Web Consortium, and provide a privacy notice on their websites. These privacy notices must notify the user as to which information is collected, why it is collected, with whom the information is shared, which 'notice' is available to the individual, and how the information is secured.[113]

Government *use* of these technological systems, standards, and protocols of data protection is, of course, not the same as regulation of the private sector, but it will help spread their adoption beyond the public sector. The large number of computers that the government can leverage can create the critical mass for their widespread adoption through network externalities, and their use by government organisations also functions as a seal of approval. The European Commission is also following this approach. In 2003, it stated that

> the use of appropriate technological measures is an essential complement to legal means and should be an integral part in any efforts to achieve a sufficient level of privacy protection.[114]

These approaches are currently being developed into more comprehensive infrastructures under the label 'Privacy and Identity Management' (PIM). They are expected to provide two features at the same time: A simple and user-friendly administration of online identities, as well as technological implementation and enforcement of data protection standards. It is not yet clear whether this will ultimately lead to better data protection or even to the end of anonymity on the net. Microsoft's heavily criticized 'Passport'/'.Net' programs with central databases are regarded as PIMs, as are other systems with decentralized online infrastructures that ensure far-reaching anonymity and pseudonymity (so-called 'federated' PIMs). Complementing the P3P front-end standard that allows the user to control which data he gives to web sites, meta-data protocols are currently being developed to ensure that once personal data has entered the corporate data warehouses (back-end), it can only be processed according to the preferences of the person it belongs to. The *Enterprise Privacy Authorization Language* (EPAL), an example of such a privacy meta-data standard, is already in use at companies like eBay. The interesting part, again, is the role of public authorities in these technical design and standardization processes. Like P3P, EPAL was developed in close cooperation with official data protection commissioners.[115] The EU has also funded a large part of the P3P development

---

112 EU Commission, *Report from the Commission. First report on the implementation of the Data Protection Directive (95/46/EC), COM*, p. 16.

113 Privacy-Times, 2 December 2002.

114 EU Commission, *First report on the implementation of the Data Protection Directive (95/46/EC), COM*, p. 16.

115 Detlef Borchers, 'Eine Sprache für den Datenschutz', *heise news* (14 May 2004), <http://www.heise.de/newsticker/meldung/47361>.

and is currently financing several PIM projects within its 6th Framework Research Programme.[116]

The state, it seems, is again starting to focus on the technological design of computers and networks and relying less on the users' self-help or industry self-regulation. Microsoft's 'Passport' program, which was redesigned after EU interventions, is a good example of how the EU is now influencing global technical developments – and thereby global data protection compliance.[117]

Legal Enforcement   The call for government regulation of private-sector privacy policies and behaviour has been growing constantly in the past few years. The FTC itself, in its 2000 report on online profiling – to the surprise of many – viewed legislation as being necessary to complement industry initiatives:

> Self-regulation cannot address recalcitrant and bad actors, new entrants to the market, and drop-outs from the self-regulatory program [...]; only legislation can guarantee that notice and choice are always provided in the place and at the time consumers need them.[118]

The FTC's call was a clear sign that the 'self-regulate, or else' approach, which has been a constant pattern in the US, is reaching its limits. The administration of US President George W. Bush has hesitated to adopt a comprehensive data protection law for the private sector, and since the attacks of 2001 is not known as a strong supporter of privacy protection in general, but Congress has seen a rising number of initiatives for data protection legislation since then.[119] Several US states have already moved further and passed laws that protect data more comprehensively than current federal legislation.[120] Even Microsoft has recently called for a comprehensive privacy law in the US.[121]

Layered Regulation and Legitimacy in the New Millennium   We have seen that even in private-sector self-regulation, there is a growing interest in pulling the state 'back in', while on the other hand the failures of purely private sector regulation have created a push momentum from official agencies and politicians towards more state control and enforcement. Whether through public funding and promotion for privacy-enhancing technologies, government oversight over private seal mechanisms,

---

116 PRIME ('Privacy and Identity Management for Europe'), RAPID ('Roadmap for Advanced Research in Privacy and Identity Management'), FIDIS ('Future of Identity in the Information Society').

117 EPIC, *Privacy & Human Rights 2004. An International Survey of Privacy Laws and Developments* (Washington, 2004), p. 131.

118 U.S. Federal Trade Commission, *Online Profiling. A Report to Congress, Part 2: Recommendations* (July 2000), <http://www.ftc.gov/os/2000/07/onlineprofiling.htm>.

119 Marcia S. Smith, *Internet Privacy: Overview and Legislation in the 109th Congress, 1st Session*, CRS Report to Congress RL31408 (Washington, 2006).

120 See <http://www.epic.org/privacy/consumer/states.html> for an older, but very comprehensive overview.

121 Brad Smith, *Protecting Consumers and the Marketplace: The Need for Federal Privacy Legislation* (Redmond, 2005). The author is Senior Vice President, General Counsel and Corporate Secretary of Microsoft.

officially certified auditing of privacy policies, or the recent US developments in favour of private sector regulation mandated by law, the state is acquiring a more prominent role again, especially if we consider the 'hands-off' approach towards the internet that was prevalent ten years ago.

However, the difference in the organizational dimension, compared to the state-interventionist approach in the early years of privacy and data protection regulation, is the more prominent role of intermediaries. The state does not regulate big databases and computer centres directly as was the case in the 1970s and 1980s. At least since the rise of the personal computer and especially the internet, this option has no longer been feasible. Instead, the state is now trying to control or steer the standards and procedures set by the important agents. These intermediaries are trade associations that have their privacy codes of conduct certified, technology companies like Microsoft that develop identity-management infrastructures, standards organizations like the World Wide Web Consortium (for P3P and EPAL) or the Canadian Standards Association (for the Canadian Model Code), and consortiums that develop new infrastructural designs under an explicit mandate of the state, like the EU's PIM projects. All this is happening under the 'shadow of the law' (in the US) or even within a legal framework (in other OECD countries). Though an important part of it still is private sector self-regulation, the emerging layered data protection regime surely is not 'governing without government'[122] or the global self-governance of the internet community. The state's efforts to regulate and certify private procedures, processes, and products more resembles what others have called 'indirect regulation through procedural law',[123] 'decentralized context control',[124] or the 'audit society'.[125]

Spatially, the new model differs from the old model of regulated self-regulation insofar as it has no clear national boundaries anymore. The goals – the principles of data protection or fair information practices – are harmonized internationally, mainly through multilateral efforts, with the EU directive being the core reference point. They are still implemented into laws with national reach– except in the US – and some of the state's oversight functions and new certification schemes only apply nationally. But the rise of indirect regulation through the control of intermediaries means that national decisions have implications with potentially global reach. This is true for the certification of corporate binding rules (the DaimlerChrysler Privacy Code of Conduct has been certified by the French CNIL agency, is automatically accepted throughout the EU, and applies to all of the corporation's data handling from Stuttgart to Bombay or Johannesburg), for the 'Safe Harbor'-certified seal and arbitration programs like

122 R.A.W. Rhodes, 'The new governance: Governing without government', *Political Studies*, 44/4 (1996): 652–67.

123 Gralf-Peter Calliess, 'Globale Kommunikationen – staatenloses Recht. Zur (Selbst-) Regulierung des Internet durch prozedurales Recht am Beispiel des Verbraucherschutzes im elektronischen Geschäftsverkehr', in Michael Anderheiden, Stefan Huster and Stephan Kirste (eds.), *Globalisierung als Problem von Gerechtigkeit und Steuerungsfähigkeit des Rechts* (Stuttgart, 2001), pp. 61–79.

124 Helmut Willke, *Ironie des Staates. Grundlinien einer Staatstheorie polyzentrischer Gesellschaft* (Frankfurt, 1992).

125 Michael Power, *The Audit Society. Rituals of Verification* (Oxford, 3rd edition 2002).

TRUSTe (which are now also being offered in Japan and other countries that are not part of Safe Harbor), and for the technical standards and systems that are designed by the W3C together with data protection commissioners, or by private enterprises like Microsoft that are under the scrutiny of the latter, or the EU Commission (both the W3C and Microsoft are standard-setters with global reach).

What about legitimacy then? In the organizational dimension, these new forms of regulated self-regulation (or better: transborder layered regulation) are certainly more representative than the international attempts of the 1980s or the industry-only approach that was dominant until the late 1990s. Especially if regulation is mandated by law or certified by national regulatory agencies, the underlying legitimacy is based on the directly elected parliaments. They are also more inclusive, as they are often developed in close cooperation with the respective stakeholders. This is also one aspect where the internet, combined with the perceived need to develop more public trust, has had an opening effect on the state's regulatory efforts. Nowadays, many of these instruments are being developed together with, or at least under close observation of, the emerging international network of privacy activists and NGOs. But these are still highly specialized expert communities; and their links to the average citizen or even to grassroots-level public-interest groups are extremely weak. So far, even the now regular EU online consultation processes have seen no significant participation by people outside these global governance networks and epistemic communities. And in the end, it is the EU Commission that decides, no matter what arguments the stakeholders submit. The participatory hopes for direct online democracy or for the internet as the space of rational deliberation of the mid-1990s have not materialized, and the biggest mistake of their holders obviously was to forget that the power relations that exist in the offline world of political institutions do not go away just because of a new mass communication medium. Technical coordination of interfaces and standards in an open, inclusive, and transparent online process might still work in internet bodies like the IETF,[126] but regulation always means there is somebody who has to make decisions against the will of others that are affected. In general, these new regulated self-regulation models of data protection are less intrusive that the interventionist model of the 1970s ands 1980s, as they give some freedom back to the regulated, who can – within the boundaries of the state-imposed principles of fair information practices – decide for themselves how to ensure data protection. On the other hand, they are more legitimate than the purely private self-regulation models of the dot-com era, as they ensure that the principles are set by democratically elected and accountable bodies.

In the spatial dimension, national standards and laws like the Canadian model code or the German certification scheme also ensure the congruence of those who set the rules and those who have to follow them. Congruence is less ensured for technological standards like P3P that are applied globally. Their adoption, like the use of other PIMs and PETs or most of the certification schemes, is voluntary for

---

126 Even ICANN has become highly politicized in the last few years, mainly because the original function of technical coordination has been supplemented with regulatory tasks like trademark protection and the discussion about who should control the country code top-level domain names.

the private sector, but network effects and the important role of intermediaries can in the end make it difficult or impossible for most internet users (companies as well as consumers) to defect from them. The third-country provisions of the EU directive are most problematic in terms of congruence. They were originally only conceived to protect the data of EU citizens, even when it is processed abroad. If global corporations like DaimlerChrysler adhered to them by applying them in all of their subsidiary companies, this might be no problem, as there is no legitimacy rule that would prohibit DaimlerChrysler South Africa from adopting higher privacy standards than mandated by local law. But the sheer market power of the EU has already made several countries outside of Europe adopt data protection laws and prevented them from making their own decision by independent deliberation. For privacy promoters, this is certainly a good development, as it shows how globalization can lead to the raising of social standards instead of the often-feared race to the bottom. The normative democratic quality of these developments is less clear, and they reflect the global power relations between the OECD world and 'the rest'. It is no coincidence that the US is the only country that has managed to negotiate a special agreement on transborder data flows with the EU, thus avoiding the need to change national legislation,[127] and other countries, such as Australia, have already complained about this unequal treatment.

Looking at output legitimacy, as most of the developments described here are very recent, it is too early to judge their effectiveness. In particular, approaches such as privacy impact assessments in the early stages of systems development, or the EU's research funding for privacy enhancing technologies, will only play out in the mid-term. But they will probably have an impact. The states are no longer willing to tolerate every use of personal data on the online environment, and the big corporations seem to have learned their lessons in terms of winning or losing consumer trust. The growing problem of e-mail spam is adding to this development. It has already been the subject of UN discussions, and even under the lax CAN-SPAM act of 2003,[128] the first big court cases have been brought against spammers in the US.[129]

---

127 Ironically, some EU member states had to change their regulations and even laws in order to make implementation of the 'Safe Harbor' agreement possible, see EU Commission, *Staff Working Paper 'The application of Commission Decision 520/2000/EC of 26 July 2000 pursuant to Directive 95/46 of the European Parliament and of the Council on the adequate protection of personal data provided by the Safe Harbour Privacy Principles and related Frequently Asked Questions issued by the US Department of Commerce', SEC (2002) 196* (13 February 2002).

128 The full title is 'Controlling the Assault of Non-Solicited Pornography and Marketing Act of 2003', Public Law 108-187. Critics say the 'CAN' refers not to canning the spam but allowing it, as only fraudulent emails and a lack of opt-out information is considered a breach of the law. For an overview, see EPIC, *SPAM–Unsolicited Commercial E-Mail* (2006), <http://www.epic.org/privacy/junk_mail/spam/>.

129 In April 2005, the first Spammer was sentenced to 9 years in prison, see 'Sie haben Post!', *Der Spiegel* (18 April 2005), p. 73.

Conclusion: The Return of the State in a Different Shape

In this chapter, I have presented a case study intended to describe the transformation of data protection governance since the 1970s. In the last three decades, the role of the state has indeed undergone significant changes.

The national data protection laws of the first generation quickly reached their limits after the rise of transnational data flows. In order to ease cross-border trade in personal information while still protecting some fair information principles, the European states started international harmonization in the 1980s with the Council of Europe Convention, and later with the EU directive in 1995. While these included binding regulation, enforcement became more and more problematic with the widespread use of computers and the rise of the internet. Private-sector self-regulation – the US model since 1974 – was therefore seen as a more appropriate way of protecting privacy online. The OECD guidelines and, more important, the 'Safe Harbour' agreement tried to link the European system, still based on proscriptive legislation, with the US private-sector and voluntary approach. Self-certification schemes, user self-help, and limited regulatory oversight became the dominant approaches to online data protection in the late 1990s. This weakened role of the state has been partly reversed in the last few years. The official data protection authorities have started certifying industry mechanisms and codes of conduct, the state is exerting more influence on how the private sector designs the systems that process personal data, and even in the US, government agencies, legislators, and even big corporations have been pushing for a comprehensive data protection law for the private sector. At the same time, public-interest groups are becoming more organized internationally through the internet, and the policy processes on the international level are becoming more open to online consultations and other forms of participation.

The case study has therefore confirmed the anticipated tendencies, namely a growth in the spatial reach of data protection arrangements and an organizational delegation of regulatory tasks to the private sector. Spatially, the advent of transnational data flows in the 1970s had already exposed the limitations of national forms of data protection. Since 1980, national laws have been shaped by multilateral agreements, such as the Council of Europe Convention and later the EU directive. As the latter also covers transactions into third countries, it created a significant momentum for the spread of data protection legislation throughout the world. Organizationally, today national laws are complemented by various types of self-regulatory procedures, and some of the oversight functions have been delegated to private agents like corporate privacy commissioners or certification and standardization bodies. Since the instances of data protection are now ubiquitous because of the personal computer and the internet, self-regulatory strategies were seen as the only way for the state to provide regulatory means for the digital age.

Insofar, both the 'Internationalists', who saw the need for global legal arrangements to regulate the global data flows, and the 'Cyber-Separatists', who saw self-governance as the only feasible model for the internet, were right – but only for a limited time. The international law approach was more dominant in Europe, and the self-governance tradition in the US prevailed for some considerable time on that side

Table 5.3   Models of data protection governance over time

specific aspects / governance model	period and region of relevance	role of the state	regulation model	basis of legitimacy
national state regulation (traditionalist)	1970s (Europe)	regulator	public intervention	democratic representation
national private governance (cyber-separatist)	1970s–1990s (US)	limited oversight through general law	national self-regulation	effectiveness, legality
multilateral regime (internationalist)	1980s–1990s (Europe)	interdependent, constrained regulator	multilateralism, national compliance	international consensus, congruence
transnational self-governance (cyber-separatist)	1990s (US, partly Europe)	none	transborder private self-regulation	effectiveness, participation
hybrid and layered global governance (new model)	2000ff (OECD and beyond)	control of intermediaries, certification	indirect state regulation, corporate compliance	consensus on principles, effectiveness, transparency

of the Atlantic. But both internationalization and self-regulation suffer from problems of compliance and legitimacy. The shift of regulatory power to the international level and the tendency towards less state-intervention were accompanied by a decrease of transparency and participation. On the one hand, international expert diplomacy lacked the accountability and visibility of national parliaments; on the other hand, private forms of regulation are difficult to control and are not accountable to the same extent as public regulation. Both suffer from weak enforcement mechanisms, while the self-regulation approach cannot overcome the defection problem, either.

Recently, we have therefore again seen a more prominent role of the state. Even in the US, the calls for binding legal regulation are getting more and louder. But the state is not returning to cyberspace in its old interventionist role, with national law as the only instrument, as the 'Traditionalists' had been expecting. Instead, we see the state setting the privacy baselines and mandating some procedures, while leaving detailed implementation and oversight to private bodies. We also find state-based certification mechanisms and more government influence on the design of the technical systems that collect and use personal data online. The state does not intervene directly anymore, or only under special circumstances, e.g., if breaches of privacy law become public. More and more, state bodies use intermediaries to influence the data handling practices of private actors. The return of the state to cyberspace is accompanied by a transformation of its role, leading to more complex, layered, or hybrid regulatory arrangements with differentiated organizational features and spatial reach.

On the regulatory side, the new model represents a nice synthesis of the cyber-separatist, the internationalist, and the traditionalist perspectives. Therefore, it does not fit into the different models of governance developed in the first part, and we have to add another row to the table – hybrid and layered global governance. We can also add a new column now to illustrate that all the different governance models were in fact relevant in data protection policy, but at different times and in different regions. The regulation of data protection has moved from the first two rows to the last row over the last three decades. Only in the recent period can we find the emergence of a new global model.

The historical reason for this was that the entry into force of the EU data protection directive coincided with the heyday of the internet economy. The 'Safe Harbour' agreement of 2000 was the first attempt to reconcile the European legal and multilateral tradition with the US approach favouring the private sector and technology, and it opened a path towards the broader use of hybrid models in general. This new regulation of data protection has had an impact on regions beyond Europe and North America, but it is dominated by a small number of countries, and direct citizen participation is still very low. New forms of an internet-based, legitimate and effective regulation of global data flows have not materialized. What we find is a bit more transparency, a bit more inclusiveness, a bit more self-regulation, and still some technical self-help on the user side. On the legitimacy side, today's governance of privacy is state-based and multilateral as far as the principles and oversight are concerned, with most of the enforcement, implementation, and compliance aspects delegated to the private sector. The citizen-consumer and his personal data are still the object of regulation. Citizens have yet to become active subjects in the politics of privacy governance, but at least they can monitor the regulation processes online nowadays.

Bibliography

Agre, Philip E. and Marc Rotenberg (eds.), *Technology and Privacy: The New Landscape* (Cambridge: MIT Press, 1998).

Albert, Mathias and Lothar Brock, 'Entgrenzung der Staatenwelt. Zur Analyse weltgesellschaftlicher Entwicklungstendenzen', *Zeitschrift für Internationale Beziehungen*, 2/2 (1995): 259–85.

Article 29 Working Party, *Working Document: Setting Forth a Co-Operation Procedure for Issuing Common Opinions on Adequate Safeguards Resulting From 'Binding Corporate Rules'*, Document WP 107 (Brussels: EU Commission, 2005).

Baer, Walter S., 'Will the Global Information Infrastructure Need Transnational (or Any) Governance?', in Brian Kahin and Ernest J. Wilson III (eds.), *National Information Infrastructure Initiatives: Visions and Policy Design* (Cambridge: MIT Press, 1997).

Barbrook, Richard and Andy Cameron, *The Californian ideology* (1995), different versions available at <http://www.hrc.wmin.ac.uk/theory-californianideology.html>, accessed 1 January 2007.

Barlow, John Perry, *A Declaration of the Independence of Cyberspace* (Davos, Switzerland, 8 February 1996), <http://homes.eff.org/~barlow/Declaration-Final.html>, accessed 1 January 2007.

Bäumler, Helmut (ed.), *E-Privacy. Datenschutz im Internet* (Braunschweig and Wiesbaden: Vieweg, 2000).

BBBOnline, *Consumer Privacy Website* (2006, constantly updated), <http://www.bbbonline.com/consumer/privindex.aspx>.

Beisheim, Marianne; Dreher, Sabine; Walter, Gregor; Zangl, Bernhard, and Michael Zürn, *Im Zeitalter der Globalisierung? Thesen und Daten zur gesellschaftlichen und politischen Denationalisierung* (Baden-Baden: Nomos, 1999).

Bennett, Colin J., *Regulating Privacy. Data Protection and Public Policy in Europe and the United States* (Ithaca: Cornell University Press, 1992).

Bennett, Colin J., 'Privacy Self-Regulation in a Global Economy: A Race to the Top, the Bottom or Somewhere Else?', in Kernaghan Webb (ed.), *Voluntary Codes: Private Governance, the Public Interest and Innovation* (Ottawa: Carleton Research Unit for Innovation, Science and Environment, 2004), <http://www.carleton.ca/spa/VolCode/Ch8.pdf>, accessed 1 January2007.

Bennett, Colin J., 'Privacy in the Political System: Perspectives from Political Science and Economics', in Alan Westin (ed.), *Privacy and Freedom Updated: Social Science Perspectives on Privacy* (forthcoming), <http://web.uvic.ca/~polisci/bennett/pdf/westinbook.pdf>, accessed 1 January 2007.

Bennett, Colin J. and Rebecca Grant (eds.), *Visions of Privacy. Policy Choices for the Digital Age* (Toronto: University of Toronto Press, 1999).

Bennett, Colin J. and Charles D. Raab, *The Governance of Privacy. Policy Instruments in Global Perspective* (Aldershot: Ashgate, 2003).

Bennett, Colin J. and Charles D. Raab, *The Governance of Global Issues: Protecting Privacy in Personal Information*, paper presented at the ECPR Joint Sessions of Workshops, Edinburgh (28 March-2 April 2003).

Berg, Terrence, 'www.wildwest.gov: The Impact of the Internet on State Power to Enforce the Law', *Brigham Young University Law Review* 25/4 (2000): 1305–62.

Berlin Data Protection Commissioner [Berliner Beauftragter für Datenschutz und Informationsfreiheit/Unabhängiges Landeszentrum für Datenschutz Schleswig-Holstein], *Neuregelungen im Bundesdatenschutzgesetz* (Berlin: Berliner Beauftragter für Datenschutz und Informationsfreiheit, 2001).

Borchers, Detlef, 'Eine Sprache für den Datenschutz', *heise news,* 14 May 2004, <http://www.heise.de/newsticker/meldung/47361>, accessed 1 January 2007.

Boutin, Paul, 'Just How trusty is Truste?', *Wired News,* 9 April 2002, <http://www.wired.com/news/exec/0,1370,51624,00.html>, accessed 1 January 2007.

Brandeis, Louis and Samuel Warren, 'The Right to Privacy', *Harvard Law Review,* 4/5 (1890): 193–220.

Brühl, Tanja, Debiel, Tobias; Hamm, Brigitte; Hummel, Hartwig, and Jens Martens (eds.), *Die Privatisierung der Weltpolitik. Entstaatlichung und Kommerzialisierung im Globalisierungsprozess* (Bonn: Dietz Verlag, 2001).

Bundesverfassungsgericht, *BVerfGE 65, 1 – Volkszählung. Urteil des Ersten Senats* (15 December 1983), <http://www.datenschutz-berlin.de/gesetze/sonstige/volksz.htm>, accessed 1 January 2007.

Calliess, Gralf-Peter, 'Globale Kommunikationen – staatenloses Recht. Zur (Selbst-) Regulierung des Internet durch prozedurales Recht am Beispiel des Verbraucherschutzes im elektronischen Geschäftsverkehr', in Michael Anderheiden, Stefan Huster, and Stephan Kirste (eds.), *Globalisierung als Problem von Gerechtigkeit und Steuerungsfähigkeit des Rechts* (Stuttgart: Franz Steiner Verlag, 2001).

Charlesworth, Andrew, 'Clash of the Data Titans? US and EU Data Privacy Rules', *European Public Law,* 6/2 (2000): 253–274.

Chaum, David, 'Achieving Electronic Privacy', *Scientific American,* No. 267 (1992): 76–81.

Council of Europe, *Recommendation No R(99)5 of the Committee of Ministers to Member States for the Protection of Privacy on the Internet. Guidelines for the Protection of Individuals with Regard to the Collection and Processing of Personal Data on Information Highways*, adopted by the Committee of Ministers at the 660th meeting of the Ministers' Deputies (23 February 1999).

Council of Europe, *Additional Protocol to the Convention for the Protection of Individuals with regard to Automatic Processing of Personal Data regarding supervisory authorities and transborder data flows (ETS No. 181), Explanatory Report* (2001), <http://conventions.coe.int/Treaty/en/Reports/Html/181.htm>, accessed 1 January 2007.

Cranor, Lorrie Faith, 'The role of privacy advocates and data protection authorities in the design and deployment of the platform for privacy preferences', in Association of Computing Machinery (ed.), *Proceedings of the 12th Computers, Freedom and Privacy Conference* (San Francisco/Ca.: ACM, 2002).

Cranor, Lorrie Faith and Joel R. Reidenberg, *Can user agents accurately represent privacy notices?* paper for the Telecommunications Policy Regulation Conference 2002, <http://tprc.org/papers/2002/65/tprc2002-useragents.PDF>, accessed 1 January 2007.

Culnan, Mary J., *Georgetown Internet Privacy Policy Survey: Report to the Federal Trade Commission* (June 1999), <http://www.msb.edu/faculty/culnanm/gippshome.html>, accessed 1 January 2007.

Cutler, A. Claire, Haufler, Virginia, and Tony Porter, *Private Authority and International Affairs* (Albany/NY: SUNY Press, 1999).

Der Spiegel, 18 April 2005, 'Sie haben Post!', p. 73.

Deutsch, Karl W., *Nationalism and Social Communication. An Inquiry into the Foundations of Nationality* (Cambridge/Ma.: MIT Press, 1953).

EPIC [Electronic Privacy Information Center / Privacy International], *Privacy & Human Rights 2004. An International Survey of Privacy Laws and Developments* (Washington DC: EPIC, 2004).

EPIC [Electronic Privacy Information Center], *SPAM – Unsolicited Commercial E-Mail (*2005), <http://www.epic.org/privacy/junk_mail/spam/>, accessed 1 January 2007.

EU, *Europe and the global information society. Recommendations to the European Council. Report of the High-Level Group on the Information Society* (26 May 1994), <http://europa.eu.int/ISPO/infosoc/backg/bangeman.html>, accessed 1 January 2007.

EU, *Directive 95/46/EC of the European Parliament and of the Council, on the protection of individuals with regard to the processing of personal data and on the free movement of such data* (24 October 1995).

EU, *Directive 97/66/EC of the European Parliament and of the Council, concerning the processing of personal data and the protection of privacy in the telecommunications sector* (15 December 1997).

EU, *Directive 2002/58/EC of the European Parliament and of the Council, concerning the processing of personal data and the protection of privacy in the electronic communications sector* (12 July 2002).

EU Commission, *A European Initiative in Electronic Commerce. Communication to the European Parliament, the Council, the Economic and Social Committee and the Committee of the Regions, COM(97) 157* (15 April 1997).

EU Commission, *Staff Working Paper 'The application of Commission Decision 520/2000/EC of 26 July 2000 pursuant to Directive 95/46 of the European Parliament and of the Council on the adequate protection of personal data provided by the Safe Harbour Privacy Principles and related Frequently Asked Questions issued by the US Department of Commerce', SEC (2002) 196* (13 February 2002).

EU Commission, *Commission Decision 2002/16/EC on standard contractual clauses for the transfer of personal data to processors established in third countries, under Directive 95/46/EC, notified under document number C(2001) 4540, with annex 'Standard Contractual Clauses'* (27 December 2002).

EU Commission, *Report from the Commission. First report on the implementation of the Data Protection Directive (95/46/EC), COM (2003) 265 final* (15 May 2003).

EU-JRC [EU Joint Research Center], *Security and Privacy for the Citizen in the Post-September 11 Digital Age: A Prospective Overview. Report to the European Parliament Committee on Citizens Freedoms and Rights, Justice and Home Affairs (LIBE)* (2003).

EuroBarometer, *E-Commerce Survey* (March 2004), <http://ec.europa.eu/consumers/topics/btoc_ecomm.pdf >, accessed 1 January 2007.

European Parliament, 'Resolution on the protection of the rights of the individual in the face of technical developments in data processing', *Official Journal of the European Communities,* No. C 140/35, (5 June 1979).

European Parliament, *Second Report drawn up on behalf of the Legal Affairs Committee on the protection of the rights of the individual in the face of technical developments in data processing.* Rapporteur: Mr. H. Sieglerschmidt, Document 1-548/81, PE 70.166/final (12 October 1981).

Farrell, Henry, 'Hybrid Institutions and the Law: Outlaw Arrangements or Interface Solutions?', *Zeitschrift für Rechtssoziologie,* 23/1 (2002): 25–40.

Farrell, Henry, 'Constructing the International Foundations of E-Commerce: The EU-U.S. Safe Harbor Arrangement', *International Organization,* 57/2 (2003): 277–306.

Fink, Simon, *Datenschutz zwischen Staat und Markt. Die 'Safe Harbor'-Lösung als Ergebnis einer strategischen Interaktion zwischen der EU, den USA und der IT-Industrie,* Master Thesis, Department of Political and Administrative Science, University of Konstanz (Konstanz, 2002), <http://www.ub.uni-konstanz.de/v13/volltexte/2003/1012//pdf/magarbsfink.pdf>, accessed 1 January 2007.

Froomkin, A. Michael, 'Habermas@Discourse.Net: Toward a Critical Theory of Cyberspace', *Harvard Law Review,* 116/3 (2003): 749–873.

Global Business Dialogue on electronic commerce, *Consumer Confidence: Trustmarks* (14 September 2001), <http://www.gbd.org/pdf/recommendations/trustmark00.pdf>.

Grossman, Lawrence K., 'Der Traum des Nebukadnezar. Demokratie in der Ära des Internet', in Claus Leggewie and Christa Maar (eds.), *Internet und Politik. Von der Zuschauer- zur Beteiligungsdemokratie* (Köln: Bollmann, 1998).

Hague, Barry N. and Brian D. Loader, *Digital Democracy. Discourse and Decision Making in the Information Age* (London/New York: Routledge, 1999).

Heisenberg, Dorothee, *Negotiating Privacy. The European Union, the United States and Personal Data Protection* (Boulder/Co.: Lynne Rienner, 2005).

Hosein, Gus, *International Relations Theories and the Regulation of International Dataflows: Policy Laundering and Other International Policy Dynamics,* paper presented at the International Studies Association 45th Annual Convention (Montreal, March 2004). <http://is.lse.ac.uk/staff/hosein/pubs/policylaund_isa.pdf>, accessed 1 January 2007.

Johnson, David R. and David G. Post, 'The Rise of Law on the Global Network', in Brian Kahin and Charles Nesson (eds.), *Borders in Cyberspace. Information Policy and the Global Information Infrastructure* (Cambridge: MIT Press, 1997).

Johnson, David R.; Crawford, Susan P., and, John G. Jr. Palfrey, *The Accountable Net: Peer Production of Internet Governance* (Cambridge: The Berkman Center for Internet & Society Research, 2004), <http://ssrn.com/abstract=529022>.

Junkbusters, *News and Opinion on Marketing and Privacy* (2006, constantly updated), <http://www.junkbusters.com/new.html>.

Leibfried, Stephan and Michael Zürn (eds.), *Transformations of the State?* (Cambridge: Cambridge University Press, 2005).

Lessig, Lawrence, *Code and other Laws of Cyberspace* (New York: Basic Books, 1999).

Lyon, David, *Surveillance Society. Monitoring Everyday Life* (Buckingham and Philadelphia: Open University Press, 2001).

Mayer-Schönberger, Viktor, 'Generational Development of Data Protection in Europe', in Philip E. Agre and Marc Rotenberg (eds.), *Technology and Privacy: The New Landscape* (Cambridge: MIT Press, 1998).

Mayer-Schönberger, Viktor, 'The Shape of Governance: Analyzing the World of Internet Regulation', *Virginia Journal of International Law*, 43 (2003): 605–73.

Mayntz, Renate and Fritz W. Scharpf (ed.), *Gesellschaftliche Selbstregulierung und politische Steuerung* (Frankfurt a. M.: Campus, 1995).

Newman, Abraham L. and David Bach, 'Self-Regulatory Trajectories in the Shadow of Public Power: Resolving Digital Dilemmas in Europe and the United States', *Governance: An International Journal of Policy, Administration, and Institutions*, 17/3 (2004): 387–413.

Newman, Janet, *Modernizing Governance. New Labour, Policy, and Society* (London: Sage, 2001).

OECD, *Declaration on Transborder Data Flows*, Adopted by the Governments of OECD Member Countries (11 April 1985).

OECD Directorate for Science, Technology, and Industry, Committee for Information, Computer and Communications Policy, Group of Experts on Information Security and Privacy, *Practices to Implement the OECD Privacy Guidelines on Global Networks, OECD Doc. No. DSTI/ICCP/REG (98)6/final* (23 December 1998).

OECD Directorate for Science, Technology, and Industry, Committee for Information, Computer and Communications Policy, *'Dismantling the Barriers to Global Electronic Commerce', An International Conference organized by the OECD and the Government of Finland in Cooperation with the European Commission, the Government of Japan and the Business and Industry Advisory Committee to the OECD, Turku, Finland, 19-21 November 1997*, OECD Doc. No. DSTI/ICCP(98)13/final (3 July 1998).

OECD Directorate for Science, Technology, and Industry, Committee for Information, Computer and Communications Policy, Working Party on Information Security and Privacy, *Ministerial Declaration on the Protection of Privacy on Global Networks, Ottawa, 7-9 October 1998,* OECD Doc. No. DSTI/ICCP/REG(98)10/final (18 December 1998).

Platten, Nick, 'Background and History of the Directive', in David Bainbridge (ed.), *The EC Data Protection Directive* (London: Butterworths, 1996).

Post, David G., 'The 'Unsettled Paradox': The Internet, the State, and the Consent of the Governed', *Indiana Journal of Global Legal Studies*, 5 (1998): 521–39.

Power, Michael, *The Audit Society. Rituals of Verification* (Oxford: Oxford University Press, 3rd edition, 2002).

Regan, Priscilla M., 'American Business and the European Data Protection Directive: Lobbying Strategies and Tactics', in Colin J. Bennett and Rebecca Grant (eds.), *Visions of Privacy. Policy Choices for the Digital Age* (Toronto: University of Toronto Press, 1999).

Reidenberg, Joel R., 'Lex Informatica: the Formulation of Information Policy Rules Through Technology', *Texas Law Review*, 76/3 (1998): 553–84.

Rhodes, R.A.W. 'The new governance: Governing without government', *Political Studies*, 44/4 (1996): 652–67.

Richardson, Lee, 'History of Self-Regulation Cast Doubt on its Effectiveness', *Privacy Times*, (12 July 2000): 7–11.

Rosecrance, Richard, 'The Rise of the Virtual State: Territory Becomes Passé', *Foreign Affairs*, 75/4 (1996): 45–61.

Rossnagel, Alexander, *Datenschutzaudit. Konzeption, Durchführung, gesetzliche Regelung* (Braunschweig/Wiesbaden: Fr. Vieweg & Sohn, 2000).

Schulz,Wolfgang and Thorsten Held, *Regulierte Selbstregulierung als Form Modernen Regierens. Report for the German Federal Secretary for Culture and Media* (Hamburg: Hans-Bredow-Institute at Hamburg University, 2002).

Schwarz, Paul M. and Joel R. Reidenberg, *Data Privacy Law* (Charlottesville: Michie Law Publisher, 1996).

Seltzer, William and Margo Anderson, 'The Dark Side of Numbers: The Role of Population Data Systems in Human Rights Abuses', *Social Research,* 68/2 (2001): 481–513.

Shaffer, Gregory, 'The Power of Collective Action: The Impact of EU Data Privacy Regulation on US Business Practice', *European Law Journal*, 5/4 (1999): 419–37.

Smith, Brad, *Protecting Consumers and the Marketplace: The Need for Federal Privacy Legislation* (Redmond: Microsoft Corp., 2005).

Smith, Marcia S., *Internet Privacy: Overview and Legislation in the 109th Congress, 1st Session*, CRS Report to Congress RL31408 (Washington DC: Congressional Research Service, 2006).

Suleiman, Ezra, *Dismantling Democratic States* (Princeton: Princeton University Press, 2003).

Swire, Peter P. and Robert E. Litan, *None of Your Business: World Data Flows, Electronic Commerce, and the European Privacy Directive* (Washington DC: Brookings Institution Press, 1998).

Teubner, Gunther, 'Globale Bukowina. Zur Emergenz eines transnationalen Rechtspluralismus', *Rechtshistorisches Journal*, 15/6 (1996): 255–90.

Teubner, Gunther, 'Globale Zivilverfassungen: Alternativen zur staatszentrierten Verfassungstheorie', *Zeitschrift für ausländisches öffentliches Recht und Völkerrecht*, 63/1 (2003): 1–28.

TRUSTe, *TRUSTe Fact Sheet* (2006), <http://www.truste.org/about/fact_sheet.php>.

U.S. Department of Commerce, *Privacy and Self-Regulation in the Information Age* (Washington DC: National Telecommunications and Information Administration, 1997), <http://www.ntia.doc.gov/reports/privacy/privacy_rpt.htm>, accessed 1 January 2007.

U.S. Department of Commerce, *Safe Harbor List* (2006), <http://web.ita.doc.gov/safeharbor/shlist.nsf/webPages/safe+harbor+list>, accessed 1 January 2007.

U.S. Department of Commerce, *Safe Harbor Overview* (2006), <http://www.export.gov/safeharbor/sh_overview.html>, accessed 1 January 2007.

U.S. Federal Trade Commission, *Online Profiling. A Report to Congress, Part 2: Recommendations* (July 2000), <http://www.ftc.gov/os/2000/07/onlineprofiling.htm>, accessed 1 January 2007.

Vogel, David, *Trading Up. Consumer and Environmental Regulation in a Global Economy* (Cambridge: Harvard University Press, 1995).

Weichert, Thilo, 'Zur Ökonomisierung des Rechts auf informationelle Selbstbestimmung', in Helmut Bäumler (ed.), *E-Privacy. Datenschutz im Internet* (Braunschweig and Wiesbaden: Vieweg, 2000).

Weinstock Netanel, Neil, 'Cyberspace Self-Governance: A skeptical View from Liberal Democratic Theory', *California Law Review*, 88 (2000): 395–497.

White House, *A Framework for Global Electronic Commerce* (1 July 1997).

Willke, Helmut, *Ironie des Staates. Grundlinien einer Staatstheorie polyzentrischer Gesellschaft* (Frankfurt a.M.: Suhrkamp, 1992).

WSIS [World Summit on the Information Society], *Declaration of Principles. Building the Information Society: a global challenge in the new Millennium* (Geneva, 12 December 2003), <http://www.itu.int/wsis/docs/geneva/official/dop.html>, accessed 1 January 2007.

WSIS [World Summit on the Information Society], *Plan of Action* (Geneva, 12 December 2003), <http://www.itu.int/wsis/docs/geneva/official/poa.html>, accessed 1 January 2007.

WTO [World Trade Organization], *General Agreement on Trade in Services (GATS)* (Geneva, 15 April 1994).

Zürn, Michael, *Regieren jenseits des Nationalstaates*, (Frankfurt a.M.: Suhrkamp, 2nd revised edition, 2005).

Chapter 6

Conclusion

Myriam Dunn and Victor Mauer

Governments derive their just powers from the consent of the governed. You have neither solicited nor received ours. We did not invite you. You do not know us, nor do you know our world. Cyberspace does not lie within your borders. Do not think that you can build it, as though it were a public construction project. You cannot. It is an act of nature and it grows itself through our collective actions.

John Perry Barlow, *A Declaration of the Independence of Cyberspace*, 1996.

Evidently, John Perry Barlow was wrong to think that governments would become obsolete and be replaced by a society of the mind in the virtual realm. However, to many observers at the time, 'cyberspace' was a highly fascinating place where almost anything could happen, and the expectations of many people concerning both the role of the internet and the speed of its evolution became detached from reality. Among other things, these inflated expectations caused a speculative bubble between 1997 and approximately 2001: the infamous 'dot.com bubble'. This period was marked by the rapidly increasing number of new internet-based companies, a subsequent rapid increase in the value of global stock markets, and finally, the spectacular and painful failure of the markets when the bubble burst.

Like in previous technology-inspired booms, speculators bought shares in anticipation of further rises, not because they were undervalued.[1] In retrospect, it is clear that most of these projections were based on the outlooks of technologists and cyber-libertarians like Barlow: people who were both adept at technology and very fascinated by it and who all succumbed to a high level of technological determinism.[2] But the burst of the bubble at the turn of the millennium entailed a harsh reality check not only for speculators, but also for many analysts that had uncritically joined the praise of the 'new economy'. Furthermore, pessimism also gradually spread to those looking at the impacts of the 'information revolution' on other aspects of life, such as politics.

While the initial enthusiasm for the networked world made sense to people who had shared in the experience of early online 'culture', and still does so to a lesser extent today, the one factor 'the internet' or cyberspace could never change is the determination of pre-existing economic, social, and political elites to perpetuate

---

1   John Cassidy, *Dot Con: How America Lost its Mind and Its Money in the Internet Era* (New York, 2003).

2   Technological determinists interpret technology in general, and communications technologies in particular, as the basis of society in the past, present, and even the future.

themselves and their position in society. We can now see that changes brought on by the information revolution are more gradual than revolutionary, mainly due to the self-reinforcing power of institutions and structures. Many of the moves that have been underway to turn the internet into something other than what it was – or seemed – in the mid-1990s have been deliberate and conscious and not in the least accidental.

Besides, out of the many possible futures that seemed possible a decade ago, the least revolutionary one has manifested itself. The 'path-dependence' generated by the persistence of institutions, whether they be social, political, or cultural, leads us to conclude that nothing, be it 'new' or not, develops in a vacuum. As one commentator noted: 'Whatever happened to the predictions for a world of unlimited communications bandwidth, where fiber-optic networks provided data at unlimited rates and at costs too cheap to meter? Well, a funny thing happened on the way to the future – economics.'[3] Indeed, as Joseph Nye and Robert Keohane stated back in 1998: 'information does not flow in a vacuum, but in political space that is already occupied.'[4]

Cyberspace has thus been demystified during the last couple of years by the realities of predefined space. This is nothing unusual: Humanity has almost always been wrong when trying to predict the future.[5] But when the future becomes the present and reality catches up with fiction, we can collect empirical evidence with which we can test or at least challenge the assumptions of the past. Seen in this light, the volume at hand addresses a timely topic: Certainly not one that has not been addressed before, but one that deserves to be monitored at regular intervals, because there is no static or final situation as long as technology, on which all information revolution arguments hinge, keeps on evolving.

While information and communication technology is generally acknowledged to be an important factor in facilitating social organization and change, most academic commentators now see it as only one factor amongst others. Close studies of particular social contexts have suggested that social change involves an interaction of social, cultural, and economic forces as well as scientific and technological influences.[6] In accordance, the general tenor of this volume is one of so-called weak (or soft) technological determinism. The weak version is less generally applicable than the 'strong case', but it is also more in accord with the available evidence.[7] Weak technological determinism claims that a technology does not create or change itself,

---

3   Del Miller in 'Difference Engine – Scarcely Believable' column in macopinion, 29 July 2003, <http://www.macopinion.com/columns/engine/03/07/29/index.html>, accessed 30 November 2006.

4   Robert O. Keohane and Joseph S. Nye, 'Power and Interdependence in the Information Age', *Foreign Affairs*, 77/5 (September/October 1998): 81–94.

5   Robert H. Cartmill, *The Next Hundred Years ... Then and Now* (Philadelphia, 2002); Laura Lee, *Bad Predictions* (Rochester, 2000).

6   Ruth Finnegan, *Literacy and Orality: Studies in the Technology of Communication* (Oxford, 1988), p. 41 and pp. 176f. See mainly Daniel Chandler, 'Technological or Media Determinism', online resource, created on 18 September 1995, <http://www.aber.ac.uk/media/Documents/tecdet/tdet11.html>, accessed 1 January 2007.

7   Chandler, 'Technological or Media Determinism'.

but rather that the presence of a particular technology is an enabling or facilitating factor leading to potential opportunities that may or may not be taken up in particular societies or periods.[8] Technology does 'constitute part of a society's core political infrastructure',[9] just as do laws regulating behaviour and taxation, but they are not likely to be any more predictable in their effects than those. Or, as the sociologist Ruth Finnegan has argued, 'the medium *in itself* cannot give rise to social consequences – it must be *used*'.[10] This use must be constantly re-evaluated. In this volume, we have looked in particular at the consequences of the information revolution for states in the field of governance.

As becomes evident from the chapters in this book, there are countless definitions for various aspects of governance. Like many abstract ideas, "governance" is a conceptually weak term, especially because it is used in many different ways. Governance emerges as a significant variable for a range of activities involving social organisation, from family life through to policy matters. Furthermore, governments and international organizations are neither exclusively engaged in governance, nor are they necessarily the only authorities to do so – firms, non-governmental organizations, and their professional associations equally engage in and create governance structures.[11] While some differentiate between domestic and global governance and point to the supposed loss of governmental control at the national level,[12] others, clearly distinguishing between governance and government, focus on 'the nature of global order and the processes through which governance occurs on a worldwide scale'[13] and therefore establish governance as a 'system of rule that is as dependent on intersubjective meanings as on formally sanctioned constitutions and charters'.[14]

In discussing the vast concept of governance and various practical attempts to translate it into reality, the volume has addressed many disparate issues. The main question that emerges is whether any such thing as 'information age governance' exists, or whether it is just an alternative term for the tentative developments in 'e-Government'.[15] More specifically, do information and communication technologies networks 'facilitate the deconstruction of national financial and cultural boundaries',

---

8   Ruth Finnegan, *Literacy and Orality: Studies in the Technology of Communication*, p. 38; Lynn White Jr., *Medieval Technology and Social Change* (Oxford, 1978), p. 28. See also Mick Underwood's online article at <http://www.cultsock.ndirect.co.uk/MUHome/cshtml/media/techdet.html>, accessed 1 January 2007.

9   Richard Sclove, *Democracy and Technology* (New York, 1995).

10   Ruth Finnegan, *Communication and Technology. Making Sense of Society: Communication* (Milton Keynes, 1975), p. 108.

11   Robert O. Keohane and Nye, Joseph S. Jr., 'Introduction', in Robert O. Keohane and Joseph S. Nye Jr. (eds.), *Governance in a Globalizing World* (Washington, 2000).

12   Ibid.

13   James N. Rosenau, 'Governance, Order, and Change in World Politics', in Rosenau, James N. and Ernst-Otto Czempiel (eds.), *Governance without Government: Order and Change in World Politics* (Cambridge, 1992), p. 1.

14   Ibid., p. 4.

15   As in fact contended by Jerry Melchling in his article, the title of which is misleading in this regard: 'Information Age Governance: Just the Start of Something Big?', in Elaine Ciulla

and is this the reason why governance in what some call 'the post-modern world' is characterised by the weakening of the nation-state through the accentuation of the local and global dimensions of human interaction?[16] Or, conversely, will global governance grow in step with economic integration and will it 'come not at the expense of the state but rather as an expression of the interests that the state embodies'?[17]

The notion that is most uncritically accepted within the overall information age debate is that state power *per se* is eroding due to the effects of information and communication technology. This volume challenges the unidimensionality of this statement. Without denying that new challenges for the state have arisen, authors in this volume argue that too much credence is often given to the spectre of an erosion of sovereignty. The influence of technology on the international system and its actors can and will not be denied. But all the authors are sceptical concerning the widespread assertions of the demise of the nation-state, and more specifically, the question the claim that the growth of the internet immediately translates into an erosion of state authority.

The volume challenges the notion that activities constrained by traditional sovereignty are fixed in space, but the activities of cyberspace flow freely and unaffected across borders. While acknowledging that the Westphalian paradigm of exclusive and all-embracing state sovereignty is challenged by a plethora of recent technological and societal developments, it is our aim to show that the traditional nation-state is about to reassert itself in, and in relation to, changing circumstances through adaptation.

We contend that cyberspace is a matter of collective and policy choice, and not some natural feature of an idealised cyber-realm. Consequently, cyberspace becomes prone to usurpation by governance structures. We argue that governments all around the world are already reacting to the information revolution and trying to redefine their role in a changing international system. The emergence of 'e-Government' ideas is just one of the visible outcomes of states' efforts to embrace new ideas and adjust their functions.[18] Other endeavours include assessments of how ICT can help mediate the communication processes that are essential to conflict management and resolution, the development of 'virtual diplomacy' abilities,[19] and of course efforts to protect vital national information infrastructures.

In this volume, Jamal Shahin has comprehensively outlined the context within which governance has become a dominant subject of discussion, in both the broader and narrower conceptualisations of the term. Furthermore, he states that global

---

Karmarck and Joseph S. Nye Jr. (eds.), *governance.com – Democracy in the Information Age* (Washington, 2002), pp. 141–60.

16 Brian D. Loader, 'The Governance of Cyberspace: Politics, Technology and Global Restructuring', in Brian D. Loader (ed.), *The Governance of Cyberspace: Politics, Technology and Global Restructuring* (London, 1997), pp. 1–19.

17 Martin Wolf, 'Will the Nation-State Survive Globalization?', *Foreign Affairs*, 80/1 (2001): 190.

18 See for example: 'A Survey of Government and the Internet: The Next Revolution', *The Economist*, 24 June 2000.

19 Virtual diplomacy encompasses social, economic, and political interactions that are mediated through electronic means rather than by face-to-face communication.

governance understood as a network relies not only upon the state as an important actor, but places the state within a network context. Therefore, we need to broaden the debate beyond such activities that are established by the state (rules, regulations, norms, and principles) to include processes that involve other actors as well (such as management, steering, and coordination) in order to fully grasp the state's role as the central point of authority in a global environment. In particular, Shahin uses the concept of 'institutional revival' to show how governments ensure that the nation-state remains crucially important in the information age, mainly in the area of e-Government. He writes that 'the liberalisation of infrastructure and subsequent reliance upon the markets is not the state giving up on regulation, but recognising that markets are more effective at delivering an efficient Information Society', an area where states have been taking action for some time already. Shahin shows that the role of government has in fact become *more*, not less important.

The often-heralded democratising power of the information revolution is also exposed as a myth in this volume. Alexander Siedschlag focuses on digital democracy as a pluralistic concept of governance transformation in the wake of internet-based communication. In order to develop models for assessing the role of online deliberation and a deliberative digital culture in governing increasingly transnationalised political communities, Siedschlag looks at how, or, respectively, to what extent, internet-based communication may lead to changes in, additions to, or substitutes for conventional patterns and repertories of decision-making in the political and in the societal arenas. His chapter shows clearly that 'any discourse within in a cultural community will primarily be *self-referential* rather than deliberative, i.e., not open to arguments and cognition, but necessarily confined to the cultural context.'

This clearly points to the fact that even though digital communication makes it possible to engage people from all over the world in dialogue, the internet allows individuals to filter and personalise information at the same time. Therefore, they might use information to reinforce existing political beliefs instead of getting to know different points of view, and it is possible to construct virtual communities where there is no interaction with people who are different from ourselves.[20] Existing prejudices will not be washed away by the internet. And even though the internet allows everyone to spread their views and opinions at little cost, attention is an increasingly scarce resource: The problem is making oneself heard, not the ability to publish. As it is, entities that are already wealthy and powerful usually gain the most attention, because they have the means to attract traffic to their sites through advertisement or special campaigns.

Many other chapters also discuss the intrinsic limitations to the information revolution's transformational force. Mika Hayashi, for example, sets out to verify whether or not rules of jurisdiction developed before the information revolution are still applicable in the cyber-context today. The principal question she addresses is whether the existing principles are retained in cyberspace, or whether they have been rejected or modified. If there are changes in these rules, she argues, we can expect the distribution of states' regulatory powers in cyberspace to be different from real

---

20 In social psychology, this is called 'selective avoidance'.

space, because the rules of jurisdiction are the rules governing the allocation of states' regulatory powers on the international plane. Hayashi examines two categories of rules of jurisdiction, namely rules found in general international law and rules found in treaties. This analysis shows that, so far, states have shown little need to be inventive concerning jurisdictions in cyberspace. Hayashi comes to the following conclusion, which is consistent with the observations in many other chapters of this book: The changes to the states' regulatory powers as a result of the information revolution are not as visible as had been predicted or advocated. She also shows that cyberspace is not inherently inimical to states' regulations. States purport to exercise their regulatory powers in cyberspace, and cooperate just as they did regarding other matters in real space before the information revolution.

With the objective of advancing our understanding of the link between the national and the transnational levels of governance, Dirk Lehmkuhl's description and analysis of the conflict between trademark provisions and the internet's domain name system reveals that the state is still a major locus of agency in creating governance. While trade names are usually issued according to national principles, the internet's architecture partly ignores governance boundaries related to national and territorial principles and, as in the case of the domain name system, requires a universal rule. In this respect, the argument goes, the case is only one example illustrating one of the major analytical issues related to the governance of the internet, i.e., questions of jurisdictional conflict. Furthermore, Lehmkuhl demonstrates that governance contributions in internationalised environments are not allocated according to a master plan. In the process, he provides insights into the dynamics of the interaction between public and private actors at the international and national levels.

Similarly, the study of data protection cases from the 1980s on that Ralf Bendrath provides in his chapter reveals that state regulation as well as public participation in regime-generating processes have increased in the last few years. Furthermore, a new mix of state-regulation, private-public partnerships, and private self-regulation can be identified. His case study supports the claim that the state, which in the globalised world has been discarded on functional grounds, is now coming back on legitimacy grounds. 'But the state is not coming back to cyberspace in its old interventionist role and with national law as the only instrument,' Bendrath writes. Rather, states use an increasing number of intermediaries to affect the data-handling practices of private actors. The return of the state to cyberspace is thus accompanied by a transformation of its role. Complex hybrid and layered global governance structures are emerging.

In conclusion, we find that we are not witnessing the end of the nation-state, but a return to overlapping authorities, and that the state must adapt its functions to the conditions of a rapidly changing international environment. This volume shows that states still possess sufficient agency to influence the extra-territorial realm of action that the internet has helped to create. Indeed, the past few years show a clear tendency towards a centralization of power, and states are becoming increasingly active in this extra-territorial space and are 'internationalizing' some of their functions. Therefore, there is no reason to assume that the internet is undermining the power of the state, while there is every reason to expect that states will collectively enforce their sovereignty in cyberspace. In this volume, the implications for the individual state, but also for the international community, have been identified. In the process, cyberspace has been demystified and set it into its proper context without belittling a phenomenon whose impact remains partly hidden from us.

Bibliography

Cartmill, Robert H., *The Next Hundred Years ... Then and Now* (Philadelphia: Xlibris Corporation, 2002).

Cassidy, John, *Dot Con: How America Lost its Mind and Its Money in the Internet Era* (New York: HarperCollins, 2003).

Chandler, Daniel, 'Technological or Media Determinism'. Online resource, created on 18 September 1995, <http://www.aber.ac.uk/media/Documents/tecdet/tdet11.html>, accessed 1 January 2007.

Finnegan, Ruth, *Communication and Technology. Making Sense of Society: Communication* (Milton Keynes: Open University Press, 1975).

Finnegan, Ruth, *Literacy and Orality: Studies in the Technology of Communication* (Oxford: Basil Blackwell, 1988).

Keohane, Robert O. Nye, Joseph S. Jr., 'Power and Interdependence in the Information Age', *Foreign Affairs* 77/5 (September/October 1998): 81–94.

Keohane, Robert O. and Nye, Joseph S. Jr., 'Introduction', in Robert O. Keohane and Joseph S. Nye, Jr. (eds.) *Governance in a Globalizing World* (Washington, D.C.: Brookings Institution Press, 2000).

Lee, Laura, *Bad Predictions* (Rochester: Elsewhere Press: 2000).

Loader, Brian D., 'The Governance of Cyberspace: Politics, Technology and Global Restructuring', in Brian D. Loader (ed.) *The Governance of Cyberspace*: *Politics, Technology and Global Restructuring* (London: Routledge, 1997), pp. 1–19.

Melchling, Jerry, 'Information Age Governance: Just the Start of Something Big?', in Elaine Ciulla Karmarck Joseph S. Nye, Jr. (eds.), *governance.com – Democracy in the Information Age* (Washington, D.C.: Brookings Institution Press, 2002), pp. 141–60.

Miller, Del, 'Difference Engine – Scarcely Believable', column in macopinion, 29 July 2003, <http://www.macopinion.com/columns/engine/03/07/29/index.html>, accessed 30 November 2006.

Rosenau, James N., 'Governance, Order, and Change in World Politics', in James N. Rosenau and Ernst-Otto Czempiel (eds.), *Governance without Government: Order and Change in World Politics* (Cambridge: Cambridge University Press, 1992), pp. 1–29.

Sclove, Richard, *Democracy and Technology* (New York: Guilford Press, 1995).

The Economist, 'A Survey of Government and the Internet: The Next Revolution', *The Economist*, 24 June 2000.

White, Lynn Jr., *Medieval Technology and Social Change* (Oxford: Oxford University Press, 1978).

Wolf, Martin, 'Will the Nation-State Survive Globalization?', *Foreign Affairs,* 80/1 (2001): 178–90.

Index